Sciences/Criminology

Ca

ion
, PO Box 3333
321

FORM 19

"This book describes an unprecedented breakthrough in our ability to understand and seriously address the fundamental problems of crime and violence. The research results are startling, but solid, providing a bold new vision of social harmony that is achievable in any community, independent of size, economics, or cultural diversity."

Dr. John Davies, Coordinator of Research
Center for International Development and Conflict Management
University of Maryland

"Thank God. Finally a comprehensive, human approach to crime with the potential for solving this massive societal problem."

Ken Blanchard
Co-Author of The One-Minute Manager ®

"This is a fascinating book that makes clear the relationship between stress and crime. It sends an unequivocal message to those concerned with public health, and all of us in business, that we have an important role to play in ending the crime epidemic. This book should be required reading by public policy makers."

Norwood H. Davis, Jr.
Chairman of the Board
Blue Cross Blue Shield of Virginia

"*The Crime Vaccine* offers a bold new approach to the causes of crime by clearly defining the stress factor. The book deserves our most serious evaluation."

James R. Graham
Executive Director
Kansas City Crime Commission

"For years, those of us who deal with drug abusers and inmates have attempted to find an alternative to incarceration and a purely punitive approach. This book shows us the way. It describes the one program that has been successful in healing the criminal mind."

Marcelino Cruces y Avila
Director of Andromeda Substance Abuse Treatment Programs
Washington, D.C.

"There is no doubt that criminology has become less than interesting. We have constantly looked for something new, and done nothing more than put the same old thing in newly labeled bottles. This book offers something new for those bottles. It is innovative and offers a unique alternative—one that deserves to be heard, tried and evaluated."

R. Dean Wright, Ph.D.
Professor of Sociology, Drake University

"Jay Marcus cogently presents a refreshing perspective on criminology in this thoroughly researched book. The profound prescriptions presented in *The Crime Vaccine* must be seriously considered by all, especially by experts and decision-makers in the field."

Ved P. Nanda
Vice-Provost and Evans University Professor
University of Denver

"In this well-researched, yet highly readable book, Jay Marcus locates the primary origin of criminal behavior and presents real solutions to the crime epidemic. Having worked as a psychiatrist in a correctional setting, I know of no other method which is so effective in rehabilitating criminal offenders. The strategies described in this book could change our approach to crime forever."

James Fleming, M.D., Co-Director
Mt. Pleasant Mental Health Institute, Mt. Pleasant, Iowa

"As an attorney practicing in the criminal area, I see our current criminal justice system failing on a daily basis. The exciting new approach described by Mr. Marcus, what he calls the crime vaccine, is a real life, workable solution to prevent crime and eliminate the stress that leads to criminal activity."

Danny Corn, Oklahoma City

"As a TM practitioner for almost 20 years, I applaud this book's theories about the connection between stress and crime. Stress affects our daily lives in countless ways, and, from my experience, is clearly associated with criminal behavior."

Richard K. Williams
Chief of Police
Madison, Wisconsin Police Department

"Congress is willing to increase spending by $30 billion on failed crime programs, which is tantamount to throwing money down the drain. Even a scant fraction of that amount can eliminate the crime problem once and for all using the enormously effective programs described in Jay Marcus' book *The Crime Vaccine*. This book could not have come too soon. It should be required reading for anyone in a position of spending taxpayers' money on crime and drug abuse programs."

Fred Gratzon
Chairman of the Board, Telegroup, Inc.
(the second fastest growing private company in America, according to Inc. *magazine)*

"*The Crime Vaccine* brings a scientifically validated holistic medicine approach to the field of crime prevention. Use of this technology would save millions of dollars now wasted in methods which have never been proven of any significant value to prevent crime."

Stokes Dickins
M.D., Neurologist, Ottumwa, Iowa
Former Director of the Sleep Disorders Center
University of Iowa Hospitals and Clinics

"I think the biggest impact of the TM program for me is when I sit in a room with anywhere from two residents to thirty residents, and we practice the TM technique. No matter what happens after that, no matter what happened before that, with the residents, you know they all feel it; you know that they can all feel the unity and the power and that peacefulness. All of a sudden, everything is forgotten; all of a sudden there is no division between who you are and who they are."

Dick Wright
former Assistant Superintendent
Rutland, Vermont Correctional Institution

The Crime Vaccine

CLAITOR'S PUBLISHING DIVISION
Baton Rouge, Louisiana

Claitor's Publishing Division, Inc.
3165 S. Arcadian at I-10
P.O. Box 261333
Baton Rouge, Louisiana 70826-1333 USA

Published in 1996
Printed in the United States of America
8 7 6 5 4 3 2 1

Publisher's Cataloging in Publication Data

Marcus, Jay B.
    The crime vaccine : how to end the crime epidemic / Jay B. Marcus.
    p. cm.
    Includes bibliographical references and index.
    ISBN 0-87511-732-5

    1. Crime Prevention. 2. Transcendental Meditation. 3. Stress management.
I. Title.

HV7431.M37 1996   364.4
                                        QBI95-20748

The Crime Vaccine

HOW TO END THE CRIME EPIDEMIC

JAY B. MARCUS

CLAITOR'S PUBLISHING DIVISION
Baton Rouge, Louisiana

Contents

Foreword

A ll societies have their share of problems, which are perceived to be basically political, social or economic in nature. To deal with these problems government has prescribed fairly uncomplicated remedies: an improved economy, improved education, and greater democracy. But while many countries, including the United States, have made large scale investments, and often significant improvements, in eliminating poverty, illiteracy, and tyranny, they still bleed from the crime problem. Crime is ubiquitous, contagious, and vicious, adapting to changing environments and spreading among diverse populations like a disease, largely resistant to any remedy regardless of the nation's increase in wealth, education, and democracy. To the author, this suggests a more basic cause of the problem, and the need for a more fundamental solution than those being offered.

This book defies the stagnant thinking of modern criminology. It is a very timely work because of the profound connection Marcus uncovers between crime and general stress, and the challenging and thoughtful inquiry into the deeper causes of crime. And unlike most books that offer only descriptions of the nature of the problem, it is persuasive in offering a fundamental solution.

The problem of crime causation is one that refuses to go away. Theories about the causes of crime abound. In evaluating the various theories, Marcus surveys the problem with remarkable skill and candor, proving himself a master of criminologic thought. His ability to point out the inconsistencies and superficial treatment of many theories is especially noteworthy since his background is outside the traditional criminological disciplines, which may in part account for the fresh perspective from which he approaches the issue.

Our current criminological theories often focus on the observable social conditions affecting those who commit crimes, without seeing the deeper causative factors in human behavior. *The Crime Vaccine* exposes the weakness of localized criminology and proposes a broader theory to fit the human experience—crime as a byproduct of general stress. Marcus provides a new perspective on Professor Robert Agnew's *general strain theory*, which holds that crime results from the strain, frustration, and anger people experience in their day to day activities, and their inability to satisfy their desires by legitimate means. While strain theory is not a new notion in positivist criminological thought, what is new is Marcus' penetrating focus on the internal physiological effect of the strain on the individual.

Marcus makes it clear that it is the internal stress and the accompanying feelings of "dis-ease," which foster criminal activity. He suggests that de-stressing individuals and the nation as a whole is the natural antidote to crime and violence. Marcus proposes strategies to change the crime prone physiology, and his *general stress theory* sees those who are stressed as contributors to a national or collective stress level, which pushes individuals who are most susceptible to crime in the wrong direction.

While this book would be important simply for the new perspective it sheds on the nature of the problem, Marcus makes a compelling case that the programs he recommends can de-stress America and produce a corresponding decrease in crime. While Marcus' views may contradict popular and "politically correct" criminological thought, the notion of a "crime vaccine" that can end the epidemic is both rationally seductive and logically formidable. When the criminal enslavement of America has resulted in 1.5 million citizens in jails and prisons, and another 3.5 million under mandatory supervision, this new perspective is timely. We can ill afford to ignore the potential for creating the more peaceful America that the author foresees.

Sam Souryal, Ph.D.
Professor, College of Criminal Justice
Sam Houston State University
Huntsville, Texas

Foreword

A century ago Emile Durkheim showed conclusively that society is an entity that exists in fact, *sui generis,* hovering above the individual. Therefore, behavior we might conceive to be primarily individualistic in origin is often instead reflective of higher level, more encompassing social realities. And as John Donne said, "No man is an island, entire of itself; every man is a piece of the Continent, a part of the main." Thus, human functioning, while biological, occurs not in a vacuum but in the social setting.

In this outstanding new work, Jay Marcus presents a fascinating biology and society-based theory of crime. Much of contemporary crime, he finds, emanates not simply from bad character but from the stresses and strains of society, which are felt by all individuals, and from poor or inadequate responses to these stimuli. Crime rises as the stresses of life rise. To truly attack crime, therefore, we must go to the roots, and develop the individual's capacity to deal with societal stress, and the stress arising from the individual's personal interaction with society.

Similarly, in an article in a medical textbook published in 1981, along with two colleagues I argued that drug dependency in the African-American community arises in great measure from the stresses—induced by economic deprivation, hopelessness, racism, poor education, and so forth—omnipresent in the ghettos of our large cities. Individual predispositions combine with cultural conditions to create drug abuse pathologies, we maintained, and drug dependency would only be fought successfully when the nation attacked these root causes successfully.

If the people of the United States really wish to conquer the mounting problem of crime, we cannot continue to use the same failing methods. Cracking down on criminals, building more jails, and executing more people won't succeed in reducing or ending crime. We need to attack the problem at its roots, and Marcus offers convincing evidence that a coordinated program of diet, exercise,

Transcendental Meditation, and the other stress reduction strategies that he describes can reduce crime and rehabilitate criminals. To ignore his proposal may be to condemn future generations to the failures of the inadequate present system. Politicians, anxious for election, may eschew the experimental as they seek to parrot what is popular, but our country will be best served when science is placed in the public interest and social pathologies addressed logically.

Joseph Drew, Ph.D.
Professor, Department of Humanities and Social Sciences
University of the District of Columbia
Vice Chair, Mayor's Advisory Committee on Drug Abuse
Director, Safe Streets Project
Washington, D.C.

Introduction

In 1994, I ran for attorney general of Iowa. I was one of those third party candidates that few people knew were running until election day, when they saw my name on the ballot. Prior to the last week of the campaign, I received brief coverage in some of Iowa's newspapers, but only two sentences of coverage from the *Des Moines Register*, the only paper that covers most of the state, and no mention whatsoever from the Associated Press, which provides stories to the print media throughout Iowa.

Third party candidates often don't get coverage owing to lack of effort or a lack of familiarity with the issues, but that wasn't true for me. I had bombarded the *Register* and the Associated Press with letters, calls, and press releases about my solutions to crime in Iowa, and I had at least a reasonable familiarity with the issues. Prior to my campaign, I had written several professional articles on crime and drug abuse, two books on stress management, and I had co-founded a prominent journal on drug abuse (*Contemporary Drug Problems*). But whether or not I had something to contribute to the issues didn't matter. In 1994, third party candidates weren't news in Iowa, no matter what they had to say, with one exception.

On one occasion, in the last week of the campaign, I was news. As a result of an eighth circuit court decision, Iowa Public Television (IPTV) was prohibited from discriminating against third party or independent candidates when it sponsored a political debate. As a result, I had to be included when IPTV introduced the Iowa attorney general candidates to its viewing audience, and, I reasoned, the newspapers would have to report my views on the issues. How much coverage I received, of course, depended on what I had to say, and that's why I was elated by the end of the debate. I came out of the studios feeling the same way I used to after scoring twenty points in an upset

Rutgers basketball victory (admittedly twenty-point performances and unexpected victories were rare events in my era at Rutgers, although I did once score fifteen in an upset win over Connecticut).

Certainly, I felt I scored enough good points to force the media to take notice; but to my surprise, the *Des Moines Register*'s article the next day had a box score that recorded none of my points. The *Register* reported extensively on the arguments of Democrat Tom Miller and Republican Joe Gunderson, and included their photos, but merely noted in the last sentence of the article that I had "also appeared on the program."

The Invisible Candidate is Born

The Invisible Candidate

"Appeared on the program?" What is this, Russia in the 1980s, or is giving me only one sentence some kind of Zen endorsement of my candidacy ("less is more")? No, I concluded that the *Register* wasn't that cosmic. It was plain and simple that the paper had intentionally ignored everything I had to say.

In his classic book *The Invisible Man*, Ralph Ellison criticized Americans in the 1950s for treating blacks as if they didn't exist. In the 1994 campaign, I didn't exist as far as the *Register* and most of the Iowa press were concerned. After enduring numerous articles and voter polls referring only to my opponents, and after reading only that I appeared at the debate, the *Invisible Candidate* was born ("funny, sad, and prophetic" said my hometown paper).

It was then that I ended my battle against Miller and Gunderson, and took on the Iowa press. I sent my "Invisible Candidate" release and faceless photo to all of Iowa's principal newspapers. In my release, I said I was in the enviable position of attacking the

Register without the paper fighting back, because to do so they would have to acknowledge my existence, which was contrary to their policy. Interestingly, my criticism of the *Register*, and my faceless photo, gave me more press than anything else during the campaign, at least from the local papers who liked the controversy over the *Register*'s reporting.

When I entered the race for attorney general, I thought I would be able to generate significant support for a new approach to crime. But the refusal of the press to look at ideas from outside the major parties gave me virtually no opportunity to be heard, and about as much chance of winning the election as Ross Perot of being elected president *and* winning the Boston marathon.

In all events, I'm now comfortable being the Invisible Candidate since the principal solutions to the problem of crime are as invisible as I was during the campaign. They're solutions that don't yet have widespread support, and they deal with how to "soften" the hardened criminal and change the criminal mind—changing what is invisible.

The New Rehabilitation Model: The Crime Vaccine

Historically, there have been two models for dealing with criminals, the punitive model favoring harsh punishment, now firmly endorsed by politicians in both the major parties, and the old medical model, recognizing that criminals are in some way ill and in need of education and rehabilitation. Unfortunately, the old medical model doesn't work, because it fails to deal effectively with the inner stress and tension characteristic of the crime prone individual. Trying to educate and rehabilitate prisoners, without first changing them from within, is putting the cart before the horse. This book presents an entirely new model, which succeeds by first dealing with the stressed criminal mind through strategies that have been scientifically proven to be effective.

The strategies described in this book are obviously different from the currently popular crime approaches, but they are also different from more politically correct, yet largely ineffective, stress reduction measures. The strategies presented here are derived from the world's oldest and most comprehensive system of *natural medicine* and human development (see chapter 5). They include Transcendental Meditation, dietary prescriptions, and traditional neuromuscular and neurorespiratory (breathing) exercises. This approach began to be used in rehabilitation when Maharishi Mahesh Yogi encouraged the use of his Transcendental Meditation program in prisons in the 1960s. This program is a primary aspect of what I am describing in this book as the "crime vaccine" because of a number of similarities between this approach and more traditional vaccines.

In disease prevention, perhaps our greatest achievements have occurred as a result of the discovery and use of vaccines. Vaccines work by stimulating natural bodily mechanisms to produce antibodies to fight the invading infection. In this process, nature is the real hero. Only nature could produce the constellation of physiological changes necessary for the body to conquer the infection. This begins to give us an insight into the inherent perfec..on in the functioning of nature. No scientist can create life in the laboratory, yet life is created naturally millions of times each day. No scientist can create food to nourish the body and allow it to grow. And no medicines can bring about the healing that the human body naturally accomplishes once the proper conditions have been established. Similarly, this new approach to crime takes advantage of this perfection in nature's functioning. It simply uses a natural medicine "vaccine" to trigger a myriad of physiological changes, with the dramatic results described in this book.

As is probably apparent, "natural medicine," as I am using the term, is not something taught in Western medical schools. The term "natural medicine" has many different meanings today, and may include vitamin therapy, macrobiotic diets, herbal remedies, luxury spa treatments, and any number of newly conceived relaxation procedures. Most of the programs and treatments that may be referred to as natural medicine, while they may in some sense be "natural," do not have any deep understanding of how to take advantage of the rehabilitative power inherent in nature; and, unlike the strategies presented in this book, they have little or no research to indicate any effectiveness.

My own training in this approach began in 1972 when I was persuaded by friends to learn the Maharishi Transcendental Meditation technique. At that time, like most Westerners, I had never heard of the Vedic literature or the Vedic tradition of knowledge, from which this technique is derived. Moreover, before learning to meditate, I would not have thought that a system of knowledge never even touched on in all my years of formal schooling could have much practical value. However, twenty minutes later, after just my first experience with Transcendental Meditation, my skepticism changed, and I have now been studying and writing about this subject for more than twenty years. Of course, the fact that a "hardened" New York City lawyer could be "softened" by this approach doesn't mean that it works with hardened criminals. This book addresses that subject, as well as how this approach can be used like a vaccine to immunize society against the crime epidemic, and whether other stress reduction strategies can have the same effect.

Interestingly, the alternative approach described in this book has significantly more research to support its use than the currently popular crime reduction strategies, but most people are totally unaware of these programs. A major reason is that politicians have not been attracted to this approach, because the major parties only advocate what is already popular or mainstream. They believe that most of the votes are in the middle, and their political ideology is to steer the safest course to win elections. And, unfortunately, the media gives serious consideration only to the programs touted by mainstream politicians. As a result, most observers see only a long history of failure in our crime strategies, and nothing new on the horizon, yet there is now more reason to be optimistic that we can end the epidemic of crime than at any other time in modern history.

This book is about what I had hoped people would hear during my campaign for attorney general, and what I hope will contribute to the end of the dark ages of criminology.

Chapter One

Running for Attorney General With a New Approach to Crime

Kingsley Brooks, Chairman of the two-year-old Natural Law Party (NLP), wants me to run for attorney general. The party has been considering potential candidates for several weeks in an effort to field a full slate on the Iowa ballot. Kingsley's proposal is not unexpected, and for several weeks I have been dreading that Kingsley will ask me to run, and occasionally feeling insulted that I have not been asked. So now he has asked, and I face my dilemma.

The Glamorous Life of Politics

There was a time in my life when politics looked glamorous, and I would have jumped at the opportunity. That was in the Jack and Jackie years, when the Kennedy clan was rich and highly visible, and I was a poor law student with a part-time job. In 1965, I sat in the audience at Virginia Law School and listened attentively to young Ted Kennedy and John Tunney when they returned to speak at their alma mater. Kennedy and Tunney won the moot court competition while law students at Virginia, and they were polished performers who charmed the audience of student admirers. They were handsome and articulate, with beautiful wives and beautiful suits, and in those days, there were as many stories about the Kennedy suits as the Kennedy women. Bobby and Ted Kennedy both studied law at the University of Virginia and were well known in Charlottesville for their shopping excursions, and for the limousine that picked them up for exotic weekends that most law students could only dream about. Since this was my idea of politicians at the

1

time, after law school, in search of those million dollar suits and
exotic weekends, I signed up for the glamorous life of politics by
accompanying my cousin Fred to one or two Democratic party
meetings on New York City's Upper West Side.

About those meetings, I can't remember much, other than that I
already had the best suits at the party headquarters thanks to the
extravagant salary a Park Avenue law firm was paying me. Also,
there was no talk of exotic weekends by the fairly ragged party
faithful who, like me, were stuffing envelopes (I should have real-
ized that the Republicans across town had the *really* nice suits and
exotic weekends). So for the next twenty or so years, except for
considering myself first a Democrat (as they say, if you weren't a
liberal in the 60s, you didn't have a heart), then a Republican (if
you weren't a conservative in the 80s, you didn't have a brain), and
voting intermittently, I did not partake of politics. And in my case,
not partaking really means not partaking. I didn't read about or discuss politics at all, except to the extent that a young associate in a
large New York law firm has to listen (and sometimes nod "know-
ingly") as the partners made statements I figured had something to
do with politics.

I've decided that this is why politics is so fascinating to me at
this time. If I had known anything about it before, I wouldn't be so
shocked now by the baseness and small-mindedness of it all.

No "Just an Ordinary Citizen" Campaign

But I wasn't fascinated with politics when Kingsley asked me to
run in May of 1994. Becoming a candidate for a new party was a
big step, especially for a party known for its bold claims to have
scientifically proven solutions to the nation's problems. There
would be no running on any "I'm just an ordinary citizen" platform.
So before agreeing to run, I decided, for one, that I had better feel
comfortable endorsing the principal programs advocated by the
Natural Law Party to prevent crime and rehabilitate criminals. Most
of the programs were not an issue. I had written and lectured extensively about them. But I supposed that the candidates in this cam-

paign would be expected to tout new research that purportedly showed significantly reduced crime in the society at large when even a small percentage of the population practiced what is known as the "TM-Sidhi" program.

Fine. But it is one thing for the research to show it, according to the scientists who could explain something called *time series analysis*, the researchers' analytical tool. It is quite another thing, however, for me to promote it, someone who didn't know times series analysis from an analysis of the clock on the wall. Moreover, I would have to describe this research in front of a live audience potentially holding live tomatoes. So I asked Kingsley for the preliminary research on the results of the most recent demonstration project in Washington, D.C. I planned to postpone my decision until I could at least review the new research (chapter 12) and ask others about it. And, of course, I had to tell my wife.

Honey, We're Moving to Pennsylvania Avenue

At least in my house it was news, big news, that I had been asked to run. My wife Susan and I both felt it was an honor to be asked to represent the Natural Law Party, but she agreed with me that it was smart to review the Washington research before deciding. Kirsi, my seven-year-old, was even more pleased. She knew exactly what this meant in terms of a change for the family—we were moving to the White House. To Kirsi, running for office meant being elected, and since the only politician she knew of was Bill Clinton, she logically deduced that we would be moving to Pennsylvania Avenue. She had seen pictures of the White House many times, and for a few days moving to the White House dominated Kirsi's little brain. My twelve-year-old daughter Emily didn't have much of a reaction, except that she liked the prospect of learning about politics more or less firsthand. Of course, it was clear to Emily and Susan that if I actually won, only one of us (*c'est moi*) would be leaving our home in Fairfield, Iowa, and commuting or moving to Des Moines, 120 miles away.

A Non-Linear Decision to Run for Attorney General

It took about ten days for Kingsley to get me the Washington research, and for me to make my decision. That's right, they happened simultaneously. While I would like it to sound as if I made a scientific decision about running ("based it on a time series analysis"), my decision was made even before reviewing the research, and had nothing to do with new suits or exotic weekends. In the ten days or so after Kingsley asked me to run, I experienced a growing realization that I would accept the offer. This one particular research study really didn't matter very much. I knew enough about the NLP-endorsed crime programs, and the research on them, to know that they worked, and I knew enough about the Republican and Democratic proposals to know that they didn't work. And twenty years from now, I didn't want to look back at this time and think that I had missed an opportunity to contribute to a party I deeply believed in. Those were, I like to think, the dominant reasons I decided to run. However, I also had less laudable reasons. The NLP was the party of choice for 90% of my clients, and my hometown was the site of the NLP national headquarters. I knew I would feel very uncomfortable explaining to my friends and clients that I was simply too busy to run (my clients, for example, could make me a lot less busy).

In all events, for the historical record, at the time I made my decision to run, I probably knew less about the attorney general's office than any candidate who had previously sought the position. I didn't know the salary, for example, or the number of lawyers in the attorney general's office, or what the job entailed, apart from handling criminal and consumer fraud cases. I couldn't even say with certainty whether the position was a two-year or four-year office, although I correctly guessed it was four. I would eventually learn these things, but in my defense, they were not of great importance to a candidate who was unlikely to be elected, and who at the time actually preferred that he not be elected. I enjoyed the private practice of law, and I initially entered the race to bring attention to the Natural Law Party ideas, not to win.

So in mid-May of 1994, I accepted Kingsley's offer, and only a few weeks later, I was at the local Best Western Hotel where I gave my first speech on the new model for dealing with criminal behavior.

The New Rehabilitative Approach to Crime

I had been given ten minutes to speak, to warm the NLP hearts, and since this was also a fundraiser, to en*lighten* their wallets. In my talk I discussed the different theories about the causes of crime, and distinguished the NLP's solutions from those of the major parties. I made the point that in contrast to the "get tough" approach, I intended to advocate a "get soft" approach (that is as politically unpopular as it gets). My approach was to soften the hardened criminal, to change his heart and mind, and make him a better person, an approach that would sound hopelessly idealistic to a different audience. But this was not a different audience, and they knew from their own experience that this new natural medicine "vaccine" could change *anyone* from within, and that the change could be dramatic. As a result, the talk was a success, but being a political novice, I never got around to soliciting contributions, and I didn't raise any funds. Nevertheless, I was strangely optimistic about my campaign, especially in my ignorance of what it takes to win an election. Tom Miller and Joe Gunderson, the major party candidates, had been working on their campaigns for perhaps a year. They're both highly intelligent, and as importantly, they had the major party networks and PAC contributions. But if I didn't have their funds or political connections, I did have new theories about the causes of crime and some new solutions.

Chapter Two

The New Crime Model: Discovering the Inner Cause of Crime

Unlike inflation and interest rates (which only Alan Greenspan understands), everyone has a theory of what causes crime. If you are a criminologist, you're almost required to have a theory. One professor I talked to at a meeting of the Academy of Criminal Justice Sciences told me he counted 252 psychological theories of the causes of crime, and this tabulation ignored the many sociological and biological theories.

How Crime Theory Begins

Theory always begins with an observation of facts, and then attempts to fit the facts into a useful pattern. Among the facts that people point to as potential causes of crime are neglectful parents, violence in the home, violence in the media, racism, urban life, overcrowding, drugs, alcohol, a lack of economic opportunities, disorganized neighborhoods, mental disorders, peer pressures, the decline of religion, and the failure of the educational system. Most of these are called the "risk factors" for crime, and the experts tell us that the more risk factors we are exposed to, the more at risk we are of becoming criminals. If all these contribute to crime, and they probably do, does this multiple factor theory end our search for the cause? Or is there a simpler way of understanding the problem?

How Do We Know if a Theory is Right?

The problem with this multi-factor theory is that, while superficially accurate, the theory doesn't get us anywhere. It is kind of like saying that living in today's world causes crime. The theory isn't simple or general enough to tell us how best to prevent crime or how to rehabilitate criminals. Also, such a theory fails to explain the exceptions. Why is it that so many kids from inner-city environments, exposed to lots of violence, don't commit crimes? And why do a significant number of surburban kids commit crimes, despite going to the best schools and having all the opportunities of modern society?

The most successful theory will be one that is the simplest and most general, needs the fewest exceptions (if any), and, of course, identifies the root cause of crime. Only with such a theory, can you do something intelligent to reduce crime.

A Brief History of the World (as it Relates to Crime Theories)

Religions have had crime theories for centuries. And modern criminologists could take a humorous angle on some of them. One friend told me that Taoists, for example, believe that "crime happens"; Buddhists, that crime happens, but it isn't really crime (the world is an illusion); and Hindus, that crime happens because it happened before (karma and reincarnation). My favorite in this category, though, could have come from my Uncle Howard from Brooklyn, who I suspect would have said that "crime happens, but does it have to happen to me?"

The early Hebrew and Christian theories gave us an explanation of crime that was largely supernatural. People were killed, for example, because God was punishing them for their sins, and miraculous signs were looked to in order to determine guilt or innocence (a heavy burden of proof). Much crime was alleged to be based on witchcraft or other demonic factors. However, despite the simplicity of these approaches, people had a hard time proving who was a witch, and the existence of demons, and the modern world has looked elsewhere for its explanations of crime.

Classical Theories of Crime

The roots of our present theories of why people commit crimes began in the mid-to-late 1700s, most particularly with the writings of Cesare Baccaria, who described the motivation for committing crime as well as methods for its control. His theories about crime derived from the earlier works of Thomas Hobbes and other philosophers, who said that pain and pleasure dictated man's actions, and that all human conduct was based on the self-interested pursuit of pleasure or the avoidance of pain.[1] This led to theories stating that human behavior is guided by choice, and that people choose between committing a crime and not committing one based on a risk/reward analysis. The rewards can be money, sexual gratification, vengeance, or the recognition of peers. The risks involve the various religious, moral or penal sanctions for violating society's rules.[2] This *classical* theory is sometimes called *hedonistic* or *utilitarian* theory, and is based on a simple view of human nature. At its core is a conception of man as a creature who can be moral or immoral, and who follows or does not follow society's rules, depending on the rewards and the risks involved. This classical school and the neo-classical school that followed in the late 1700s is still the basis of modern criminology.

Unfortunately, too many crimes are unexplained by the pleasure/pain or risk/reward analysis of classical theory. A typical homicide, for example, is said to result from people who know each other arguing over some relatively minor matter that they have argued about frequently in the past.[3] In the past the argument may have led to physical violence, but this time the situation escalates into a homicide. The notion that the homicide would produce so much pleasure that it outweighs the risk misses the essential nature of the crime, which is impulsive and self-centered, and grows out of a reaction to a stressful situation. Classical theory does not adequately explain the irrational, impulsive crimes that are said to be so common today. It is also based on a misconception of human nature. Our everyday experience is that many people do not commit crimes irrespective of how great the reward may be and how little the risk.

In all events, classical theory (which still guides the U.S. criminal justice system) has been around for centuries, but it leaves us with little more in the way of a solution than attempting to counterbalance the rewards of crime with increasingly heavy penalties. And, if numerous crime experts are correct, many criminals are blind to penalties, because they never expect to get caught. A young man imprisoned at the Ventura School for Delinquents, one of seventeen juvenile prisons in California, said:

> You never think you're gonna get caught. I didn't get caught for anything. I was doing little crimes, I never got caught. And then it just progressed . . . shoplifting, and then maybe stealing a bike, then a car. You know going on a joyride, robbing somebody. And I never got caught . . . until this, the one that I'm locked up for now, and that's murder.[4]

Even if criminals can conceive of getting caught, they often can't discount the present gratification expected from the crime by the potential punishment sometime in the future. This is the nature of crime. The reward is now and the punishment, if it comes at all, is later. Unfortunately, impulsive people aren't deterred by what can happen in the future, and the inability of classical theory to explain the many exceptions to the risk/reward analysis of crime has led to an increasing number of theories in the quest for a deeper explanation.

The Positive School of Crime

One hundred years after the birth of classical theory, Cesare Lombroso (1838-1909), a physician born in Venice, founded what is now referred to as the *Positive School of Crime*. The Positive School developed as the scientific method spread through Europe, and it attempted to apply science to human behavior.[5] The Positivists were themselves divided into those who favored biological theories and those who favored psychological theories of the cause of crime. Lombroso's original theories were biological, but his early crude attempts to identify criminals based on the shape of their skulls or the length of their arms (criminals were thought to be a savage relic of the past) didn't work. Lombroso's students, however, gave Positivism an expanded basis, and modern day Positivism now includes theories that use mostly psychological factors to explain personality, aggression, and deviance.

The earliest of the psychological views coincided with the religious views—criminals were possessed by evil spirits. Later theories suggested that deviants were mentally deranged, usually by reason of an inferior genetic makeup, and that crime was an outlet for their abnormal tendencies. When too much crime was left unexplained by an insanity theory and the early theories of defective intelligence, a psychologist named Gabriel Tarde came up with one of the forerunners of modern crime theory. He said that people learn from one another through a process of imitation, and that activity or behavior seen in others either reinforces or discourages previous habits.[6] Tarde's ideas are expressed today in the belief that family interactions and observed behavior (such as television violence) influence crime, and his views can be seen underlying many of the behavioral theories.

Behavioral Approaches to Crime

Psychology has its different branches, one being the behavioral psychologists who view crimes as learned responses that aren't necessarily abnormal responses. For example, one group within the behaviorists, the *social learning theorists*, argue that "people are not necessarily born with a tendency to act violently, but [as Tarde suggested] they learn to be aggressive through their life experiences."[7] According to a number of experts, these learning theories are probably the most popular crime theories today because research shows that associating with criminal friends has a strong correlation with delinquency. Others question whether the association of criminals is just "birds of a feather flocking together," motivated by an underlying factor.

Cognitive Approaches to Crime

Then there are the *cognitive psychologists*, who explain criminal behavior as resulting from faulty perceptions and a faulty analysis of situations. According to this theory, when people make decisions they engage in a sequence of thought processes, relying on mental "scripts" learned in childhood that tell them how to interpret events. Decisions that lead to criminal conduct are based on thought processes that use information incorrectly. Violence, it is said, becomes a continuing behavior because "the scripts that emphasize aggressive responses are repeatedly rehearsed as the child matures."[8] Also, as a result of a faulty analysis ("cognitive lapses"), others seem more aggressive than they actually are, and this theory says that criminals often react in a volatile manner to slight provocations.

And All Crime Theories are Supported by Research

Virtually all the psychological theories have some research to support their viewpoints. Studies show, for example, that violence is impacted by both early childhood difficulties as well as the mass media. One researcher found that the homicide rate increased significantly after a heavyweight championship prize fight. Another showed that at least forty-three deaths had been linked to the movie *The Deer Hunter*, in which the main character kills himself playing Russian roulette. Studies also show that violence in the home tends to result in anti-social behavior among youths. And simple common sense tells us that young people imitate those with a higher status in life; as a result, repeatedly observing violence in elders would also be a causative factor. Finally, it should also be obvious that disorderly thinking (cognitive flaws) can cause crime and, of course, substantial research shows that kids with delinquent friends are more likely to be delinquent (the learning theories).

While all the psychological theories have some research to support them, they're incomplete because they miss the underlying thread that can tie together apparent inconsistencies. For example, some crime is caused by a *logical* risk/reward analysis, but isn't that inconsistent with the cognitive view that a faulty or *illogical* analysis causes crime? And don't both the cognitive and the risk/reward approaches consider crime to be based on a reasoned approach (albeit flawed reasoning in the case of the cognitive approach), which is inconsistent with the view that impulsive behavior causes crime?

The picture drawn by crime theorists only becomes more complex once we add the sociological theories.

Sociological Theories of Crime

The *Sociological School* developed from the theories of sociologists who, in the modern era, have had an even greater influence on criminology than psychologists. Interestingly, sociologists often define crime as a normal social event. Crime is seen as part of human nature because it has existed in every age, and crime is "normal" to at least some sociologists because it is impossible for them to imagine a society without it. Sociologists emphasize interpersonal relationships as the source of crime. They believe that understanding the interactions between individuals in our primary social institutions (families, peers, schools, and jobs) will allow us to understand crime.

Sociological theories include *economic theories* that crime is caused by the unequal distribution of wealth and power. Economic disenfranchisement leaves those of lower economic status, including many minorities, with inadequate housing and health care, high unemployment, and few opportunities for success, all of which, taken together, can lead to criminal activity. And certainly there is research to support this view.

Social disorganization theory is another sociological theory, which links crime rates to disorderly neighborhood characteristics. These theorists point out that neighborhoods with a heavy transient population are often unable to provide their residents with essential education, health care, and proper housing, and are found to be high in crime. Residents in these neighborhoods are uninterested in community matters, and the sources of control within the community are said to be disorganized. Many studies have linked life in depressed or transient areas to crime, giving support to these theories. Disorganized neighborhoods have gangs, graffiti, noise, congestion, and, of course, crime.

Another sociological theory is *cultural deviance theory*, which holds that criminals have learned their values from deviant persons who reinforced the notion that crime is worthwhile. For example, in a gang culture, aggression and even criminal behavior are reinforced and result in peer approval. Again, the advocates of this theory have research to help them make their case.

Many Theories: Right, Wrong, or Incomplete?

Is crime caused by psychological factors, or is it caused by a lack of economic opportunities, social disorganization, or association with deviant persons? And if these are all causes, aren't they inconsistent with one another, or are we just back to a multi-factor theory that essentially says the complexities of life cause crime? And again how do we explain poor people, from bad neighborhoods, with bad friends, who grow up to be good citizens?

A Gardener's Theory of Crime

As Chauncey Gardiner (the Peter Sellers character in the movie *Being There*) might have explained, if the soil that sustains a plant lacks water or nutrients, some of the leaves will turn brown, while others initially remain green. Evaluating the plant's health from the level of the leaves can be very confusing, because we get inconsistent information. However, if we could examine the "invisible" root, we would see that it is diseased, even though some of the leaves haven't yet been affected because of the nutrients remaining in those particular limbs.

Inconsistencies among crime theories arise due to not seeing the root cause of crime. When we look at outer activity (seeing violence in the home, or on TV), or when we look at the environment (for example, whether the community is disorganized), and we try to determine whether that activity or environment causes criminal activity, we are going to get inconsistent information. An experience "causes" subsequent activity, only because the initial situation has an impact on the deeper, invisible levels of human life—on the functioning of the brain and the nervous system, which are at the basis of our thinking and behavior. In the same way, destroying one branch of a tree affects other branches only because its destruction affects the underlying "nervous system" of the tree. There is an inner source of the problem, at the level of the "root," or nervous system.

Biological Theories: Looking for the Root Cause of Crime

Biologists are one group looking at the inner causes of behavior. Unfortunately, the biologists haven't been very well appreciated by the psychologists and sociologists, although biological factors, at least theoretically, are now gaining greater respect. Biologists like Cesare Lombroso originally gave undue attention to craniology and other crude physical differences in criminals, and they were ridiculed for it. Later, however, as their ability to distinguish more subtle physical causes emerged, an increasing number of researchers began to identify deeper biological factors contributing to crime.

In many studies researchers have now found rather remarkable correlations of low serotonin (a brain chemical) with increased violence. Other researchers have said that up to 25% to 50% of violent individuals may have abnormalities in brain functioning, as reflected in abnormal EEG (electroencephalographic) activity, while still others have observed evidence of genetic factors in criminal behavior.[9] Many of these researchers come from the physical sciences (although a growing number of psychologists and sociologists are now investigating the biological factors), and occasionally the biological research is seriously evaluated by criminologists. But more often than not biological factors are still ignored, despite persuasive evidence that these factors influence criminal behavior.

One reason biological influences are ignored is the tension these theories create with our traditional notions of free will and criminal responsibility. Our legal system assumes that criminal acts are voluntary acts to be punished, absent a severe mental disease or defect interfering with the ability of the criminal to know right from wrong. If biological factors influence criminal decisions, many people fear that individuals may not be held fully responsible for their criminal acts.

Another difficulty with the biological approaches is that the studies are perceived by most criminologists as pure research rather than applied research. In other words, even if a biological factor predisposes to crime, it's irrelevant because the traditional thinking is that you can't change biological factors, except perhaps through pharmacology, which has its own problems and will be offensive to many. Minority groups especially react against any effort to locate genetic differences that may predispose to crime.

Moreover, the biological studies are highly technical and depend on familiarity with the physical sciences. The research is often simply unfathomable to psychologists and sociologists, and can only be evaluated by persons outside the traditional criminological area. When a sociologist, for example, learns that cortisol hypersecretion may predispose to crime, he's more likely to look at other factors because he will have great difficulty explaining the importance of how excess cortisol "breaks down the amino acids which are precursors for the monoamines," and how only "one of these enzymes, tryptophan pyrrolase, breaks down the serotonin precursor, L-tryptophan," as one chemist described it.[10]

In all events, if there are important biological factors predisposing to crime, are they inconsistent with the psychological and sociological theories? What's the root cause of crime?

The Root Cause of Crime

Of the existing crime theories, one that is growing in popularity comes closest, I believe, to being a general explanation of crime. It was conceived by Professor Robert Agnew from Emory University and is known as *general strain theory*. The original strain theory has been around for many years, and in its earlier form held the view that crime resulted from the frustration and anger people experienced over their inability to achieve success in life, either in financial or social matters. Agnew broadened the theory because the original theory neglected to consider that there were many other forms of strain, like the strain or tension of urban life, or the strain from the loss of a parent, or the strain of child abuse, or other such life events. Agnew expanded strain theory into his *general strain theory*, and his work is starting to be recognized as a major contribution to criminology. It also starts to provide a basis for understanding what should be the most successful crime interventions. Professor Agnew's theory is simple, and it brings together many of the existing psychological and sociological theories, although based on what I have read, it may not address biological factors.

Professor Agnew's theory eliminates many of the inconsistencies in the various sociological and psychological theories by pointing out that economic inequalities, disorganized neighborhoods, violence in the home, and violence on television all cause crime because of the strain and negativity they produce. This can be better understood, and virtually all the theories can be tied together, if we focus not just on the social interactions that cause strain, as Professor Agnew does, but on *stress,* which is the internal physiological effect of strain on the individual. If we focus on the internal stress and the feelings of "disease" that accompany it, this new or modified theory says, for example, that if cognitive defects (cognitive theory) cause crime, the defective thinking is itself the result of stress in the nervous system; and that young people who imitate violence in their elders (social learning theory), or who learn their values from deviant persons (cultural deviance theory), or who live in disorganized neighborhoods (social disorganization theory), all act violently or choose to associate with deviants as a result of the internal stress they developed growing up in an unhealthy environment. Even the biological theories are rooted in an understanding of stress. EEG abnormalities and low serotonin, inappropriate cortisol responses, and autonomic nervous system instability are all factors that predispose to crime (see chapter 5), and it has to be more than coincidence that they are all byproducts of stress in the nervous system.

Viewed from this inner perspective (and based on the understandings I have gained from studying Maharishi's teachings), general strain theory becomes what I would call *general stress theory*.

This theory focuses on the causal element deep within the individual, at the level of the root. Often when people talk about the causes of crime, they are unclear about what they mean by a "cause." There can be many factors, for example, that have some causal influence, but the necessary condition for crime to occur (lawyers may like to think of it as the *proximate* cause), is stress in the brain and nervous system, and the deficiencies this physiological stress produces in mental and emotional functioning. This inner dimension of the individual dictates how he perceives the world and how he reacts to stressful circumstances, and is the critical factor that determines the emergence of either criminal or law-abiding behavior. The value of this shift in focus is the practical one of more successfully being able to reduce crime, because we have learned so much in the past twenty years about how to eliminate stress.

Chapter Three

General Stress Theory: Dealing with Criminals and Carriers of "Dis-ease"

General stress theory looks at Professor Agnew's general strain theory from a new *psychophysiological* perspective that takes into account the interdependence of the mind and body. General stress theory says that all the risk factors for crime (e.g., abusive parents, a lack of economic opportunities, overcrowding, poor housing) are influences that are likely to produce stress in the individual. These outside influences, using the language of physiologists, are termed "stressors" and the disorder that they produce in the body is the "stress." Because the mind and body are interdependent, these outside stressors also produce mental stress, which is found to an extensive degree in the stressed criminal mind. The mind and body are like two sides of a coin that are inexorably bound together, jointly affected by the environment. That is why mental and physical stress can result not only from purely physical means—what we eat, how rested we are, whether we exercise during the day, and even what music (sound waves) bombards our auditory senses—but also from mental or emotional circumstances. As Dr. Kenneth Walton, a biochemist at Maharishi University of Management in Fairfield, Iowa, points out, "everyday experiences such as frustration, anger, fear, humiliation . . . . and even apparently neutral or positive experiences, such as a change of residence, marriage, promotion, or outstanding personal achievements, cause the stress response . . . ."[1]

What is the Stress Response of the Body?

The concept of stress was first identified as a specific syndrome in 1935 by the noted physician Hans Selye, a professor at the University of Montreal. Researchers everywhere now devote more than 1,000 articles per year to a discussion of stress and its effects. The technical term Dr. Selye used for stress was the *general adaptation syndrome,* which he described as often developing in three stages: the alarm reaction, the stage of resistance, and the stage of exhaustion. In the initial alarm reaction, sometimes called the *fight or flight* reaction, the body reacts to meet the stressor. Adrenaline is produced, hormones are released from the pituitary gland, and the individual adapts to the situation. During the second phase, Selye noted that some of the body's reactions persist until the stressful situation has abated. The expenditure of energy and resources may then lead to the third phase, exhaustion.[2] As a result of frequent stressful experiences, individuals may persist in the third stage as stress becomes a chronic condition that gradually destroys one's well-being.

Professor Agnew's general strain theory incorporates all these concepts and recognizes that the emotions produced by the different "strains" in life can be "a predisposing factor in delinquency when it is chronic and repetitive and creates a hostile, suspicious, and aggressive attitude."[3] As a sociologist, Agnew looks at the more observable effects of stress or strain (hostility and aggression), whereas Drs. Walton, Selye, and other researchers in the physical sciences look at the internal physiological and biochemical effects.

Since Dr. Selye's early work, the stress response has been studied extensively. Today, it is more accurate to say that a whole constellation of physiological changes take place in the body, as a result of stressful circumstances (not just the alarm or fight-or-flight reaction). Different people respond to stressors differently. For some it leads to ulcers, for others anxiety and tension, for still others the inability to sleep, or irritability over minor events. The underlying physiological changes may also be somewhat different—decreased serotonin, decreased autonomic stability, increased cortisol, irregular brain functioning, or all of the above. But in every case there is a fundamental abnormality in the functioning of the basic root system (the brain and the nervous system), and both the mind and body are affected.

Does Everyone Who is Stressed Commit Crimes?

If this is to be a general theory to explain all crime, one issue is why everyone who is stressed doesn't commit crimes. But that actually depends on how you define a "crime." If crime is only behavior that the law makes punishable by incarceration or a fine, then everybody who has a stressed inner state doesn't commit crimes. However, if crime is more broadly defined to include violations of the social order like "flying off the handle" at your kids or your wife, or drinking to excess, engaging in insulting behavior, conspiring to get even with the boss, or infidelity, then it is likely that everyone with stress gets included. As Professor Agnew suggests, the level of strain (stress) may determine the level of antisocial behavior.

In addition, some people who are stressed turn their anger or anxiety inward, while others unleash their anger in all directions. Those in the first group suffer from headaches, insomnia, indigestion, heart disease, alcoholism, anxiety states, and other stress-related disorders, but may avoid activities that the law labels as a "crime," or at least their crimes are minor. Others externalize this stress and commit crimes, and of course many people fall into both categories (they have both stress-related health disorders and they commit crimes). General stress theory says that the underlying mechanism is the same, only the expression is different.

From the perspective of general stress theory, the reason some people don't commit crimes, despite being exposed to many risk factors, is that their nervous systems are healthier and more resilient than others, and thus they have more stable minds and emotions. This allows them to lead relatively productive and law-abiding lives, despite their exposure to potentially stressful situations. Stressors may cause stress and strain for some, but others are unaffected, in the same way that some trees have stronger root systems than others, which allow them to survive the strain of insufficient water or sunlight. This should not be surprising since crime experts acknowledge that "protective factors" such as an easygoing disposition (caused by a healthier or more resilient nervous system) help many high-risk youth resist succumbing to the criminal lifestyle.[4] On the other hand, lower-risk youth may engage in criminal behavior because of their internal disposition, and the absence of a more stable and flexible inner state.

The functioning of the nervous system (and the parallel functioning of the mind and emotions) can be influenced by hereditary factors, which is why chromosomal or genetic conditions can predispose a person to crime or to law-abiding behavior; or by environmental or nurturing factors, such as whether one has supportive parents, a good neighborhood, and proper rest, exercise, and nutrition. Psychologists and behavioral scientists often spend inordinate amounts of time trying to determine why one person subjected to the risk factors commits a crime, while another resists gang membership and graduates from high school or college with honors. It is simply a function of the different factors (nature and nurture) and how they contribute to the individual's ability to resist the disordering effects of stress.

A Theory With Its Roots in the *Milieu Intérieur*

If the nineteenth century French physiologist Claude Bernard (a founder of experimental medicine) had been a criminologist, I suspect he would support general stress theory. Dr. Bernard said that environmental challenges, and even germs, only cause disorder or disease when the body's interior balancing mechanisms cannot cope with the outside influence. Consistent with Dr. Bernard's findings, general stress theory says that the seeds of crime, like germs, are everywhere, but they only become crime based on this *milieu intérieur* of the body. Crime is a violation of the social order, but it results from an interior state that is in disorder, based on the stresses or strains in the offender's life. If crime has existed in virtually every age, stress has existed in virtually every age, although the members of some societies have had very little stress (and thus produced very little crime). Following this line of thinking, however, crime is not "normal," because it is caused by stress which, by definition, is an abnormality in physical functioning. Based on modern medical knowledge, Dr. Bernard would probably also tell us that it will be more effective to inoculate the individual against all the germs than to try to prevent the germs from ever reaching him. This is the practical value of this theory. It allows us to focus on those strategies that strengthen the *milieu intérieur,* strategies that change the deepest levels of the physiology, with corresponding changes in our mental and emotional states.

For the purpose of constructing a crime strategy, there is no reason why we shouldn't consider stressful situations to be like germs. As with germs, if the interior state cannot effectively resist the stressors, it creates the conditions for disorder or "dis-ease" in the physiology. Moreover, stress is often transmitted by social interactions, just as "carriers" transmit germs. And in order to end an epidemic, whether of disease or crime, we can't focus only on those who are sick or have already committed crimes; we need to inoculate carriers and others in the general population.

The Carrier Concept in Crime

There is a shorter answer to the earlier question of whether everyone with a stressed inner state commits a crime: yes! Everyone who is stressed *at least indirectly* commits crimes and contributes to the crime epidemic. This can be understood by reference to the carrier concept in epidemics. Beginning in the late 1800s physicians studying epidemics showed that in the spread of disease, virulent bacteria were carried by individuals who displayed no symptoms, or barely recognizable ones. For example, with cholera and typhoid fever, the German physician Robert Koch discovered that simply looking for typhoid cases was not enough, and that only a bacteriological investigation could identify those who had been exposed to the infectious disease and could transmit it to others. When eight cases of typhoid fever broke out in a German village, Koch undertook a systematic examination of family members and others who had contact with the eight and found seventy-two persons who were infected. The carriers were then treated, and the epidemic in the village was stopped.

The carrier concept in disease recognizes that there are many times more the number of carriers (who are infected with the virulent microbe; but don't have the disease), as those who contract the disease and become medical cases. The number of carriers who don't have the disease is said to vary greatly for different diseases. For example, from 20% to 50% of the population are estimated to be carriers of influenza, and the number of carriers of meningitis is said to be "ten to thirty times as numerous as the number of cases."[5]

In crime, as with disease, many people who don't commit crimes are carriers. They are stressed and carry around a stressful influence in society, infecting others with their negativity and dis-ease, even though we may consider many of them to be normally functioning individuals. Carriers include those who abuse drugs and alcohol, parents who abuse their children, employers who intimidate their employees, and even politicians who conduct intensely negative campaigns. In general, carriers are those who, by virtue of the stress and strain in their own lives, make life unpleasant for those with whom they come in contact. But the carrier concept extends even beyond spreading stress through social interactions.

Everyone radiates an influence in society that is either stressful or coherent, and the society has a *collective consciousness* and *collective stress* level that is based on the functioning of its individual members. This concept of a collective consciousness, and of stress in collective consciousness, was introduced about twenty years ago by Maharishi Mahesh Yogi, the founder of the Transcendental Meditation program. It arises from an understanding of consciousness as the basis of all thinking and behavior (see chapter 5). Maharishi explains that "just as the consciousness of an individual determines the quality of his thought and behavior, so also there exists another type of consciousness for a society as a whole: a collective consciousness," which he said was a "direct and sensitive reflection" of the level of consciousness of the individual members.[6] In this explanation, as individuals we influence the collective consciousness (causing it to be more or less stressful) and are also influenced by it. And owing to what I call the carrier concept in crime, if the collective stress level is high, it creates an atmosphere that can lead to those most at risk committing crimes, just as being surrounded by carriers of germs causes an increase in disease among those who are most at risk.

By reference to the physical principle of a *critical mass* (the point at which an accumulation becomes explosive), this concept predicts that if the collective stress level in the community gets too high, it also causes an explosion, which may manifest as gang warfare or other violent eruptions, in the same way that the accumulation of plutonium can detonate a nuclear weapon due to the mass action principle. Anyone who has spent time in prisons has experienced that collective stress and collective consciousness are not just abstract concepts. At times the primary objective of the prison staff is just "to keep a lid on" the tension level, and prevent the rioting that would otherwise erupt. And, unfortunately, even if violent outbreaks are prevented, if the stress in prisons isn't eliminated, the atmosphere undermines any rehabilitation efforts.

In crime prevention, the carrier concept means that if we are serious about eliminating crime as a major problem, we have to "inoculate" the carriers of stress as well as those who are criminals, thereby reducing or eliminating the high stress levels, not only in prisons, but in many segments of society. The preventive and rehabilitative strategies in this book, therefore, are really for everyone, not merely those who are incarcerated or who have drug or alcohol problems. The carrier concept also means that we can't just blame our youth (see chapter 4), or even criminals, for causing crimes. Each of us with stress bears some responsibility for contributing to societal stress, which creates a climate in which those who are most susceptible are pushed in the wrong direction. As the late Professor Charles Edward-Winslow of the Yale School of Medicine said in his important treatise on epidemics: "any scheme of prevention which fails to take into account carriers and missed cases is doomed to partial and perhaps complete failure."[7]

Is General Stress Theory Too Simple?

The situation now in criminology is much the same as in other sciences before a real breakthrough occurs. As quantum theory resolved many of the complications in physics, and as Copernicus' theories resolved many of the difficulties in astronomy, a simple theory of crime can pave the way for a new era of success in dealing with the problem. While many people attached to their own theories may say this theory is too simple (they will undoubtedly call it "simplistic" to give it a derogatory spin), simplicity is a characteristic of most important changes in science.

Before Copernican astronomy, the Ptolemaic theory made the earth the fixed center of the universe, around which all other heavenly bodies revolved. The earth wasn't thought to move because of the invisibility factor—people didn't see it moving. Similarly, stress in the nervous system isn't seen as the cause of crime because of the invisibility factor.

In Copernicus' time, if you examined the movement of the stars and assumed that the earth didn't move, you wound up with a very complicated theory about how the stars moved in the heavens, which postulated that some stars wandered about aimlessly. Copernicus' faith in an inherent *simplicity and order* throughout the universe led him to reject the notion that planets executed reverse maneuvers, grew in size and wandered about. He constructed a simple theory that placed the sun at the center of the solar system, with the earth and other planets moving around the sun. Once he advanced his theory, people started to look at the observable data (the movement of the planets and stars) in a new way, and others came forward claiming that the new theory was correct.

In this same way, a great deal of observable data (including the results of scientific research) substantiates this theory of crime. This data shows the connection between stress and crime in society (chapter 4), and most importantly that a vaccination against stress reduces or eliminates crime (chapters 5 through 7).

Chapter Four

The Connection Between Stress and Crime: Parallel Epidemics

Dr. Deborah Prothrow-Stith, a pediatrician at the Harvard School of Public Health, is attempting to develop a successful violence prevention program. In an interview with Bill Moyers for a TV special on the subject, she said:

> We are a country that—that's infatuated with violence. We really like violence a lot. Some of us are in love with violence or addicted to it. We celebrate it. We're entertained by it. We applaud it. We run to read about it, to see it. We encourage our children sometimes to fight. We don't want a wimp for a child.[1]

Why is violence so much a part of our lives? Life involves a series of stresses and strains to the nervous system that sow the seeds for future criminal outbursts. Psychiatrist Harold Bloomfield says stress blocks a person's ability to enjoy quiet pleasures. Instead, it results in a quest for excitement, especially for the young. Dr. Bloomfield characterizes society as having a "raised mental temperature" that makes it difficult to enjoy the ordinary events of daily life, or even mildly exciting experiences. Bloomfield says that "when a person's mental temperature gets high enough, he becomes almost exclusively dependent on strong excitements as his primary source of pleasure."[2] As a result, youths enjoy the excitement of fighting. Violent movies and television shows simply give people what they want, and in a real sense what they need, to experience satisfaction. An inmate at the Ventura School in California stated:

> We used to love violence, you know. I did myself. I
> loved it. Before, when I saw a fight, I didn't know
> who was fighting, I would try to jump in there.
> Somehow, I would end up in that fight.[3]

Dr. David Sands, a pediatrician who has studied the way stress
affects young people, says the inability of youths to cope with the
stressful events of life causes many to be chronically angry and to
lash out with the slightest provocation. This is reflected in the statement of another inmate at the Ventura School who was jailed for
murder. He explained what caused him to be sent to prison:

> I was in a real bad mood that day. And someone
> was in the wrong place at the wrong time. It could
> have been anyone at the time. Someone just said
> something to me—and I have no idea what the per-
> son said. I just unleashed every—all the anger I had
> inside me. I did it with a piece of wood . . . . I was
> just in a bad mood. It, it, it, was years of violence,
> years of being violent, just built up . . . . It started
> when I was a little kid, when my parents got
> divorced . . . . I was eleven. I thought that my whole
> world had gone to hell. Before my parents got
> divorced, I thought we had the perfect family, you
> know, I had everything I wanted, and I was real
> happy. But they got divorced, and it was like some-
> body dropped a bomb.[4]

"Bombs" from stressful family experiences or other painful situations reinforce the chronic stress cycle. They keep the nervous system pumped up, which, at least for the moment, inhibits chronic
tension, anxiety, or mild depression, according to Dr. Bloomfield.
Millions of people in our society literally lust after increased excitement, whether it is violence or sex in the movies, the noise and glit-
ter of the next rock concert, alcohol, marijuana, drugs, the gang life
style, burglarizing a store, or jumping into a fight to get your
"juice" as it is known on the streets.

The Parallel Epidemics

The widespread epidemic of stress in America suggests its connection to crime, which is also approaching epidemic proportions. Despite huge government investment in an attempt to reduce crime, on a per capita basis violent crime has increased 38% since 1984 (even though it was down 1.5% in 1993) and 51% on an overall basis, according to the FBI's Uniform Crime Reports published by the U.S. Department of Justice. Similarly, Americans are more aware of the ill effects of stress and spending more and more dollars to combat it, but it is our common experience that life has become no less stressful in the past ten years.

In 1993, 14,141,000 FBI Index crimes (murder, rape, robbery, aggravated assault, burglary, larceny, motor vehicle theft, and arson) were *reported*, and almost two million of those were violent crimes. These statistics do not include millions of other reported crimes such as sexual assaults, kidnapping, simple assaults, drug violations, weapons violations, vandalism, and a host of frauds and thefts. And because so many crimes go unreported (especially domestic abuse, sexual offenses, and drug crimes), the real extent of criminal activity is largely unknown. Some experts estimate that reported crimes account for about 50% of actual crimes, and others suspect actual crimes could be higher.

As for stress, 44% of all Americans are known to suffer from stress-related health problems.[5] The stress and strain in the lives of these "carriers" could certainly be the "germs" that are responsible for our expectation that about one in twenty Americans will be the victim of some serious crime (violent or property) next year.[6] A family of four has a one in five chance that someone in the family will be the victim of a serious crime next year.[7] Moreover, the odds of being a victim increase if you move to an urban area,[8] in the same way that the odds of your suffering from a stress-related disorder increase as a result of the fast pace of urban life. The odds of being victimized are even greater for urban dwellers if they live in disorganized neighborhoods that are a breeding ground for stress, just as your odds of getting an infectious disease increase if you become surrounded by carriers.

Apart from the epidemic nature of both stress and crime, some of the well-known statistics within the overall crime picture also show the stress-crime relationship.

Age, Stress and Crime

One of the fundamentals of crime is that it is highly age-specific. Crime, in essence, is a game for the young. Careers in most crimes terminate at a relatively young age. Murderers, robbers, and burglars are at their peak at ages 17 to 18, while few people age 45 or older are still at it. For all crimes, only 8% of arrests in 1993 involved persons 45 or older, and only 2% of arrests involved persons 55 or older (see chart below).

Total Arrests by Age—1993

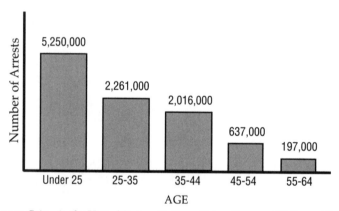

Reference: *Crime in the United States: Uniform Crime Reports*, 1993, pp. 227-228.

The age-specific nature of crime is explainable by how stress affects daily living. As Professor Larry J. Siegel of the University of Massachusetts states, "Crime peaks during late adolescence because this is a period of social stress caused by the weakening of parental supervision and the development of relationships with a diverse peer group."[9] Professor Siegel, the author of a textbook on criminology, points out that crime drops in adulthood as these sources of stress or strain are reduced, and as new sources of self-esteem become available. Underlying Professor Siegel's explanation is our common experience that a stressful event is likely to cause a stressful outburst relatively soon after the event occurs, rather than at a later time. Since young adolescence is a highly stressful time, it isn't surprising that adolescents would be prone to committing crimes. Stress builds as a result of early childhood and adolescent traumas, which lead to more chronic stress states in the high crime ages of fifteen to twenty-four. Then crime starts to get "old" as people age, and as they start to internalize their stress (i.e., direct it against themselves rather than others) due to increased coping mechanisms and societal restraints.

In addition, certain statistics show how the stress factor affects the younger generations, ultimately leading to crime. If stress is the causative factor, this model would suggest that youths, more than adults, would be involved not just in crime, but also in certain accidents associated with stress. For example, motor vehicle deaths bear similarities to the age-specific crime rate and seem to support this model. Youths fifteen to twenty-four experience the greatest percentage of motor vehicle deaths, and the rate declines with age until the mid-sixties, similar to the crime rate.

MOTOR VEHICLE DEATHS PER 100,000 POPULATION	
Age	**1990**
15-24 years	35.5
25-44 years	20.8
44-64 years	15.9

Reference: *Health, United States*, 1992, U.S. Government Printing Office.

Gender, Stress and Crime

The data also show that crime is largely a man's game. Of all arrests made in 1993 for the FBI Index crimes, 78% were of males. And when it comes to the violent crimes of murder and robbery, about 91% of arrests were of males.[10] Among federal prison inmates in 1993, 92.3% were male, and 7.7% were female.[11]

Total Arrests By Gender

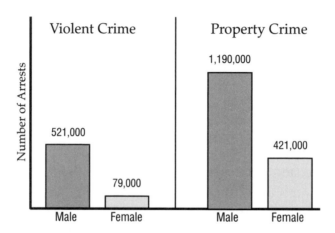

Reference: *Crime in the United States: Uniform Crime Reports*, 1993, p. 222. Based on arrests for the FBI Index crimes.

Many of the prevailing crime theories have difficulty explaining gender differences. For example, it was routinely assumed that with greater equality of status between men and women, there would be greater equality in crime rates. This has not proved to be the case, however, nor can it be said that males have more opportunity to commit crime, accounting for the difference. Women, for example, outnumber men in many white-collar occupations (e.g., clerical workers and bank tellers), yet even in such instances, where the opportunity for crime is controlled, there is a higher rate of fraud among males as compared to females.[12]

The stress model, and underlying differences in the psychophysiology of men and women, may also explain why men commit so many more crimes than women. In general, women are ill more often and for longer periods than men, but men have higher mortality rates for all the leading causes of death.[13] In other words, when men become ill, it tends to be more serious (the physiology seems to be more acutely stressed) and, as a result, they die at a higher rate. In 1980, men, in general, were 1.8 times as likely as women to die from cardiovascular illness and pneumonia, 2 times as likely as women to die from ulcers and liver disease, and 3 times as likely as women to die from accidents and chronic pulmonary disease.[14]

And in looking at specific events that bear a relationship to stress, it's interesting that males are involved in significantly more accidents than females, including drowning, burning, and falling, and men are also much more likely to abuse alcohol and drugs.[15] Furthermore, in looking again at motor vehicle deaths, this time by gender, females have far fewer accidents than males.

MOTOR VEHICLE DEATHS PER 100,000 POPULATION BY GENDER (1988-1990)		
Age	Females	Males
15-24 years	19.0	51.4
25-44 years	10.7	31.0
44-64 years	10.0	22.2

Reference: *Health, United States*, 1992, U.S. Government Printing Office.

Another difference between males and females is the differing degree to which they exhibit the "hyperactive child syndrome." Hyperactive children exhibit the traits of seriously stressed individuals. They have short attention spans and are easily distracted. They are restless, irritable, and impulsive, and have associated behavioral and learning problems. And to an alarming degree they grow up to be psychopathic criminals.[16] Interestingly, the disorder is said to be four to nine times more frequent in boys compared with girls.[17]

Overall Health, Stress, and Crime

Researchers at Harvard have estimated that 60% to 90% of all visits to physicians are related to disorders caused by stress. Because stress directly causes numerous health disorders, and indirectly contributes to others, the stress-crime connection should reflect a more stressed or less healthy criminal population, compared with a national sample of individuals, and most experts recognize that to be the case.

One important study on prisoner health was reported in the book *Stress, Crowding, and Blood Pressure in Prison.*[18] Researchers from the Yale School of Medicine examined 568 male inmates of the Middlesex County House of Correction in Billerica, Massachusetts. Their study was conducted from 1975 to 1978 and found that approximately 53% of the inmates had significant psychological disorders, most of which seemed connected with stress— 40% of the inmates experienced frequent anxiety, and 29% had insomnia (both recognized stress disorders). In addition, 26% had neurological disorders, the most common being frequent headaches (18%) and frequent dizziness (almost 9%). Twenty-two percent had various cardiovascular disorders, including frequent chest pain or high blood pressure, and 36% had respiratory disorders, including pneumonia, asthma, and chronic coughs.

The authors of the study stated that the inmates were much less healthy than a typical sample of young men. The inmates reported symptoms of chronic stress to a much greater degree than national averages. For example, they had from two to twenty times more incidence of ulcers and asthma as the national sample, and they were attempting to cope with their stress in ways that only threatened their future health and exaggerated their condition. They were three to sixteen times as likely to use illicit drugs, and twice as likely to be cigarette smokers and problem drinkers or alcoholics as the national averages.

The Best Evidence

While there appears to be considerable evidence showing the connection of stress to crime, the best evidence for general stress theory is the changes that take place in people once they begin to use effective anti-stress techniques (see chapter 5), including the changes in prisoners (chapter 6) and drug abusers (chapter 7).

Chapter Five

How the Crime Vaccine Changes the Crime Prone Physiology

One of the principal reactions of the body to stressful situations is the classic fight-or-flight response, where the body gears up to meet the stressor. As Dr. Hans Selye pointed out many years ago, the alarm reaction of the physiology includes a pounding heart, an increase in adrenaline flowing into the bloodstream, pituitary changes, increases in the hormone production of the endocrine glands, and blood lactate increases. While this response is part of the body's natural adaptation processes, when people are repeatedly subjected to stressors (without a means of revitalizing themselves), the effects of this chronic overload on the system build up over time, and the body's resources for dealing with stressful situations become depleted. This is reflected in behavior as anger, irritability, hot tempers, and, in general, a loss of control and an impaired ability to make good decisions.

Excessive stress responses of the body are generally considered not to be treatable by surgery or pharmacology. But they have been successfully treated by the strategies of natural medicine that are addressed in this book. Sometimes these strategies are referred to as psychophysiological approaches because they affect both the mind and the body.

There are many psychophysiological approaches being used today to treat stress. Among the most widely used are relaxation and meditation procedures, because they are understood as giving the mind and body deep rest, and it is known that rest produces the opposite physiological reaction from the fight-or-flight response.

During rest, the heart and breath rate slow, skin resistance increases, and, if the rest is deep enough, the body is revitalized and natural repair mechanisms correct the harmful influence caused by stress. Stress has a disordering effect on the physiology, while deep rest has an ordering effect. The body tries to "normalize" (that is, restore itself to a state of normal functioning) or heal itself whenever it can as, for example, when antibodies automatically gather to heal an infection. When we become ill, we may relieve the symptoms with medicine, but as Sir Hans Krebs, a Nobel prize-winner in physiology, says, "The physician and the patient can do no more than assist nature, by providing the best conditions for your body to defend and heal itself."[1]

Rest is the most important requirement for "assisting nature." In fact, the deep rest of sleep is so crucial to the proper functioning of the mind and body that it's every doctor's natural medicine prescription for virtually every disorder. And not only physical disorders can be remedied by sleep. Since every physical state has its corresponding mental state, the anxiety that occurs during the fight-or-flight response can be tempered by a good sleep, resulting in an elevated mood, and feelings of self-control and well-being, at least for a time.

Unfortunately, the rest gained by sleeping is often not enough to normalize the physiology, given the stressful occurrences of modern life. As a result, if a procedure can produce a more profound rest than deep sleep, it offers great promise for reducing stress, and, because of the stress-crime connection, for advancing the war on crime. This is one factor behind the success of the Transcendental Meditation program, which has been the most extensively researched procedure for combating the damaging effects of stress.

A Comprehensive Approach From the World's Oldest System of Medicine

Ayurveda is the traditional system of medicine that originated in ancient India. As is the case with many ancient systems of knowledge, over time certain critical aspects were lost, in particular the understanding of Ayurveda as a holistic *prevention-oriented* approach to health. In 1980, Maharishi began his comprehensive revival of Ayurveda, to restore this age-old system of natural medicine to its original purity. The body of knowledge that has emerged is today known as "Maharishi Ayur-Veda," which is part of the traditional Vedic knowledge. "Veda" itself means "knowledge" in Sanskrit, and the Vedas are the oldest records of human experience.

At its core, this system of natural medicine is based on a deep understanding of the most fundamental laws of nature that promote healing and evolution. This is the body of knowledge from which Maharishi's Transcendental Meditation program derives, and this Vedic approach to the problems of crime includes not just the TM program, but numerous strategies that take advantage of the body's natural ability to correct mental and physical imbalances and promote health and well-being. Included among these strategies are dietary recommendations; natural food supplements that promote stress reduction and rejuvenation; neuromuscular techniques; neurorespiratory (breathing) techniques; behavioral strategies; and the advanced TM-Sidhi program, which accelerates the benefits of the Transcendental Meditation program.

Many of these strategies as they relate to crime prevention and rehabilitation are described in a later chapter (see chapter 10). This chapter focuses on the Transcendental Meditation technique, the most extensively researched of these strategies, because the changes it produces in the mind and body counteract the crime prone physiology.

Counteracting the Crime Prone Physiology

The Transcendental Meditation technique is a simple, natural procedure, distinctly different from other practices that share the name "meditation." It is practiced twice daily for fifteen to twenty minutes in the morning and evening, while sitting comfortably with the eyes closed. During the practice of this technique, the individual's mind naturally settles down and "transcends," or goes beyond, all mental activity to experience a perfectly settled state, called *tran-*

scendental consciousness. Maharishi explains that this is the experience of the fundamental level of the mind, which is at the basis of all thinking and behavior. During this process, because the mind and body are intimately connected, the body becomes deeply relaxed, dissolving stress and accumulated fatigue. Over 500 research studies conducted at more than 200 independent research institutions in 27 countries have described the changes that occur in the mind and body during the practice and, most importantly, the practical benefits of this experience in daily life. *This particular procedure has been more extensively researched than any other relaxation or meditation technique for two reasons.* First, it is so simple to practice. One inmate said it was as simple as falling off a log; another said it was a simple as robbing a candy store (apparently he had not yet been rehabilitated). And because it is such an effortless procedure, the research instruments such as EEG electrodes attached to the scalp don't interfere with the process or results. Second, this technique has been researched so extensively because it works; in fact, it works much better than other procedures to counteract stress (see chapter 9). Scientists continue to conduct research on the Transcendental Meditation program because they continue to make significant discoveries. It's tough to get excited about a lack of results (and even tougher to get published), which is why other programs have not generated anywhere near this same degree of research.

The research on Transcendental Meditation shows that, during a twenty-minute session, profound physiological changes take place. The TM meditator experiences a markedly increased basal skin resistance (skin resistance is low when a person is stressed),[2] oxygen consumption declines precipitously (much faster than during sleep),[3] blood lactate levels decrease significantly (high concentrations of lactate are associated with anxiety and high blood pressure),[4] the hormone cortisol (found in large concentrations during stress, fasting or dehydration) decreases,[5] serotonin increases (low serotonin is associated with aggression and violence),[6] and the EEG brain wave patterns become coherent,[7] among other changes.

Physiological Indicators of Deep Rest Through Transcendental Meditation

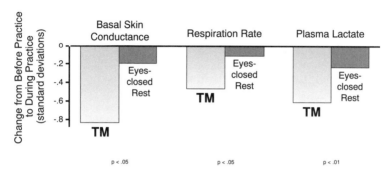

References: 1. *American Psychologist* 42 (1987): 879-881. 2. *Science* 167 (1970): 1751-1754. 3. *American Journal of Physiology* 221 (1971): 795-799.

The various changes lead to the unmistakable conclusion that an *integrated* or *holistic* physiological response is occurring, itself suggesting that the deepest levels of human functioning are being affected. Moreover, many of these changes are vitally important because they are in the opposite direction of what researchers have found to be associated with criminal behavior.

But before we look at specific physiological changes, there is another general aspect of the physiological state produced during the Transcendental Meditation technique that is very important. The decrease in oxygen consumption, for example, doesn't cause a deficiency in the oxygen being supplied to vital organs and tissues of the body. The deeply rested style of functioning simply allows the body to operate more efficiently. If there were oxygen starvation during the Transcendental Meditation technique, it would show up in blood analyses and result in compensatory "overbreathing" in the minutes following meditation, but this does not occur. Also, while the heart rate slows during meditation, there is no shortage of blood flowing through the body. We might expect that if the heart were to beat more slowly, there would be a reduced blood flow. Researchers have found, however, that there is an increase in cardiac output and a large increase in blood flow to the frontal cerebral areas, apparently because of the balancing effect of the restful state on the autonomic nervous system.[8] In short, the changes produced are not simply a slowing of metabolic activity, but indicate that the physiology is becoming more orderly and balanced in its functioning.

The Restfully Alert State

One last general component of this meditative state is that, unlike sleep, where you become unconscious, during the practice of the Transcendental Meditation technique you are mentally alert. For example, even though the mind becomes deeply settled and silent, you would be aware of surrounding noise and have the awareness to check your watch to see if it was time for the meditation session to end. Because of this unique combination of deep physical rest with mental alertness, the state is often described as one of "restful alertness," and it results in a physiological state that is more orderly than at any other time.

The Link Between Serotonin and Crime

To crime researchers, among the most important changes brought about by the practice of the Transcendental Meditation technique may be those in levels of the neurotransmitter serotonin. Research has consistently shown *low* levels of serotonin linked to aggression, violence and even the inability to control the sex drive in primates, rats, and humans. And if violence is associated with low serotonin, one reason people tend to calm down in their 40s, according to Dr. Markku Linnoila, who was scientific director of the National Institute on Alcohol Abuse and Alcoholism in the late 1980s, is "primarily because their serotonin levels go up with age."[9] The TM technique, then, should be especially interesting, since its practice has been found to naturally *increase* serotonin.

In 1993, the *Chicago Tribune* summarized some of the most interesting studies on serotonin in a series of articles. As the *Tribune* stated, the first indication that violence was influenced by serotonin occurred in 1976 when the chief of neuroscience at a hospital in Stockholm found that patients with low levels of serotonin had a significantly greater risk of violent suicide. The findings were initially ridiculed, but in the late 1970s and early 1980s, researchers at the National Institutes of Health found that people who repeatedly committed violent criminal acts tended to have low serotonin.[10] Then in the late 1980s, Dr. Linnoila, referred to above, discovered that violence associated with low serotonin was impulsive and hot-blooded,[11] and another study of fifty-eight prisoners convicted of manslaughter predicted with an 84% degree of accuracy who would kill again after they were released, just based on their serotonin levels.[12] By 1989, more than a dozen studies directly connected abnormally low serotonin levels with aggression, including studies on individuals with personality disorders, those with a history of alcoholism, homicide offenders, arsonists, mentally retarded patients, and males at a juvenile detention center.[13]

To show that virtually anyone can become violent as a result of a decrease in serotonin, researchers at McGill University in Montreal conducted a study with their students. The first student to push a button when the light flashed punished his partner with a charge of electricity. In the initial phases of the game, each student typically gave his opponent mild charges that were no higher than he had received. But when the scientists had some students drink a concoction that lowers serotonin levels, the subjects developed a mean streak and began inflicting more pain on their partners, despite receiving lower-level charges themselves. Then the students were given a large dose of tryptophan, which the brain uses to make serotonin. As the serotonin increased, the amount of punishment they gave their partners decreased.[14]

One caution has to be noted in looking at the serotonin experiments. Although many studies have now shown a correlation between violent behavior and low levels of serotonin, in humans it is difficult to directly measure the serotonin levels in the brain, so the studies typically have to be conducted on what is known as 5-HIAA, the major metabolic byproduct of serotonin. These studies have typically measured 5-HIAA levels in the fluid bathing the brain or its rate of excretion in the urine. Some researchers have questioned the accuracy of these indirect measures in predicting actual levels or function of serotonin in the brain. Since only 2% of the body's serotonin is in the brain, the question arises whether the increased 5-HIAA found to be associated with the practice of the TM technique could come from areas of the body exclusive of the brain. However, Dr. Kenneth Walton, a biochemist at Maharishi University of Management, says that a number of studies have now found low 5-HIAA associated with a wide variety of criminal activities *and* with pronounced changes in mental functioning (likely caused by changes in brain chemistry), thus allaying much of the concern.

A Natural Means of Increasing the Offender's Serotonin

Research on the Transcendental Meditation program and serotonin was initially conducted by scientists at the Institute for Neurochemistry at a hospital in Vienna, Austria.[15] In 1976 they studied eleven healthy practitioners of the TM technique and compared their data with data from a control group of thirteen members of the clinical staff, chosen to approximate the age and sex distribution of the experimental group. The age of the TM practitioners ranged from nineteen to sixty-one years and, on average, they had been meditating for more than two years. The researchers state that the selection of the meditators was essentially random. The results showed that the meditators had significantly higher urinary excretions of 5-HIAA than the control subjects, and that 5-HIAA excretion increased directly following the practice of TM, a further indication that the TM technique was responsible for the change. The higher 5-HIAA excretion was said to be "well above controls" and statistically significant at the $p = .01$ level, indicating odds of one in 100 that the results were due to chance.

To be sure that the Transcendental Meditation technique was responsible for the increased indications of serotonin activity, a later experiment collected urine samples from the heroic subjects at three-hour intervals, twenty-four hours a day over several days ("wake up Joe, it's time again"). And in another study, six subjects were tested for 5-HIAA levels over a period of eighty-nine consecutive days.[16] These studies also found a rise in the urinary excretion of 5-HIAA following the practice of the technique. Further studies on the ability of the Transcendental Meditation program to increase excretions of 5-HIAA were reported at the annual meeting of the Society for Neuroscience in Toronto in 1988, and at the International Journal of Psychophysiology meeting in Budapest in July, 1990.

If serotonin levels are so important in relation to crime, one obvious question is why not give patients drugs that may increase serotonin levels. Prozac, Paxil and Zoloft are drugs known as selective serotonergic uptake inhibitors (SSRIs) that increase the availability of serotonin in the brain, and can result in mood elevations. But all synthetic drugs (no exceptions) have side effects, and SSRIs may have to be taken for years or even a lifetime, which results in drug tolerance, the necessity of higher doses, and an increased danger from side effects. According to psychiatrist James L. Fleming, Co-Director of the Mt. Pleasant Mental Health Institute in Mt. Pleasant, Iowa, the side effects of SSRIs include what are known as "vegetative symptoms," such as insomnia, fatigue, and loss of appetite, as well as "cognitive symptoms," including low self-esteem. Dr. Fleming, who was formerly a psychiatric consultant to the District of Columbia correctional system, gave me his perspective on the efficacy and safety of the TM technique compared to SSRIs:

> The use of drugs should be limited in a correctional setting because most psychiatric disturbances in the prison setting are stress-related. Also, Prozac and the other SSRIs were really designed by researchers to deal with major depressive disorders, and it is inappropriate and potentially harmful to use them for other disorders. On the other hand, having seen how the Transcendental Meditation technique naturally improves an individual's mood and self-esteem, it would be a serious mistake not to use this procedure.

Reducing Cortisol (a Stress Hormone)

Dr. Kenneth Walton, a biochemist referred to earlier in this chapter, has conducted a number of studies on serotonin as well as cortisol (a stress hormone). He says the effect of the Transcendental Meditation program on cortisol levels is remarkably similar to its effect on serotonin, except in the reverse direction. The evidence indicates that cortisol drops markedly during individual TM sessions and averages lower over long periods of time in regular meditators.[17]

Biochemistry of Reduced Stress

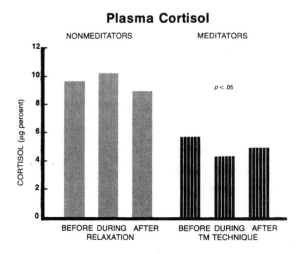

Reference: R. Jevning, A.F. Wilson, E. VanderLaan, and S. Levine, "Plasma Prolactine and Cortisol during Transcendental Meditation," The Endocrine Society Program 57th Annual Meeting, New York City, 18-20 June 1975, p. 257.

Walton's studies show that when the physiology starts to function more normally through the deep rest of Transcendental Meditation, the meditator experiences both low cortisol and increased serotonin, reflecting a less violent and more adaptive individual.

Dr. Walton has pointed out what he considers to be the connection between cortisol and serotonin. Walton's studies show that chronic stress results in chronically high cortisol. He also says that numerous studies on animals show that chronically high cortisol is actually responsible for chronically reduced serotonin; and that, conversely, reduced serotonin secretion prevents the body from stopping the secretion of cortisol into the bloodstream. Thus, according to Walton, "if the mechanisms in humans are the same as in animals, we are left with a vicious cycle that quickly gets out of hand as the elevated cortisol reduces serotonin, and the reduced serotonin leads to increased cortisol."

One other aspect of the changes in the body's production of cortisol is important to crime researchers. Researchers at Rockefeller University in New York first demonstrated that animals who were not stressed and were leaders in the group had low cortisol levels. Yet, when the animals in leadership roles experienced stress, their cortisol rose appropriately to meet the challenge. This is probably the most important finding to criminologists, and is similar to what Walton and his colleagues found in the meditators they studied.[18]

In one study, Walton and his co-researchers examined twenty-nine males who were randomly assigned to either a TM group or a stress education class. Cortisol was measured in all the subjects before they learned the TM technique or began participating in the stress class, and again after four months of either regular practice of meditation, or daily sessions spent analyzing the stressful experiences and planning how to deal with them in the future. After four months, the TM group experienced significant decreases in cortisol compared with the stress education group. Just as importantly, the TM group's cortisol levels rose higher than those of the controls during a stress response.[19]

When I first looked at the cortisol research on criminals, what was perplexing (and potentially a challenge to general stress theory) was that a number of studies have shown that habitually violent offenders and impulsive people actually have *lower* cortisol levels than non-violent offenders or a less impulsive group.[20] This low cortisol finding (described as *low arousal* levels by criminologists) in certain criminals shows how complicated this area can be. Since low cortisol is associated with relaxation and a lack of stress, this finding seemed at odds with this book's perspective on criminal conduct. However, what distinguishes the criminal low arousal state from the physiology of the relaxed individual is that habitually violent criminals consistently show low arousal states along with *low* responses to stress. This is thought to cause their lack of fear and inhibition in committing crimes. On the other hand, those practicing the Transcendental Meditation technique display a low cortisol state, but as Dr. Walton has found, their cortisol levels rise rapidly and appropriately in response to stress. This is the critical aspect of the cortisol finding that is in the opposite direction from the crime prone physiology.

Improving Autonomic Functioning

The same physiological profile of a relatively stressless state in TM meditators, followed by an appropriately high response to outside stimuli, is also found in studies measuring the electrical conductivity of the skin (electrodermal activity). Skin resistance is determined by what is known as the galvanic skin response (GSR), and is a highly accurate measure of relaxation. GSR is measured by placing electrodes on the skin's surface and measuring the resistance to a mild electrical current. This easy-to-measure change has been used in law enforcement and is the basis for the "lie detector" test. If, for example, after answering a particular question the individual's skin resistance decreases, this indicates that he is anxious, possibly because he is lying. If skin resistance increases, this indicates that he is more relaxed, which is felt to be some indication of truthfulness.

Research on TM meditators shows that they have consistently high skin resistance (meaning that they are more relaxed). And one study showed that it only took about *one minute* of the practice to gain a profound state of relaxation. In a study of eight subjects, a marked increase in skin resistance to approximately 400% of the prior level was found in the very first meditation after learning the Transcendental Meditation technique.[21] The mean skin resistance for the eight subjects during a resting period with the eyes closed before they learned to meditate was 107 kilohms. One hour later, the subjects learned to meditate, and during the first minute of the first TM session, the mean skin resistance jumped to 461 kilohms, giving an indication of the simplicity and effectiveness of the technique.

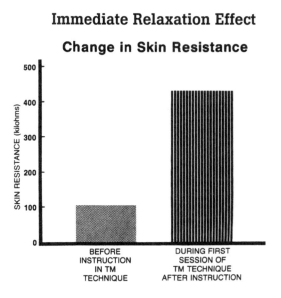

Immediate Relaxation Effect

Change in Skin Resistance

GSR also has been used to measure the number of spontaneous fluctuations in skin resistance that occur independently of any external stimulation. This is said to be a good index of a person's general anxiety level and the degree to which he has a stable nervous system and is resistant to situations that might otherwise lead to stressful outbursts, criminal or otherwise.[22] In a study reported in *Psychosomatic Medicine*, Dr. David Orme-Johnson compared non-meditating control subjects to those who had been practicing the TM technique regularly an average of fifteen months. The non-meditators showed much less stability in the functioning of their autonomic nervous systems. They produced an average of thirty-four spontaneous GSRs (about normal for an adult population) during a ten-minute rest period compared to ten GSRs for the meditating group. But just two weeks after the non-meditators learned TM, they produced an average of only fifteen spontaneous GSRs during the ten-minute period.[23] Similar findings of low anxiety as measured by GSR were found in subjects who had learned TM by experimenters at Rollins College in Florida, and at Eastern Michigan University.[24]

Again, as important as the meditators' relaxed state, as measured by GSR, is that when challenged by a stressor, they respond appropriately. Dr. Orme-Johnson's study showed that despite lower levels of spontaneous fluctuations in skin resistance, the meditators' initial response to a stressor (a loud tone) was at least as great as the non-meditating controls. Then Goleman, in a study at Harvard, conducted further research on this point, which has important implications for criminology. Goleman showed TM meditators a movie of gruesome shop accidents. Compared with controls, the meditators' hearts started beating faster and their skin resistance responses were stronger, but then they relaxed more quickly after each incident had passed.[25] This is in sharp contrast to what we know about criminal psychopaths, who don't respond approximately to what should be a stressful or fearful situation.

The Paradox of the Psychopath

A perplexing question for criminologists, and again what seemed to be a potential challenge to general stress theory, is whether psychopaths are stressed and whether they can therefore be helped by classical "anti-stress" techniques. The psychopathic personality was first described in the early nineteenth century as an individual who repeatedly involved himself in aimless anti-social behavior. Psychopaths are also sometimes referred to as sociopaths, and one classic work by Cleckley described their major characteristics. They are generally intelligent with a superficial charm, relatively free of apparent anxiety or nervousness, and yet they are habitually untruthful and unreliable. They lack remorse, exhibit poor judgment, and show an inability to learn by experience. They have an incapacity for love, and are highly self-centered. They engage in continuous criminal activity, and typically *they have no fear of punishment.*

Physiological research conducted on psychopaths using skin resistance tests, hormone evaluations, and tests of EEG brain wave activity has generally found that psychopaths have low arousal states. In other words, they tend to appear relaxed, with a physiological profile of high skin resistance, low cortisol, and slow brain wave activity. On the other hand, as stated earlier, they don't respond appropriately to stressful situations, which is likely the physiological counterpart of the emotional "fearlessness" they exhibit. Highly maladjusted youths, for example, show a minimal adrenaline output when confronted with what should be a stressful situation,[26] and psychopaths are said to merely pantomime "feelings, but they don't have fears because they have so much difficulty feeling things emotionally."[27] As one writer said, psychopaths "hear the words, but not the music."

The unusual physiological functioning found in adult psychopaths may have existed for many years, since a similar physiology is also found in hyperactive children, who are found to be at high risk for turning into delinquents and psychopaths in their later years. For example, in a thirty-year follow-up study, one researcher found that approximately one-third of those children showing symptoms of hyperactivity were later diagnosed as psychopathic, and 59% of eighty-three teenage hyperactive subjects were later found to have had some run-in with the police.[28] Hyperactive children also have a low central nervous system arousal level and abnormal brain wave patterns, which also indicate low cortical arousal.[29]

What is so interesting is that when you look at the behavior of the hyperactive child, it seems to be wholly at odds with a low-arousal internal state, since the hyperactive child is a whirling dervish of nonstop motion. Hyperactivity is characterized by excessive motor activity or restlessness, a short attention span, impulsive behavior, irritability, and associated learning problems.[30]

These behavioral problems allow us to see more clearly that the hyperactive's low arousal state is just a different form of stress and physiological disorder. Paradoxically, hyperactives respond favorably to medication that stimulates their nervous system, such as certain forms of amphetamines. Consequently, the hyperactive child's excessive motor activity is now believed to be caused by an inadequacy in the functioning of the part of the brain and nervous system that controls these motor functions. It is said that the hyper-active child has a lack of *inhibitory control*, and the stimulation caused by amphetamines is thought to restore the central nervous system to a more normal state in which the child is better able to control motor activity.[31] The excessive motor activity and restless-ness actually represent the child's attempt to raise his low internal arousal levels, consistent with the current belief that these children have a pathological need for stimulation. In later years their impul-sive behavior and need for activity and excitement, coupled with their intolerance of routines and boredom, often result in the contin-uous anti-social behavior that we define as psychopathy.

Research on psychopaths and hyperactives seems to indicate that their low arousal levels are much different from the low stress levels of relaxed individuals. Professor Sarnoff Mednick from the University of Southern California Psychology Department, who has written extensively on biomedical factors in crime, has found that psychopaths and others exhibiting anti-social behavior don't recover well from stressful situations, as measured by skin resistance stud-ies.[32] This contrasts with healthy individuals, including (as we've seen) those who practice Transcendental Meditation, who recover quickly. Moreover, recent research looking at different types of stress scales suggests that the question is not whether psychopaths have low or high stress, but really what type of stress. Researchers have found that psychopaths may be low in psychological anxiety so they don't worry much, aren't self-conscious and may have self-confidence. But their stress makes them feel panicky and ill-at-ease for no reason, they have difficulty collecting their thoughts, and they experience physical anxieties such as weakness in the legs, burning sensations, irregular heartbeats, frequent headaches, and other aches and pains in the body.[33]

In summary, the foregoing research indicates two distinctly dif-ferent states of physiological functioning, with some superficial similarities. There is a *low arousal state* associated with a need for stimulation, an attraction to the excitement of the criminal lifestyle, and a lack of fear. It is a state of inactivity that could be described as a dull state, which is why habitual criminals are unresponsive to the environment. Then there is the *restfully alert state* that is experienced during the practice of the Transcendental Meditation technique, which over time becomes the characteristic style of functioning of the TM meditator. This is a relaxed state, but one in which the individual responds appropriately to stressful situations. Interestingly, as we will see in the next chapter, the restfully alert style of functioning actually counteracts both the high anxiety state that characterizes some criminals (the researchers from Yale found that 40% of the inmates they studied experienced frequent anxiety—see chapter 4), and the low arousal state that characterizes others. It counteracts vastly different criminal profiles in a way that no drug could ever do, because both criminal profiles are abnormal styles of functioning caused by stress. The profound rest produced during the Transcendental Meditation technique gives the body the maximum opportunity to repair itself and correct the disorder, whatever the disorder may be.

The technique's ability to create order or coherence can also be seen by looking at the EEG brain wave patterns.

Enhancing EEG Brain Wave Coherence

Brennan, Mednick (referred to above), and Volavka, researchers who have long studied the physiology of anti-social persons, state that "a large number of studies . . . conclude that there is strong evidence for EEG abnormalities in criminal offenders, and especially violent offenders."[34] Some reviews, they point out, suggest that from 25% to 50% of violent individuals may have EEG abnormalities, whereas in normal populations the figure is 5% to 20%, at least based on clinical judgments of abnormalities rather than computer scoring.

Most of the studies involving EEG measures in deviant individuals report that criminals show high levels of slow alpha wave activity. This was found in a study of 129 males, whose criminal arrests by age eighteen were predicted at age twelve, based on their brain wave data. These findings were duplicated in a larger sample of 571 subjects in Sweden.[35]

EEG frequencies are classified as delta, theta, alpha, and beta, with delta being the lowest arousal level and beta being the highest. Individuals with slow alpha activity show essentially a drowsy pattern,[36] and are unresponsive to the environment. In contrast, during the practice of the Transcendental Meditation technique, the background noise or chatter in the mind settles down, and the individual is deeply rested, alert, and also responsive to the environment. Because, as indicated above, there are different states of rest (drowsy or dull, as compared to restfully alert), both of which may show an increase in slow alpha activity, it is important for future researchers to look at more sophisticated EEG measurements than those indicating simply whether slow alpha activity is present. One suggestion would be to look at the degree to which a criminal's brain functioning is orderly, since this should be the basis of orderly thinking, free from deviant tendencies.

Coherence of Brain Waves

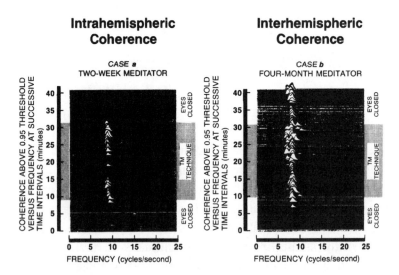

Jean-Paul Banquet, a neurophysiologist at Massachusetts General Hospital, found that the Transcendental Meditation technique produced a unique orderliness in the functioning of the different hemispheres of the brain. He described it as "an increased synchronicity in brain wave frequency, phase and amplitude." Frequency indicates the number of waves recorded in a given time period. Phase indicates whether the waves are in step with one another (whether the crest of one wave coincides with the crest of another at a particular point in time). Amplitude refers to the peak height of the wave. During the practice of the technique, Dr. Banquet found that the brain waves measured by all the electrodes on both sides of the brain became more ordered in frequency, phase, and amplitude.[37]

Brain Wave Coherence
15-Year TM Meditator

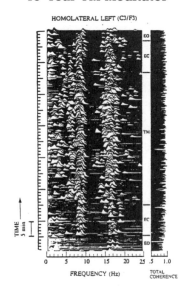

HOMOLATERAL LEFT (C3/F3)

TIME 5 min

FREQUENCY (Hz)

TOTAL COHERENCE

Banquet's early findings were duplicated by Dr. Paul Levine and other researchers at Maharishi European Research University.[38] Levine used a mathematical technique that allowed a computer to provide a simple picture of brain wave orderliness by focusing on the brain waves that showed a strong similarity to other brain waves. Levine used the concept of coherence to describe the relationship. His most common finding was coherence in alpha waves during and after the practice of the TM technique. The findings are presented in a vivid, computer-generated picture called a COSPAR (coherence spectral array), with the "peaks" indicating strong coherence. The experiments begin at the bottom of the chart while the subjects sit with eyes closed. After a few minutes, they begin to practice the TM technique for twenty minutes. For the more experienced meditators, coherence persists after meditation during the second eyes-closed period. For the fifteen-year meditator, the coherence is much stronger, has spread to much of the brain, and continues after the practice, in the eyes-open period. These charts (see prior pages) graphically indicate the growing coherence in brain wave functioning as a person continues to meditate.

The Development of Consciousness

In the ancient Vedic civilization, the physiological changes caused by meditation were not evaluated by objective measurements. The focus was on the development of consciousness produced by the regular experience of transcendental consciousness, the most settled state of mind. This was classically understood to lead to many benefits in the mind's functioning, including increased alertness, clarity, comprehensiveness, and creativity, improved memory, and the growing ability to fulfill one's desires. Moreover, the experience of transcendental consciousness was understood to create orderliness not only in the mind, but also in the body. The development of consciousness was therefore seen to bring a corresponding development of physiological functioning, which would support the continued development of consciousness, as well as create a more ideal state of health and increased longevity.

In the past twenty-five years we have made significant progress in studying the physiological correlates of changes in consciousness, and we now know that the real development of consciousness produces corresponding changes in the functioning of the brain and nervous system. Many programs of development may talk about "raising" a person's consciousness or expanding his awareness, but this is often a loose use of terminology. A fundamental change in the mind's capacity to engage in pro-social behavior requires fundamental changes in physiological functioning. And while we can't physically touch or see consciousness, what we see in the physiology can allow us to make accurate assessments about the person's inner state of mind.

From a theoretical standpoint, the general stress theory of criminality could also be called *consciousness theory*. In fact, this would actually be a better description of the theory, but one that would be subject to more misinterpretations because of the abstract nature of consciousness, and the varied use of the term. However we express the theory, though, it recognizes the interdependence of the mind and body; but calling it consciousness theory would acknowledge what the Vedic tradition has maintained throughout the millennia —that consciousness is *primary,* and because it is the most fundamental level of an individual's existence, consciousness and the mind have a profound influence on physiological functioning.

Modern science, to the extent it has concerned itself with consciousness at all, has typically held the viewpoint that consciousness is a mere byproduct, or artifact, of the functioning of the brain and nervous system. But Maharishi explains that the field of transcendental consciousness which underlies the mind's activity is also at the basis of the inner intelligence which gives orderliness and structure to the functioning of the body. Now, years of research on the Transcendental Meditation program seem to uphold the Vedic understanding. In the final analysis, however, it doesn't matter so much whether we look at crime as being caused by a failure in the development of consciousness, or as a result of the impact of stress on the brain and nervous system. Both perspectives are supported by the evidence of pro-social changes that result once the individual begins to experience this distinct inner state in the mind and body.

Optimization of Brain Functioning

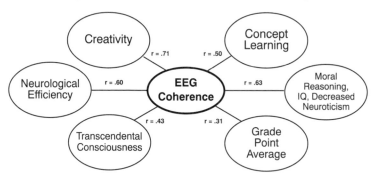

The chart above was constructed with data from the following four studies: 1. *International Journal of Neuroscience* 13 (1981): 211-217. 2. *International Journal of Neuroscience* 15 (1981): 151-157. 3. *Scientific Research on the Transcendental Program: Collected Papers,* Volume 1 (Livingston Manor, NY: MERU Press, 1977), paper 21, 208-212. 4. *Scientific Research on the Transcendental Program: Collected Papers,* Volume 4 (the Netherlands: MVU Press, 1989), paper 294, 2245-2266.

A number of carefully conducted studies now show the relationship between the orderly brain wave activity resulting from the
practice of Transcendental Meditation and better mental functioning in activity. In one paper, significant positive correlations were
shown between coherent EEG brain wave activity, the experience of
transcendental consciousness, increased creativity, improved moral
reasoning, enhanced concept learning, and decreased neuroticism.

In another study, of fifty-eight students at a traditionally African-
American university,[39] EEG coherence was measured along with
moral development and other personality factors. Fifty subjects
were randomly assigned to either learn TM, progressive muscle
relaxation, or cognitive therapy, and another eight selected to learn
TM. There were fifty African-American and eight Caucasian subjects. The groups were tested before learning their meditation or
other program and again afterwards, using the EEG measurements
and a self-concept scale. The research demonstrated that the two
TM groups improved significantly compared to the progressive
relaxation and cognitive therapy groups. The TM groups were more
self-satisfied, showed a greater sense of moral or ethical self,
increased in all the social scales, and decreased in maladjustment
and personality disorders. Real change of this kind must be accompanied by underlying physiological changes, and the TM group also
showed strong increases in EEG coherence, whereas the progressive relaxation and cognitive groups showed no such change.

Improving Psychology and Reducing Aggression

Many of the psychological studies on the TM program show that
meditators develop into what Abraham Maslow calls more "self-
actualized" people. Maslow studied exemplary individuals and
found they had common characteristics. Self-actualized people uniformly exhibit an easy, positive attitude about life. They have higher
self-esteem and enjoy warm personal relationships. They are also
self-sufficient, cheerful and caring in attitude.

One of the first psychological studies on the TM program was
conducted at the University of Cincinnati and reported in the

Journal of Counseling Psychology in 1972.[40] The researchers questioned both meditators and non-meditators to determine changes in twelve personality characteristics associated with self-actualization. They found significant changes among the meditators in six characteristics, including greater spontaneity and self-acceptance, and an increased capacity for warm personal relationships. The non-meditating control group showed no changes. These findings were later duplicated in a study at the University of Cincinnati, which found significant changes in ten of the twelve self-actualizing characteristics, including an increased capacity for warm personal relationships after only ten weeks of meditation.[41]

Increased Self-Actualization

Northridge Developmental Scale

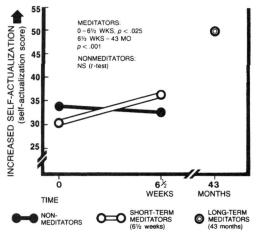

Self-reported studies like those above are vulnerable to the criticism that subjects may try to appear changed in positive ways when they really haven't changed. This is especially true when dealing with prisoners. If you ask a prisoner if he's changed, he swears he's a different person. Another possible objection to these studies is the particular personality inventory used (Shostrom's Personal Orientation Inventory), which has been criticized as too general and abstract. Clearly, no individual study should be regarded as conclusive. Taken collectively, however, these and other studies make a convincing argument that the TM program promotes real change.

Numerous psychological studies have now been conducted using a variety of personality inventories. An earlier book of mine described more than twenty such studies.[42] Some of these studies circumvent tendencies to exaggerate by comparing long-term and short-term meditators. If you assume a tendency to exaggerate, you would have to assume it for each group of meditators. Therefore, if you find the long-term meditators to be psychologically healthier than the short-term meditators (see chart on prior page), it adds to the credibility of the study. Moreover, if you find psychological health to vary in direct proportion to the length of time practicing the Transcendental Meditation technique, as has been consistently shown, it's likely that the TM program is responsible for the psychological growth.

Changing the Criminal Mind

Most of the Transcendental Meditation studies on psychological health and aggression have been conducted on the so-called "normal" population, rather than criminal populations. The results, however, on prisoner populations have not been significantly different, as indicated in the next chapter.

Chapter Six

Rehabilitation That Works: Reducing Stress in Prisons

Historically prisons have vacillated between a "medical model," which views the offender as ill and needing treatment and rehabilitation, and a punitive model, which emphasizes hard labor and punishment. A labor philosophy, hard or otherwise, dominated corrections until the late 1800s when opposition to a work orientation came from private manufacturers and labor unions, who objected to the manufacture of competing goods with cheap prison labor.[1] With the decline of a hard labor model in post-depression America, the rehabilitative model came into favor from around 1940 until the 1970s. Then, conservative politics and Robert Martinson's famous "nothing works" study of rehabilitation efforts in prisons caused a renewed emphasis on a punishment model, which is now a firmly ingrained part of the "get tough" approach favored by Republicans and Democrats.

In 1994, the *New York Times* reported on the numerous proposals throughout the country to make hard time harder, by taking away basketball courts, and bringing back chain gangs and striped uniforms.[2] *The Times* reported that state Representative Billy W. Joye, Jr. of North Carolina, said he received "a heck of a response" to his bill to ban televisions and make prisons a place of punishment, not joy. Mississippi's Governor Kirk Fordice said he wanted to make his state the "capital of capital punishment," and the legislature banned private televisions, radios, and computers for inmates. Wisconsin's Governor Tommy Thompson also joined in, and he ended weightlifting and tennis.

But prison experts repeatedly warn about get tough approaches. According to the same *Times* article, Don Cabana, a former

Mississippi warden and now a professor at the University of Southern Mississippi, said, "We're only taking a step back about sixty years." And a national survey conducted by Senator Paul Simon's Subcommittee on the Constitution questioned 157 wardens from eight states, and found them nearly unanimous in calling for an expansion of rehabilitation programs, including literacy and other educational programs. Nevertheless, those who favor more education and rehabilitation are fighting an uphill battle because of the difficulty of pointing to any program that has been consistently effective in rehabilitation—any program, that is, other than a true stress reduction program that "immunizes" the physiology.

The Importance of Stress Reduction in Prisons

In an effort to find out whether anything works in rehabilitation (other than the programs I was already advocating), I attended the 1994 annual meeting of the Academy of Criminal Justice Sciences in Boston to hear the latest in criminology research. At one session, Professor Kevin Ryan of Norwich University in Vermont presented his recent paper describing the illusion of change in prisons. Ryan distinguished between "false" or "pseudo" change, which involves a mere verbal pronouncement of change (where individuals pretend to have changed because they stand to benefit), and individuals undergoing a real inner change. Ryan pointed out that a mask of change is often donned by prisoners simply for the thrill of "running a con" on some gullible person. Prisoners, for example, often tell others that "they have found Jesus," knowing that this is simply a line.

At the end of his talk, I asked Professor Ryan whether he was aware of any program that had been found to produce real change, or what he called a "veridical" conversion, as opposed to a mere "narrative" conversion. Ryan said that his review of the literature took note of two programs that at least took an "inside out" approach emphasizing inner change—Alcoholics Anonymous and Transcendental Meditation. His report states that "despite the almost universal belief that Twelve Step [Alcoholics Anonymous] programs are effective, extraordinarily little research has been done

to evaluate the effectiveness of such programs." Citing a 1989 summary of the AA research, Professor Ryan stated in his paper that
"not one study has ever found AA or its derivatives to be superior
to any other approach, or even to be better than not receiving any
help at all . . . ."

In contrast, Professor Ryan noted that Transcendental Meditation
had been well researched and had been taught to approximately
2,700 inmates and more than 250 correctional officers in 28 facilities in the United States. Yet Ryan reported that despite the positive
results of these research studies, the "standard reviews of effectiveness research fail to mention TM." This unconventional approach
gets ignored, the typical fate of new knowledge (see chapter 9),
despite the promise it offers for effective rehabilitation.

The Problem with Recidivism:
Putting the Cart Before the Horse

The problem with the old medical model is that it doesn't effectively deal with an offender's stress. Prisoners are painfully aware of
the stress and tension in their lives, and any decrease in stress is
much sought after. Butch Evans, an inmate at the Augusta
Correctional Center in Georgia, writes articles on stress and health
for the prison newspaper. In one article he states:

> Stress. A daily part of our lives . . . . Stress is espe-
> cially high for us due to our environment, concerns
> for the family's health and finances, our loved ones,
> will they wait for me, be there for me when I get
> out, and when am I getting out? This high level of
> stress will follow us into freedom as well . . . . How
> we manage stress, control it (and it can be done
> effectively) will make all the difference in our qual-
> ity of life, now and in the future.[3]

The old medical model tries to reeducate an offender before it
treats the underlying stress that makes him uninterested in education
or incapable of being educated. Yet virtually every psychologist

knows that when you decrease tension and anxiety, the individual begins to think more clearly, concentrates better, and often begins to succeed where previously he experienced only failure.

Professor Ryan states that the debate over prison rehabilitation considers it successful if we reduce recidivism, and that the ultimate goal of prison rehabilitation is increased public protection. In other words, the goal is to seek change in the offender only to the extent that it facilitates public safety. But this puts the cart before the horse. Public safety and improved recidivism rates will be the result of changing the individual offender, and Professor Ryan calls for prison programs to be evaluated on this basis.

The Crime Vaccine in Prisons

The first research on the use of the Transcendental Meditation program in a rehabilitative setting was conducted in 1971 at the La Tuna Federal Penitentiary in La Tuna, New Mexico. Since that time, other programs in prisons and juvenile centers have been conducted in the U.S. and elsewhere, many with research components.

Reducing Hostility, Aggression, and Violence

Folsom State Prison. In 1971, Pat Corum was the first inmate to learn the Transcendental Meditation technique in the California prison system. He was then serving two life sentences at Folsom State Prison, one of the most repressive, stressful prisons in the California correctional system.[4] After Corum, other inmates at Folsom learned to meditate in what proved to be one of the most rewarding experiments in U.S. correctional history. On being asked by a reporter whether the use of this technique had changed things at Folsom, Corum said:

> Inside at Folsom, just numerous murders have been stopped. It's because the people no longer feel the inside tension, the hostility within, and the need to strike out. These men are just mellowed out. They're calm. They're thinking for the first time in

their lives. And you get a man that thinks, he's not going to be in trouble.

*Once rival factions, eyes closed, practicing Transcendental
Meditation. Pat Corum is seated in the front row (with beard).*

It may seem like an exaggeration to think that numerous murders were prevented by the Transcendental Meditation program, but others felt the same way about how Folsom was changed. Ernest Merriweather also learned to meditate at Folsom shortly after the TM program was introduced. He said:

> We had some of the toughest groups, or gangs I
> guess you could call them, in the world at Folsom
> Prison. There was the Aryan Brotherhood, the Black
> Gorilla Family, the Mexican Mafia and others . . . .
> They were bent on destroying themselves and
> everything else around them . . . . Prior to [the
> Transcendental Meditation program] coming to
> Folsom Prison, if you looked at some of these peo-
> ple the wrong way, you were dead the next morn-
> ing, or if you talked to someone the wrong way, you
> were dead, or if you borrowed a pack of cigarettes

from someone and didn't give it back, you were
dead. And [the TM program] brought us all together
. . . . It really was a miracle to see some of these
tough groups getting together in the same room and
embracing one another . . . . It's still hard to conceive, but it happened.

Group meditation in California's Folsom State Prison.

Research conducted on the Transcendental Meditation program
at Folsom in the 1970s verified the effects described by these men.
In their studies, researchers used what is known as random assignment cross-validation designs. Using this methodology, the same
study is conducted twice on two independent samples that are randomly assigned to different groups, in an attempt to substantiate the
results. In a study involving 115 inmates, the researchers found that
the Transcendental Meditation program significantly reduced anxiety
and neuroticism. The first group showed reduced negativity and
suspicions and the second group showed reduced assault, irritability,
negativity, and verbal hostility.[5]

Hoyt S. Chambles, the supervisor of the Correctional Education
Programs at Folsom, described the reduced hostilities he observed:

> The small group of inmates who are now receiving
> Transcendental Meditation instruction appear to
> have better control over their emotions and lives
> within a very few weeks. I have personally

observed two situations that would have led to physical confrontation before having TM instruction. However, these two different inmates not only controlled themselves but also received apologies from the other inmates involved after a cooling-off period . . . . Of other inmates that I have knowledge of before and after the TM instruction, there is a calmness and ability to discuss and talk a problem out rather than using physical means to achieve their goals. My observations of the inmates taking TM instruction showed there has been a measurable accomplishment, that these men are willing to meet life head-on, but without any physical or violent confrontation.

Reports such as these led other prisons to provide Transcendental Meditation programs for some of their inmates.

Milan Michigan. In 1975, a researcher at Indiana University conducted an extensive study of sixty-eight prisoners at the Federal Correctional Institution in Milan, Michigan.[6] The Milan study involved random assignment to either a TM group that also participated in other unit therapy programs, a TM group that participated in no other therapy programs, or a control group. All were drug offenders, with an average incarceration of seventy-five months, an IQ that ranged from 80 to 128, and an average education of 10.8 years.

The groups were tested using five different personality inventories to measure a broad range of psychological factors, including aggression, self-esteem, emotional stability and maturity, and over-concern with physical symptoms. The groups were tested before learning the Transcendental Meditation technique and again approximately two and a half months later. For aggression, the Buss-Durkee Hostility Inventory and the MMPI (Minnesota Multiphasic Personality Inventory) were used. The results were striking.

Those who meditated *regularly* showed significant changes on nine of the ten aggression indices, including reduced psychopathic tendencies, and reduced hostility, irritability, resentment, and suspicion. The *irregular* TM subjects improved significantly on four of the ten aggression indices, whereas the controls improved on only two of the ten indicies.

Decreased Hostility in Prisoners

Reduction in Hostility (Buss-Durkee Hostility Inventory)

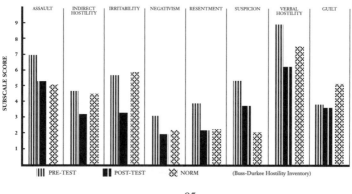

$p<.05$

Walpole, Massachusetts. Another study showed a reduction in aggression in the minimum security prison at Walpole in Massachusetts, in research funded by the Massachusetts Department of Mental Health.[7] The researchers at Walpole administered the Buss-Durkee Hostility Inventory to forty-five inmates who learned the Transcendental Meditation technique. At the start of the program there was considerable apprehension and mistrust of the meditation program because the inmates thought it might be behavior modification. Once they learned to meditate, however, the prisoners became less tense, and continued with the program. The study showed a statistically significant decrease in hostility in a post-test approximately ten weeks after the group learned to meditate. And in a follow-up evaluation a year and a half after the program was introduced, of the fifty-seven inmates who learned TM, forty-seven were still meditating with some degree of regularity.

Another study at Walpole recorded the disciplinary infractions of three groups of inmates who learned the Transcendental Meditation technique. Infractions were recorded during the period before the inmates learned the technique (the pre-testing period) and for an equal period after they learned it (the post-testing period). For the two groups that had repeatedly broken the rules, there was a significant decrease in disciplinary reports after learning TM. For those who already received few reports, there was no significant change.

Reduction in Disciplinary Infractions

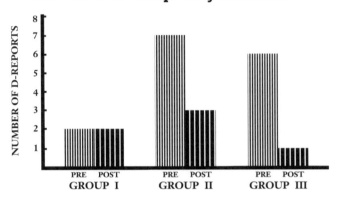

Often prisoners may seem quiet or peaceful when, in reality, they just have a difficult time expressing themselves verbally. Then, one day, what is mistaken for relaxation erupts into violence. On the other hand, when inmates experience a real reduction in their inner tensions, they may become more amiable and outgoing, and gain the ability to resolve matters without violence. Jose Melgar, an inmate at a different prison, said:

> Our yard has changed a lot. As for me, I can say that before TM I was very quiet and shy. I didn't communicate very much with other inmates. But now it is totally different, because I am chatting very often and my personality has grown enough to allow me to face problems with dignity. And I have not had to resort to violence.

Oscar Curry was incarcerated at Folsom State Prison when he learned to meditate. Curry said:

I was accused of making a third party call, which is against the rules here, and I didn't make the call. And before, if I would have been accused like that, I would have been all over him. But instead, this time I talked with him and in a decent manner.

Reduced Anxiety

Numerous studies have looked at the effects of the Transcendental Meditation program on anxiety in prisoners. For example:

Stillwater Prison. One study was conducted in the 1970s at Stillwater in Minnesota. Thirty inmates were randomly assigned to a Transcendental Meditation group and another twenty to a control group that was not taught Transcendental Meditation until after the experimental period. Another control group consisted of sixteen inmates who did not want to learn Transcendental Meditation. Anxiety decreased significantly in the TM group compared with the control groups (at the $p = .001$ level, indicating odds of one in 1,000 that the results could have been due to chance). The Stillwater meditators shifted from being one of the most anxious populations to being one of the least anxious.[8]

Lompoc, California. At the Federal Correctional Institution in Lompoc in the 1970s, thirty inmates who began the TM program were measured by the standard State-Trait Anxiety Inventory, a self-report measure, but one that has been found to be extremely reliable. The meditators showed a dramatic decrease in anxiety as well as an increased optimism about their future.[9]

Vermont. Improvements in anxiety were also found in several studies in the Vermont Department of Corrections (see page 75). Ron Perry, an assistant professor at Norwich University and a correctional consultant when TM training was provided at the St. Johnsbury Community Correctional Center in Vermont, noted how prisoners who were previously anxious and gloomy changed their outlook. He said:

When the men first start the TM program, I see a spark of life returning. I see smiles and laughter. I see a real sense of accomplishment in their eyes, and from the applause of others when they complete [TM] instruction. I see they become more involved —working on GEDs, taking leadership roles in the therapeutic community, getting actively involved in the TM educational lessons, and making future plans. I see a respectful type of relationship forming with the correctional officers, especially with those who have also begun the TM program, based on just seeing growth with each other . . . . Probably the best reflection of my experience working at St. Johnsbury is what I feel during group practice of the TM technique [the inmates and staff meditated together]. These sessions are as powerful as any I've experienced in the community. Despite the boundaries of the walls, the inner quality of each of these men still begins to flow freely.

Increased Interest in and Effectiveness of Education and Vocational Training

Reduced anxiety may be the catalyst for the renewed interest in education found with the Transcendental Meditation program. The Stillwater study described above helped quantify this increased interest in education. After learning the Transcendental Meditation technique, the meditators participated in twice as many recreational and educational activities, and spent three times as many hours per week in these activities compared with the control groups.

Bill McCuiston, a correctional counselor at San Quentin State Prison, watched the meditation program at his institution grow from 35 meditators to 200, with more wanting to learn. McCuiston said that after learning to meditate the inmates would want to know how their families could get involved, and they discussed with him "their increased interest in education, setting goals for the future, and the lessening of stress in a hostile environment."

Improved Social Behavior

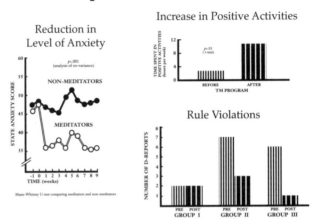

Pat Corum, who was at both San Quentin and Folsom, says he spent a lot of time conning people before his stress levels changed. Only then did he become interested in the educational programs that were available. Corum told a remarkable story of his experiences both before and after learning the Transcendental Meditation technique. He said that in a period of seven and a half years of incarceration at San Quentin, he saw twenty-two psychiatrists, psychologists and counselors, and spent hundreds of hours in group therapy, group counseling, and individual therapy. Finally, he says he was able to "con the psychs into giving him clearance" and he was paroled. Then after shooting a policeman and assaulting several more, he was again incarcerated at Folsom State Prison, and was into his fourteenth year of prison when he learned to meditate. Corum said:

> Within a year [after learning the TM Technique] I was out from the maximum security side, and in two years I was transferred into San Quentin. From

Pat Corum giving lecture after completing college program.

there, I completed a college program, and was transferred to a medium security institution . . . . After eleven years of meditation, I was released back into society. From the time I was instructed in meditation I have not found it necessary to put my hands in anger on another human being. I have completely gotten away from all uses of mind and mood altering chemicals. My stress levels, those that caused me to strike out, to shoot people, to commit homicides, are not here today . . . . Without the introduction of Transcendental Meditation to the system, it's going to continue to get worse because there are no other answers. I know. I have been through all the little programs the Department of Corrections had. None of them worked until I got into Transcendental Meditation. Once I was able to experience living without stress and stop being involved in the insanity, then some of the other programs did work because I did complete a college program, I did complete a vocational program, but nothing worked as long as there were those high levels of stress where I couldn't function.

Increased Optimism

William Clark, a staff psychologist at the Walpole prison in

Massachusetts where a number of studies were conducted in the late 1970s, encouraged the Massachusetts Department of Corrections to expand a small TM program that involved about sixty inmates. He said that in a number of confidential interviews, inmates told him that the Transcendental Meditation program freed them from long standing drug addictions, and they reported "being immensely reassured in their belief in themselves." This is important because one cause of stress and crime that criminologists have long recognized is the tension that results from a lack of optimism, and the ensuing difference between what someone wants and what he thinks he can obtain through lawful means (original *strain theory*).

In explaining the results of the Walpole Transcendental Meditation program, Clark said that at first there was considerable skepticism toward the meditating inmates, but this changed to respect and questions of how others could get involved in the program. Having seen many of the TM group in his counseling sessions before their TM training, and again afterwards, Clark recommended that Transcendental Meditation be made available to all the inmates and staff at the prison.

Enhancing Self-Esteem and Emotional Maturity

In the extensive study at the Federal Correctional Institution in Milan, Michigan (described earlier in this chapter), the researchers looked at the inmates' self-esteem and emotional maturity, as well as aggression and other personality factors. Those individuals who practiced the Transcendental Meditation technique *regularly* showed a highly significant increase in self-esteem (with a statistical significance of $p = .0001$, indicating odds of one in 10,000 that the results were due to chance). The TM subjects who practiced meditation *irregularly* also increased significantly in self-esteem, but not as much as the regular TM subjects, a further indication that the Transcendental Meditation technique was responsible for the change. The control group showed virtually no change in self-esteem.

In addition, the TM subjects who were *regular* in their meditation showed significant decreases in all negative measures of emotional stability and maturity, whereas the controls remained at the same levels. The regular meditators became significantly less neurotic, guilty, depressed, manic, obsessive-compulsive, and schizophrenic. The *irregular* meditators were also significantly less neurotic and obsessive-compulsive; they showed decreases in guilt, depression and schizophrenia, although these changes were not statistically significant.

Immediate and Lasting Improvement

Vermont. From 1982 through 1984 more than 700 inmates and correctional staff learned to practice the Transcendental Meditation technique in programs at several institutions in the Vermont Department of Corrections. The inmates also participated in related educational programs to gain an understanding of the positive changes they were experiencing. Several studies emerged.[10]

In the first study, after only a four-week period, physiological tests indicated greater relaxation in the inmates, reduced sleep disturbances and paranoid anxiety, and significantly increased control. This test was designed to evaluate the immediate results from TM in a short period of time. During the first four weeks, however, the inmates' consumption of cigarettes and caffeine, and their levels of hostility, did not change significantly.

In the second study, 129 inmates were pre-tested and subsequently post-tested up to fourteen months following instruction in TM. This longitudinal study showed continued improvements in sleep disturbances, paranoid anxiety, and anger control. In addition, hostility was also found to decrease in the subsequent testing, presumably because the inmates had been meditating longer. The researchers analyzed the results using various statistical procedures and stated their conclusion that the "progress [from the Transcendental Meditation program] persists over time" and that the improvement is brought about by the practice of the technique itself rather than, for example, the level of motivation of the inmates who decide to participate.

This process of continuing change as the inmates continued to meditate contrasts sharply with results of conventional programs. With most self-improvement programs, the results decline over time. Initially, inmates may be inspired and motivated to behave better, but "pep talks," and purely psychological approaches, don't often produce lasting results. In contrast, the deep inner changes in mind and body from the Transcendental Meditation program have a lasting effect on the individual, which is the prerequisite for public safety and lower recidivism rates.

What, then, can we expect from this new approach in the way of reducing recidivism?

Dramatically Reducing Recidivism

Catherine Bleick and Allan Abrams conducted recidivism research on 259 male parolees of the California Department of Corrections who had learned the Transcendental Meditation technique, and their findings were published in the *Journal of Criminal Justice* in 1987.[10] They found that in comparison to matched controls, the Transcendental Meditation group had consistently more favorable recidivism outcomes in every year from one to six years after parole. Controlling for twenty-eight social and criminal history variables in what is known as "stepwise multiple regression," the Transcendental Meditation program significantly ($p = .001$, indicating odds of one in a thousand the results were due to chance) reduced recidivism, at one year and up to six years after parole, while prisoner education, vocational training, and psychotherapy did not consistently reduce recidivism.

The researchers found that those men paroled within five months after TM instruction tended to have a worse recidivism profile than those paroled later, who had more time to practice the technique. This was one indication that the Transcendental Meditation program was responsible for the change. In addition, the average recidivism rate was significantly lower for the meditator group every year after release compared with controls. Recidivism will naturally increase over time (more people will have been returned to prison four years after their initial release, compared with three years). But as both the Transcendental Meditation group and the control group increased in recidivism over the years, the groups did not converge, and the meditators consistently stayed out of trouble compared with the controls. As an indication of the lasting impact the Transcendental Meditation program had on the inmates, 55% of those who began the program were found to still be meditating, and about 42% were still meditating very regularly, up to six years after they learned the technique. Actually, even more may have been meditating, since of those surveyed, 10% said they had stopped and the others simply did not respond.

Reduced Recidivism

p < .001   p < .005   p < .01   p < .05   p < .025

Dr. Charles Alexander and his co-researchers at Harvard came to similar conclusions about this program's ability to reduce recidivism in a carefully controlled study at the minimum security prison at Walpole in Massachusetts.[12] Dr. Alexander's study followed the released inmates for more than three years and used not only a random sample of inmates as a comparison group, but also four different treatment groups: those in drug rehabilitation, a counseling group and inmates involved in two self-improvement programs. The fifty-three prisoner Transcendental Meditation group showed consistently lower recidivism rates when compared to the random sample controls, and those in treatment.

How much better in terms of recidivism were the Transcendental Meditation groups compared with the control groups in these studies? Unlike conventional education programs, where the Bureau of Prisons is excited about a 4.2% difference in recidivism (see next chapter), the Bleick and Abrams study with the Transcendental Meditation program found that the difference was 30% to 45%. One year after parole, 7.4% of the Transcendental Meditation group returned to prison compared with 13.8% for the controls. This constituted an absolute difference of 6.4% and a relative reduction by the TM group of over 45% (the 4.2% Bureau of Prisons statistic was also a relative rate of comparison). Overall, looking at up to six years after release in the Bleick and Abrams study, 19.8% of the Transcendental Meditation group returned to prison versus 34.5% for the controls, an absolute difference of 14.7%, and a relative reduction of over 40%. Controlling for other potential variables, the meditator group had a 40% better recidivism rate after one year and approximately 30% as an overall percentage for the period for from six months to six years after release.

In the Alexander study, when controlling for the time of release (to avoid the potential bias caused by groups with later dates of release having less time to recidivate), after thirty-six months the Transcendental Meditation recidivism rate was 48% lower than the entire group involved in other treatment programs.

The results, to date, are extremely encouraging, and should be even better when the experiments are on a larger scale and have the full support of the therapeutic community. They will also be better once the full complement of natural medicine strategies is applied (see chapter 10).

The Need to Immunize Correctional Officers

People in stressed occupations get burned out, quit, or fall prey to any number of stress-related disorders. And perhaps no group in society works in a more stressful occupation than the correctional officer. Studies show that correctional officers, to an alarming extent, are prone to heart attacks, high blood pressure, and ulcers (even more so than police officers).[13] In fact, the average life span of the correctional officer is said to be sixteen years less than the national average.[14] The carrier concept in relation to stress (see chapter 3) may explain this phenomenon, at least in part. Correctional employees, even those who may not have face to face contact with prisoners, work in a stressed environment. The prisoners are stressed, and they radiate that influence in the prison environment, creating an unmistakable atmosphere of tension. As a result, the failure to immunize the staff against this stressful influence seriously undermines their health and effectiveness.

Bill McCuiston, the correctional officer from San Quentin mentioned earlier, summarized the reaction of many correctional staff after learning to meditate.

> Prior to meditating I was unaware of the stress I was exposed to. Many times I had trouble resting in the evening, and always seemed tired and irritable . . . . Since I began TM I have experienced restful nights. I fall asleep as soon as I lie down. My awareness of myself and others has increased. After a period of time I became aware that I had been fooling myself concerning my lack of stress, and being all together . . . . I became more at ease with myself and others. Changes within myself were noticed by others. So not only have I observed changes in the inmate group, but I was able to experience similar changes within myself.

Bill McMullen, another correctional officer at San Quentin, said:

> I started TM in approximately 1981, and that was a time of unrest here at the prison where we were having numerous assaults and gang wars. And as a stress reliever, I found that TM, which I came upon quite accidentally, worked very well for me. At first . . . I was concerned as to whether or not it was something that had to do with religion, and I was pleased to find out that it did not, and I've just really been able to operate at peak efficiency with the help of TM.

One inmate commented on the changes he observed in the attitude of the prison staff.

> I have seen staff after they've learned to meditate talk about "man, I got up this morning, looking forward to going to prison." And that's a difference in attitude. They weren't calling in sick all of the time. They enjoyed who they were.

Farrokh Anklesaria, who was trained as a barrister in England, has directed prison programs involving the Transcendental Meditation program throughout the world. He says teaching the staff to meditate is crucial to a successful program.

> Teaching the inmates is simple. But if you don't instruct the wardens and staff, your program can be sabotaged. Everything in prisons is under lock and key, and if the staff wants to undermine your program, they can. Inmates, for example, have to come to a lecture room for educational sessions, or for their exercise classes, or to have their meditation checked, and to answer their questions about the practice. A meditating staff knows that the program works. They help you, and are supportive of the inmates' participation. Without learning the technique themselves, the staff is cynical, and they spread their negativity to everyone. Forty or fifty years of failed attempts at rehabilitation makes correctional officers disbelievers in rehabilitation *until* they experience it for themselves.

At the Vermont Department of Corrections, 200 members of the staff learned the Transcendental Meditation program. One phase of the Vermont research evaluated changes in the staff. In this aspect of the study, a randomly selected group of eighteen correctional personnel showed significant decreases over a four-month period in the same measures as the prisoners—hostility, paranoid anxiety, and sleep disturbance. After the program, Dick Wright, who was the Assistant Superintendent of the Rutland, Vermont Correctional Institution, said:

> I think the biggest impact of the TM program for me is when I sit in a room with anywhere from two residents to thirty residents, and we practice the TM technique. No matter what happens after that, no matter what happened before that, with the residents, you know they all feel it; you know that they can all feel the unity and the power and that peacefulness. All of a sudden, everything is forgotten; all of a sudden there is no division between who you are and who they are.

Positive Experiences in Other Countries

When this approach has been introduced in other countries in prisons or to correctional or police personnel, the results have been even more dramatic for several reasons. For one, these programs utilized Transcendental Meditation, as well as certain of the complementary approaches described in chapter 10 (especially neuromuscular and respiratory techniques). There was also a strong educational component, to make sure the prisoners were meditating properly and that they understood the changes taking place in themselves.

Moreover, many of the programs in foreign countries have been much larger, involving thousands of individuals. These, of necessity, have had the support not just of the staff, but usually of government officials who supervise the activity of the prison directors. The inmates also enjoy their practice more in larger groups. Those who practice the Transcendental Meditation technique in groups often find that they have more settled experiences in meditation in direct proportion to the size of the group. This may be one reason for this important finding of the research over the last fifteen years—the more substantial the prison program, the more beneficial the results.

Spanish inmates performing neuromuscular stretching exercises.

Inmates meditating in Senegal.

Senegal

In 1987, this approach was used by two prisons in the West African nation of Senegal. The Director of the Camp Penal Prison in Dakar, Ilbrahima Sy, said that the penology experts in Senegal had long been searching for an effective rehabilitation program. His country's efforts had been modeled earlier on those of the Western nations. In a search for genuine rehabilitation, his administration attempted to institute the so-called progressive or enlightened reforms used in the West, since repressive measures, he said, "turned out to be a fiasco everywhere, even in countries referred to as the most civilized."

When the experts decided that only through work and the teaching of trades could a prisoner rediscover his value and become rehabilitated, some Senegal prisons, Mr. Sy said, offered farming, carpentry, masonry, automobile repair, and other workshops for the training of inmates. As in the U.S., the goal was to teach the prisoner a trade so he could continue in it after release and earn a

Guards and TM instructors outside the group meditation hall in a Senegalese prison.

decent living. However, Mr. Sy said the experience showed that inmates in the work programs "who were thought to be well rehabilitated, constitute the biggest number of recidivists." But once the Transcendental Meditation program was tried, Mr. Sy's inmate population changed dramatically for the better, and he felt he had finally found the key to rehabilitation.

The positive results convinced Mr. Sy and the director of the Senegal penitentiary system that the Transcendental Meditation program should be brought to the remaining prisons. As a result, except for a few prisons in outlying areas, the program was introduced in all Senegalese prisons. *Eleven thousand* inmates and 900 correctional officers and administrators were instructed in the Transcendental Meditation technique, and in neuromuscular and neurorespiratory exercises, and received related classroom instruction, a program taking about two hours a day. Mr. Sy said:

> One has only to refer to the registers to find that
> there are less escapees, less punishments, less fights

among the prisoners, and less medical consultations today, than in the past. Only a few months ago it would have been unthinkable to have 250 prisoners led only by three or four guards, move in perfectly orderly lines from the inner courtyard to the Transcendental Meditation hall in the administrative part of the prison, without there being serious risk of escape or uprisings. Today, this movement takes place without any problem, twice a day for group meditation. Even the families of prisoners no longer look upon the guards as tormentors, but rather as educators and advisors.

Happier and more relaxed inmates after learning Transcendental Meditation.

Top right: "The last time my parents visited me, they were amazed at how well and happy I looked. I told them that I had started Transcendental Meditation. Now, they too want to learn it." Lamin Gueye, juvenile inmate, Dakar, Senegal.

Bottom right: "I meditate for twenty minutes and always when I come out of meditation I feel calm inside. I feel really relaxed. It is as if inside me there is a flowing river but without waves." Moussa Diop, inmate, Dakar, Senegal.

Two years after the program was introduced, Colonel Mamadou Diop, then director of the penitentiary administration of Senegal, wrote a letter describing the overall results:

An immediate improvement in the inmates' sleep • A sharp reduction in irritability and aggressiveness • Greater confidence among the inmates • Improved relationships between inmates • A marked decrease in drug consumption • Almost a complete cessation of fights between inmates.

Colonel Mamadou Diop, Director of Penitentiary Administration, Senegal

Colonel Diop said that before the program was instituted Senegal prisons had an especially high recidivism rate since "there is no structure or scheme for the reintegration of inmates into society, nor is there any provision for work or jobs for those released." As a result, he estimated that in Senegal usually about 90% of inmates released after serving their sentence returned to prison within only one month. Every year in Senegal there is a presidential pardon for some of the inmates. Six months after the June, 1988 amnesty, in which 2,390 inmates were released, there were less than 200 recidivists, and 80% of those consisted of the group that had not participated in the meditation program because their prisons were in such remote regions of the country. In other words, only about forty of those who participated in the program returned to prison. This allowed the country to close three prisons for lack of inmates, and in others there were sharp reductions in the number of prisoners.

After this experience, the Senegal prison directors were no longer skeptical that prisoners could be rehabilitated. In fact, thirty prison directors signed a proclamation asking, among other things, that words like "penal," "penitentiary," and even "prison" be discontinued and replaced by expressions referring to the "re-education" and "rehabilitation" that was possible.

Other Countries

Successful TM prison programs involving more than 30,000 inmates have also been conducted in Sri Lanka, India, Kenya, Chile, Spain, Paraguay, Mexico, Korea, and elsewhere.

In Brazil, the program was taught on a large scale at the police academies. In 1987 and 1988, 26,000 military police learned the Transcendental Meditation technique. A number of studies were

*Top left: "The police lead a hazardous life; they have to constantly interact with the public. That is why I consider TM an indispensable subject in our training courses."
Sergeant Roberto Silva, Bahia Military Police Training Academy, Bahia, Brazil*

Top right: "Transcendental Meditation brought about a dramatic decline in recidivism. It transformed the once tense camp—due to gang rivalry — into a friendly and livable environment." Remigio Araya, Superintendent, Camp Sampaguita, Manila, Philippines

Bottom left: "I can testify from personal experience that no better recipe than the TM technique can be prescribed to steady the nerves of tension ridden police personnel and to increase their morale." V.N. Rajan, Inspector-General of Police (Retd.) Kerala, India

Bottom right: "Statistical studies from the Military Police Operations Center have shown many positive changes in the behavior of the police. There has been a significant drop in disciplinary measures taken against police personnel." Major Arcanjo Mendez, Director of Police Academy, Bahia, Brazil.

conducted showing decreases of 31% to 65% in disciplinary measures taken against the police as compared with the pre-TM experience, and a highly significant improvement in community relations as measured by a more than tenfold increase in positive reports about the police from the citizens of Salvador. Other results included sharp reductions in tension, a significant decrease in physician visits, and greatly improved relationships with others.

Improvements at Police Academy
Military Police of Piaui: Center for Education and Training of Policemen—289 Students

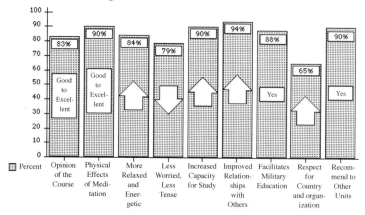

Improved Health and Discipline
Military Police of Bahia
6,300 Police Officers, 100 Cadets in Training

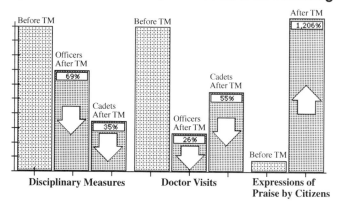

Politics and Prisons:
No Way to Run a War Against Crime

Almost everything about prisons is highly political. This often makes it difficult to get unconventional programs, even proven ones, to be utilized. When a warden becomes interested in any unconventional program, he worries whether his job will be jeopardized if the program doesn't "sit well" with the head of corrections or the governor. And even if the head of corrections and the governor aren't afraid of an unconventional approach, the corrections head may worry how long the existing governor will be in office, and what his replacement may think. As a result, despite the often dramatic results of this new approach, almost none of the prison programs described in this chapter (not even the Senegal program) were funded by governments. They were funded by private contributions, usually by meditating donors eager to prove that this approach could work in a rehabilitation setting. After a time, however, the money runs out, and the programs stop, until private donors can be inspired again. This is no way to run a war against crime.

Chapter Seven

The Enjoyable Antidote to Drugs and Alcohol— And 12 Times More Effective than DARE

If we are going to significantly reduce crime, we have to signif cantly reduce the demand for drugs and alcohol, which are intimately connected with our high crime rate. The U.S. Department of Justice's Bureau of Justice Statistics tells us that 57% of jail inmates (jail is a short-term detention facility; the term excludes state and federal prisons) in 1991 reported they were under the influence of drugs or alcohol when they committed their offense.[1] Drug offenders in 1991 constituted 56% of federal prison inmates and over 25% of state prison inmates.[2]

Drug arrests accelerated greatly in the mid-1980s, primarily of nonwhite youths recruited into the drug trade. Juveniles make good recruits because they work cheaply and are often able to avoid adult punishments. Standard practice is for drug dealers to arm these kids with guns, since they often carry substantial cash and drugs, and they can't complain to the police if someone steals their property. Guns from the drug trade probably account for much of the increase in homicides by youth eighteen and under in the last ten years, either directly, or as the guns make their way from drug sellers into the rest of the community.[3]

Youths, of course, don't just sell drugs, they use drugs. Surveys conducted by the University of Michigan reported that the number of high school students using marijuana at least once a month jumped from 11.3% to 15.6% from 1993 to 1994, and that 25% of eighth graders have used some illicit drug at least once. And youth use alcohol even more than illicit drugs. Almost 30% of the nation's high school seniors and 44% of college students participated in binge drinking, defined as downing five or more drinks in a row in the two weeks prior to being questioned by the Michigan researchers.

In my state of Iowa, which is somewhat worse than the national average on alcohol and somewhat better on illicit drugs, about 10% of the population is addicted to either drugs or alcohol and another 19% indulge to the point that they could become addicted.

Nationally, including alcohol, drugs and tobacco, the cost to society of substance abuse is estimated at $238 billion per year (about $1,000 per person). This includes the amount spent on law enforcement, prevention, treatment, higher health care costs, lower productivity, increased sick leave, and industrial theft and damage. Other estimates go as high as $550 billion. Whichever figure you choose to believe, either one indicates we are a stressed nation, seeking chemical relief, which only compounds the drug-crime problem. As one columnist said, "The drug war is over, we lost. Now what do we do?" In our frustration, the approach that is becoming a more acceptable solution is decriminalization.

Is Decriminalization the Answer?

Decriminalization has now gained some eminent advocates, including conservative columnist William F. Buckley, Jr. Even Newt Gingrich recently expressed his frustration with the drug problem, saying he wants to consider decriminalization if an increased use of the death penalty for some drug sellers fails to remedy the situation. Decriminalization of drugs is also an approach promoted by the Libertarian Party.

During my campaign in 1994, I thought this would be an interesting political issue. The Republicans in Iowa, like me, were against decriminalization, while the Democrats called for studies on the issue. When James Flansburg, a senior columnist at the *Des Moines Register*, wrote a column supporting decriminalization during the

1994 campaign, I wrote to him setting forth my opposing views in the hope that this would trigger more discussion. Unfortunately, since only the Libertarian and NLP candidates were interested in debating this issue at the time, the papers in Iowa dropped the subject in favor of endless articles on the death penalty.

Decriminalization is a solution that derives from the inability to control the supply of drugs, and the ineffective solutions aimed at decreasing the demand. The huge demand for illegal drugs, and the profitability of supplying them, leads those advocating decriminalization to conclude that the simple way to end the problem is to take the profit out by decriminalization. They would decrease the demand for *illegal* drugs, by making the drugs *legal*. Advocates of decriminalization reason that, since the cost to society of drug crimes and drug enforcement should then decline, the money can be spent on prevention (which hasn't worked very well) or else on other things. In addition to reducing costs, many believe that the strongest argument for decriminalization is a moral one—that the enforcement of drug laws violates an important principle of a free society: that those who do no harm to others by their drug taking (a highly debatable point given the drug-crime statistics) should not be harmed by the government.[4]

Decriminalization theorists state that the vast majority of the Americans who violated the drug laws in recent years have done no harm to others, and in many cases they believe they have not even harmed themselves (also highly debatable). Decriminalization advocates argue that the violence caused by the drug-crime connection would greatly diminish, and that there would be far fewer illicit drug traffickers and far less violence resulting from drug wars, which often claim the lives of police and innocent bystanders. They point out that drugs are more dangerous because they are illegal, not regulated, and, consequently, often polluted by poisonous substances.[5]

All the experts, whether they are in favor of decriminalization or not, recognize that law enforcement has but a small effect on the drug problem, as a result of the nature of the market for drugs, and its profitability. Drugs can be grown and processed virtually anywhere, and if we succeed in preventing their importation from one area of the world, it only results in an increased flow from another area. The same multiple source principle that prevents an international solution also prevents effective street level enforcement. If drugs are not available for a time in New York's East Village, you can find them in the West Village, Harlem, Coney Island, or Sutton Place, or on Locust Street in Des Moines, Iowa. Most observers say the estimated $20 billion a year spent in enforcing drug laws has done little or nothing to alleviate the problem.

The Problems of Decriminalization

But as bad as the drug problem is, Mark Kleiman from Harvard's John F. Kennedy School of Government suggests that decriminalization carries with it such grave risks that its implementation may be a cure that is worse than the illness.[6] For example, Kleiman points out that if we decided to make a drug like cocaine legally available for at least some "recreational" use, we would still regulate it by controlling the age of its users. But, as Kleiman suggests, in view of the large percentage of cocaine users under the age of twenty-one, decriminalization would not result in much of a decrease in illegal trafficking to underage youth.[7] Moreover, we should expect that the availability of "legal" cocaine would result in more youths experimenting with the drug, in the same way that twelve and thirteen-year-olds now experiment with alcohol. There is virtually no way to enforce laws against adolescent drinking, and similar problems will exist in enforcing laws against adolescent drug use.

The legalization of hard drugs would also reduce their price. And a lower price, coupled with legalization, and a trickle down to underage youth, would result in increased consumption. Increased consumption occurs with every commodity if you lower the price, make the access easier, and relax the social restraints.[8] Therefore, while decriminalization could solve some problems, it may leave us with more insidious ones, as more young people harm themselves by taking illicit drugs the way they now use alcohol.

Why People Take Drugs — The Source of the Problem

Why do people use marijuana or crack? For the same reason news reporters, stockbrokers, and football coaches have a scotch and soda or a couple of beers. They enjoy it. They unwind with it.

To understand what is behind the drug problem, it helps to compare data on drug abuse with the percentage of people who know that they seriously risk harming themselves with drugs. For example, of young adults (high school graduates one to twelve years beyond high school) who smoke marijuana or use crack or cocaine regularly, 72% of the marijuana users, 92% of the cocaine users, and 96% of the crack users perceive it as a great risk to their health.[9] And most people today are well aware of the problems that result from tobacco use or frequent social drinking, but people continue these behaviors because they enjoy them (or have enjoyed them so much in the past that they are now addicted), even though they realize they're harmful. Classroom instruction about the dangers of drugs or alcohol, and how to resist saying "yes," pale in the face of peer pressure to go along, and the reality that most people who use drugs or alcohol enjoy the experience.

Nancy Tobler, a prominent drug researcher affiliated with the School of Social Welfare at the State University of New York, cites figures from the National Clearinghouse for Alcohol Information.[10] showing that having fun or celebrating is the dominant reason for drinking according to 61% of those surveyed. And if you add reasons such as forgetting problems and relieving stress (both of which represent a search for greater satisfaction), the percentage is probably close to 100%.

Recognizing that drugs and alcohol bring enjoyment to those who use them is critical to solving the problem. This doesn't mean that we need a new strategy of realism that lets kids know that drugs are fun but dangerous. Kids already know that. The true "get real" message needs to be addressed to those who insist on continuing with current drug education strategies. The message is that prevention and rehabilitation are going to be an uphill battle if our drug reduction efforts consist of trying to convince kids to resist what is fun, without offering a healthy alternative.

DARE — The Failure of the Popular Strategies

Perhaps the most vivid illustration of a politically popular—yet unsuccessful—drug strategy is the DARE (drug abuse resistance education) drug prevention program. Its political history was well chronicled by a recent article.[11] DARE began in Los Angeles in 1983 as a joint project of the Los Angeles Police Department and a Los Angeles school district. It grew dramatically after President Reagan declared a national "War on Drugs" in 1986, because DARE pushes all the right political buttons. It is action oriented, and satisfies the demand to "do something" for our kids. It involves the police, who teach the seventeen-lesson program, and the schools, where it is taught, and it's popular with parents who hear their sixth-grade kids warbling anti-drug messages at the dinner table. For politicians, DARE represents the classical affirmation of traditional values, and in the mid-1980s DARE promoters started appearing at Congressional hearings arranged by politicians who liked all the politically correct associations. The DARE leaders promoted the DARE drug prevention program, and a new respect for authority that would result from police interaction with youth.[12]

In 1986, LAPD chief Daryl Gates obtained U.S. Department of Justice funding for his department "to share [the] unique DARE program with other communities," and before long, the Justice Department funded DARE Training Centers for police officers (it now costs up to $90,000 per year for each full-time officer-instructor), and began appointing members of a national DARE advisory board. The U.S. Department of Education then provided funding through the 1989 Drug Free Schools and Communities Act, but only if DARE programs or similar programs involving the police are used.

Despite all the political acclaim, there have long been serious questions about DARE's effectiveness, and the recent long-term studies uniformly show either exceedingly small positive effects, no positive effects, or even potentially negative effects. Getting on the DARE bandwagon has now resulted in the use of the program by 50% of all school districts in all fifty states, making it the biggest and most expensive failure in drug prevention history.[13]

In 1994, a long term evaluation of the program in thirty-six Illinois schools[14] concluded that there was little evidence of its effectiveness in decreasing drug use one or two years after the students received their instruction. The researchers from the University of Illinois pointed out that DARE's rapid growth was inconsistent with the modest prior evaluations of DARE by only a handful of states, and that the prior evaluations were largely unpublished reports that had inadequate research designs or analytical strategies.

In 1994, researchers at Indiana University came to similar conclusions. They published their carefully controlled research which showed that there were no long-term effects in either drug use, self-esteem, or respect for the police. Unfortunately, they even found significantly higher hallucinogen use among the DARE group, suggesting (as does other literature) that such programs may lead to a greater interest in experimentation.[15]

With a vested political interest in DARE, and in response to the early rumblings about DARE's ineffectiveness, the Justice Department decided to fund its own comparison of DARE to other prevention programs using *meta-analysis*, a potent new research tool. Meta-analysis is a scientific procedure for drawing conclusions from large bodies of research, systematically combining the results of many studies. It is thus a highly sophisticated method of comparing the relative effectiveness of different programs. Without meta-analysis, comparisons of programs are difficult and have to be based on subjective factors, producing judgments that could be misleading. Meta-analysis takes into account the number of participants in a study, and statistically controls for the strength of the research design, the kind of persons involved in the study, and other factors.

When the researchers hired by the Justice Department conducted their meta-analysis they weeded out poorly designed studies without a control group, and finally selected what appeared to be the eight best DARE studies involving 214 schools, 5,898 DARE students and 3,419 non-DARE students. These studies were then compared to studies on twenty-five other drug prevention programs. The results showed that DARE was less effective than the comparison programs, and had only a small effect in preventing drug use.[16] How small? Really small!

According to statistical analysis, in dealing with these kind of behavioral studies, an *effect size* (the measure of the effectiveness of a program) of .80 is considered large, .50 medium, and .20 is considered small.[17] Taking all the studies into account, DARE had a .06 effect size on drug abuse, which was about one-third of the .19 effect size (also small) for the best of the other programs.

Politics at least being predictable, the Justice Department refused to accept the findings and tried to prevent publication of its own study, in the same way that Robert Martinson's report twenty years ago (that "nothing works" in rehabilitating prisoners) was suppressed by the State of New York, which had funded Martinson (legal action had to be taken to obtain its release). It is well known that politicians attach themselves to popular crime approaches, then refuse to alter their positions, even in the face of hard evidence, for fear of losing political popularity.

Is it DARE or Something Deeper?

As for other approaches that are supported by our tax dollars, Tobler, in 1986, used meta-analysis to evaluate 143 adolescent drug prevention programs. Her study of the mostly school-based programs involved an analysis of individual studies conducted from 1972 to 1984. All studies involved control groups that didn't participate in any program. Tobler's study evaluated whether the programs changed the student's (1) knowledge about drugs, (2) attitudes, (3) use of drugs, (4) refusal skills (the ability to say "no" when pressured), and (5) behavior, as measured by reports of principals, parents, police, or others, depending on the particular study.

Tobler's study concluded that there was solid evidence to discontinue programs that involved only knowledge about drugs or attempts to change attitudes about drugs.[18] In other words, the assumption that knowledge of the harm caused by drugs will discourage drug use is erroneous. In all the "knowledge only" programs, there were substantial gains in knowledge without significant decreases in use.

When measuring changes in the use of drugs, the effect sizes varied significantly depending on the "drug" involved. Remembering that a small effect is .20 (which Tobler translates to a 10.6% success rate when compared to the control group), a moderate effect is .50, and a large effect is .80, the programs averaged an effect size of .17 for alcohol, .14 for soft drugs, and .21 for all drugs including hard drugs.

Tobler updated her meta-analysis in 1993 and evaluated 120 programs, including 81 located after the 1986 study. The results showed that the knowledge, self-esteem, and attitudinal programs (which Tobler termed non-interactive) had a small effect size of .075, compared with the still small effect size of .164 for the interactive programs. The latter were peer programs that attempted to develop refusal skills and more generic skills such as communication, assertiveness, problem solving, and coping. The least effective non-interactive programs were the DARE programs and such well-known school programs as "Here's Looking at You" and its offspring "Here's Looking at You, Two" (a cute name is a definite aid to funding). The best of the peer programs had an effect size of .21 (about an 11% success rate), which is perhaps not as bad as it seems, considering that the program may involve only about ten hours of time. However, Tobler warns us to beware of the sleeping giant, because these programs only address peer pressure to take drugs, and a program's effectiveness typically declines over time. This is especially true in the face of what is perceived as the enjoyable alternative—taking drugs or drinking with a "designated driver" attitude, courtesy of the beer companies.

In reality, the problem isn't just DARE, it's the approach. As one researcher funded by the National Institute on Drug Abuse said in describing our current programs, "we want the person to give up something that gives him pleasure and/or relieves stress, while offering little in return except vague, distant promises of a better life and improved self-esteem."[19]

The More the *Inner* Effect, the Better the Results

The better results of peer and interactive programs among the current prevention efforts are due to their relatively greater impact on the target population. Students identify with their peers more than with authority figures, and interactive programs (compared with straight lectures) facilitate the mind's understanding. In other words, there is a greater *inner* effect. The peer and interactive programs probably work well enough to continue their use, but our experience tells us that they don't work well enough to dramatically change the demand for drugs. They don't have greater success because they don't offer adequate compensation for giving up the pleasure kids find through drugs (imagine your son asking his buddies if they want to practice drug resistance role playing on Saturday).

How do we make a dramatic change? Management experts say that if you want a company to improve by 10% or 20%, then you do the things you have been doing, but do them better (i.e., more sophisticated peer and interactive programs). If, however, you want a 500% change, then you have to do things in a completely different way.

Same Underlying Problem as Crime, Same Inner Solution

The Transcendental Meditation program has been found to be remarkably successful in preventing and treating drug abuse. Its success was chronicled in late 1994 in a special double issue of the *Alcoholism Treatment Quarterly*,[20] which contained seventeen articles describing its effectiveness, and that of the Maharishi Ayur-Veda program, in dealing with substance abuse. This new approach works because drugs and alcohol abuse represent a search for relaxation, a means of avoiding pain or responsibility, or a coping mechanism—in other words, relief from stress. General stress theory states that the root cause of both crime and drug abuse is the stress in people's lives, which makes them unhappy, tense, and dependent on an artificial coping mechanism. Relieving stress through the natural strategies described in this book gives the drug abuser something positive in return for giving up drugs. It also works far better than conventional programs to prevent the misery either of drug abuse, or of trying to live life without drugs.

Catherine Bleick of the Institute of Social Rehabilitation in California has worked to rehabilitate many drug abusers. One of those she helped told her:

> TM has removed on numerous occasions over-whelming urges for me to "just have one drink," or "one Valium" to calm down. I go to many AA meetings and I see what I call toxic stress messes—individuals who are haggard, worn out, living off coffee, cigarettes, lack of sleep and compulsive attendance at AA meetings, forever searching for a scrap of serenity, relief and release—and I must state emphatically that most of this type of misery in sobriety is nothing but stress and TM removes the stress . . . .[21]

The Crime Vaccine Meta-Analysis: 12 Times More Effective Than DARE

One of the articles in the 1994 special issue of *Alcoholism Treatment Quarterly* is a meta-analysis of nineteen studies on TM and drug abuse (all studies which provided sufficient data to undertake a meta-analysis).[22] The studies involved 4,524 subjects, 3,249 of which were Transcendental Meditation participants and 1,275 were inactive controls or participants in other treatments. The studies included populations of high school drug users, college drug users, adults at an industrial work site, elderly African-Americans, teenage drug users in Sweden, Vietnam veterans with alcohol problems, and skid row alcoholics. Six of the studies involved random assignment to the Transcendental Meditation program or comparison groups involved in relaxation techniques, and a number were longitudinal studies that tracked meditators over varying periods of up to twenty-four months. Unlike the *small* effect sizes for the conventional programs described above, this meta-analysis showed that the Transcendental Meditation program produced *large* effect sizes.

In studies involving preventing substance abuse in the general population (these are more comparable to the Tobler studies previously discussed), the effect size (weighted, as is customary, for the size of the study and its design, among other factors) for the Transcendental Meditation groups was .42 for alcohol and .74 for illicit drugs. (Remember that for DARE, the effect size was .06 and for the interactive programs in Tobler's 1986 study it was .164.) For illicit drugs, this is more than twelve times the effect of DARE and 4.5 times the effect of other interactive programs. In measuring the Transcendental Meditation program's effectiveness in treating heavy users of alcohol and drug abuse, the effect sizes were greater. In populations being treated for substance abuse with Transcendental Meditation, the effect size was 1.35 for alcohol and 1.16 for illicit drugs. All these effect sizes were significantly greater than for the control groups. In most instances, the control group was an untreated, substance abusing population, although in five of the nineteen studies the control group was actively involved in some therapeutic program. Tables 1 and 2 summarize those studies with control groups of either kind, treated or untreated, that were analyzed by Dr. Charles Alexander and his co-researchers, the authors of the report.[23]

In summarizing the findings, the authors conclude that the Transcendental Meditation program produces better results because it works at a deeper level of mind and body than conventional treatments. Such treatments, they say, often employ several modalities, but generally target more superficial levels of functioning such as attitudes and behavior. The Transcendental Meditation program, in contrast, eliminates the deep imbalances in mental and physiological functioning (stress), the prerequisite for total recovery. As the authors point out, "if the deeper imbalances are not eliminated, initial effects may only be temporary, with addictive behaviors re-surfacing again and again despite numerous attempts at abstinence. This may account for the rapid decline in abstinence following completion of most standard treatment programs."[24]

Table 1

META-ANALYSIS ON EFFECTS OF TM IN PREVENTING SUBSTANCE ABUSE

Author of Study	Sample Size	Alcohol Effect Size	Other Drugs Effect Size
Shafii (1974)	216	0.43	0.75
Myers (1974)	180	0.45	0.39
Friend (1975)	193	0.84	0.42
Monahan (1977)	415	0.33	0.75
Katz (1977)	467	0.20	1.36
Farinelli (1989)	207	0.58	(not measured)
Nidich (1989)	51	0.41	1.00
Thrall (1989)	46	0.37	1.25
Schneider (1992)	112	0.62	2.29
Alexander (1993)	86	0.89	2.29

Table 2

META-ANALYSIS ON EFFECTS OF TM IN TREATING DRUG ABUSERS

Author of Study	Sample Size	Alcohol Effect Size	Other Drugs Effect Size
Schenkluhn (1977)	115	(Not measured)	1.10
Brautigam (1977)	20	(Not measured)	1.23
Taub (1982)	108	0.54	(Not measured)
Brooks (1985)	18	2.28	(Not measured)

The Crime Vaccine Used with Heavy Drug Users

In the nineteen studies evaluated by Dr. Alexander and his colleagues, one particularly noteworthy study was conducted in West Germany by two researchers who followed over one hundred fifteen late-teen drug users attending an outpatient drug rehabilitation center in Germany.[25] All were serious drug users, with the majority using multiple drugs. The drugs of choice were marijuana, hallucinogens, amphetamines, barbiturates, and opiates. The Transcendental Meditation group consisted of seventy-six subjects who learned to meditate in addition to receiving outpatient drug counseling, while the control group (thirty-nine students of comparable demographics) received only the outpatient drug counseling.

Reduced Drug Abuse

Drug Use

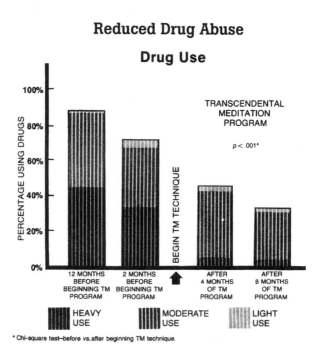

After four months practicing the Transcendental Meditation technique, the number of heavy drug users in the TM group fell from 44.6% to 4.6%. After eight months of TM practice, the use of amphetamines and barbiturates decreased 96% ($p = .001$), the use of hallucinogens decreased 91% ($p = .001$), and the use of opiates decreased 78% ($p = .001$). The Transcendental Meditation group also showed enhanced psychological health relative to controls on multiple measures of a personality inventory. This study also illustrates how the results from this particular meditation program increase over time, as the individual continues to gain a natural sense of inner fulfillment. For most programs, the results decline over time because they don't provide a healthy inner experience that substitutes for the enjoyment or relief the abuser derives from drugs. This study with late-teen, heavy drug users is especially important because of the age-crime connection (see chapter 4). Because so many crimes are committed by young drug users, a treatment program that is effective for this age group saves not just their lives, but the lives of many others.

Chapter Eight

The Failure of Crime Strategies That Don't Immunize the Physiology

A research report from the Federal Bureau of Prisons on recidvism acknowledges that the Bureau's staff is "greatly interested in the effects of correctional operations on recidivism." At the same time the report admits that there are presently only a few formal programs explicitly aimed at "rehabilitating the criminal offender."[1] When the Bureau attempts to rehabilitate, the report says that it favors programs that attempt to "normalize" life, such as educational programs and social furloughs to overcome the debilitating effects of prison. Underlying this approach is a theory of the cause of crime that fails to deal with the underlying stress factor, except in superficial ways that don't change the functioning of the brain and nervous system of the offender.

The Crime Theory of the Bureau of Prisons

The approach to recidivism of the Bureau attempts to reduce what is known as "prisonization," the sense of alienation and isolation that inmates experience while in prison. The Bureau policy makers acknowledge that the programs they favor derive from the late Edwin H. Sutherland's *differential association* theory of the cause of crime, which was formulated in the late 1940s. Sutherland, a leading sociologist, did not believe crime was caused by individual traits, but was a learning experience (a sociological explanation) that could affect anyone. While Sutherland is correct that crime can be a learning experience, one prerequisite is a stressed nervous system that allows the individual to be attracted to the excitement of

105

the criminal lifestyle and leaves one open to "learning" this behavior.
The Bureau states its bias against psychologically-based rehabilitation efforts, which it says have not been shown to be effective, and
it doesn't consider a natural procedure like Transcendental
Meditation, despite its proven effectiveness.

The federal programs aim at replacing the norms that support
prison misconduct, such as prison gangs and the inmate's alienation
from the staff and prison rules, with activities that are intended to
support law-abiding behavior. These programs were described by
the Bureau research report, as follows:

> The normalizing policies, operations, and programs,
> to which we refer, facilitate the humane treatment
> of inmates; open lines of communication between
> staff and inmates, which allow inmates to express
> their needs, and staff to provide guidance on meet-
> ing those needs in a law-abiding manner; and pro-
> vide opportunities for diversion from the pains of
> imprisonment and for acquiring law-abiding habits,
> skills, norms, and attitudes (accompanied by
> rewards for taking advantage of these opportunities
> and sanctions for not doing so.)[2]

This is a laudable description of a hoped-for effect of prison programs, but the real issue is how to achieve the goal of increased
communication and openness to education and to others. The
Bureau cites support for its current policy in the positive recidivism
findings on the effect of social furloughs (time allowed with family
away from the prison) and prison education programs. The research
cited, however, only minimally supports the theory. The research
merely suggests that Sutherland's learning theory is but one of
many crime theories that have some research to support them, but
which don't meet much success because they don't address the
underlying stress factor. The Bureau research estimated that 4.2%
fewer inmates recidivated who successfully participated in at least
one education course for every six months of their prison term,

compared with those who did not. For social furloughs, the Bureau reports 13.4% fewer inmates recidivated who received a social furlough, compared with those who received no such vacation. Furloughs are a difficult variable to evaluate, however, and of limited usefulness since only extremely low-risk prisoners are given furloughs. As for educational programs, a 4.2% better recidivism rate isn't going to win the war on crime (the Transcendental Meditation program reduced recidivism by 30% to 45%), and new research raises serious questions about the value of conventional education that doesn't address the prisoner's stress.

Conventional Education: Does it Help the Criminal or is it a Liberal Myth?

Professor Daniel Lockwood, of the Criminal Justice Department at Clark Atlanta University, presented a paper at the 1995 meeting of the Academy of Criminal Justice Sciences, which undertook an exhaustive analysis of the education of U.S. prisoners and its effect on recidivism. His study used data developed by the Bureau of Justice Statistics based on state and federal criminal histories for a large random sample of released prisoners from eleven states. The sample consisted of 7,126 cases chosen randomly from a prison population of approximately 37,000 former inmates. His data defined recidivism as arrest for a felony or misdemeanor within three years after release. His research showed some revealing statistics that could cast serious doubt on the liberal belief that educating prisoners along conventional lines will have any significant impact on recidivism.

Lockwood found that for those who entered state facilities with a high school diploma, the rate of re-arrest within three years of release was over 62%. For those with some college, it was 61%. For those who had less than a tenth grade education, there was essentially no difference. It was only for those who entered with a college degree that the recidivism rate was markedly lower. For those few, only 38% were re-arrested within three years.

Professor Lockwood then evaluated the effects of educational programs within correctional institutions. He evaluated forty studies which reported on the recidivism of prisoners who participated in such programs. He noted, first, that many of these studies were conducted by individuals who were highly uninformed about recidivism theory. Since factors such as age at time of release and race tend to be predictors of recidivism, a sound evaluation of educational programs needs to be based on an analysis that takes those variables into account. In his paper, Professor Lockwood pays particular attention to several studies that were important because of either the careful design or the large number of individuals studied. Referring to the GED (general equivalency diploma program) in New York State's prison system, Professor Lockwood states that of the more than 4,000 people who completed the GED program in prison, 34% returned to prison, compared with what he considers a very close rate of 39% for those who did not earn the GED. (The small difference is especially striking if you factor in the higher motivation to change among those who decide to get a GED in the first place.) Similarly, for vocational training, Professor Lockwood found that there were insignificant differences between those that received correctional education and those that did not. Lockwood stated that "the notion that delivering increased amounts of education to persons in trouble will solve their problems may be a liberal myth . . . ."

The Failure of Conventional Education Without Stress Reduction

Julio is a good example of an educated prisoner who still couldn't cope with the stress outside the prison walls. While incarcerated at the Augusta Correctional Institute in Georgia, he told his own story in a prison newsletter.

In 1974, Julio was sentenced to life in prison for murder. While in prison he participated in all the conventional self-help programs and earned a GED, a BA, and five vocational certifications. He won local and national awards for his academic achievements. The goal of living a normal life and returning to freedom motivated him to modify many negative behaviors and "to walk the chalkline," as he puts it.

In 1987 he was paroled, but he says he lacked the "coping skills which would be required in normal everyday life." When released, he said he was "the Boy Wonder of the Georgia Penal System with a BA and an overly inflated ego," and he thought he would never return to prison. He described his first two years outside as turbulent times, even with the support of his wife and children. By his third year he was making good money in two legitimate businesses, but his wife left him, and he returned to drugs and a criminal lifestyle. In 1991, he was convicted of armed robbery and sentenced to prison for the remainder of his life.

Obviously, "education" is valuable, but what kind of education? Prisons don't offer effective stress reduction programs or character education (see chapter 11). Even when they recognize the debilitating effects of stress, they offer purely psychological approaches that do little, if anything, to correct the problem. They may tell prisoners to count to ten when they feel stressed, or to take a time out, or teach them to intellectually recognize stressful occurrences. Stress, however, is not just intellectual or psychological. It produces a physical abnormality in the nervous system, and approaches that don't deal with this concrete physiological aspect of stress won't succeed. *It's like trying to overcome a polio epidemic with words of caution, rather than a vaccine.* Unfortunately, some academics and others who promote the existing strategies have been endorsing them for so long that they can't admit that these strategies don't work, in much the same way that many politicians can't admit that DARE is a failure. Education, counseling, behavior modification, and group therapy (the typical strategies that try to produce an "inner change") can have some benefit, but their effects will be severely limited without also making concrete changes at a deep level of physiological functioning.

Counseling

The aim of counseling is to motivate and to teach people something, typically about themselves. Counselors tell prisoners that they must want to change their lives, become less bitter, and bring out the best within themselves. Counselors tell prisoners that they need to ask themselves if they have thought about stopping their irresponsible behavior, and the homework they give prisoners requires them to describe the reasons they want to change. They are told they need to examine whether they want freedom or the kind of life that has resulted in their imprisonment. Ultimately, counselors encourage prisoners that change is possible and that "none of us need be victims of our past."

Counseling sessions in Iowa prisons often include work-sheets, reading sessions, and videos attempting to motivate prisoners to change. The encouragement to change often revolves around attempting to convince prisoners that they may be dissatisfied with their situation, but not with themselves, and that they need to see how *they* are the source of their problem. This basic attitude was expressed in a few paragraphs of a worksheet I was given by one of the counselors in charge of drug programs at the medium security prison in Mount Pleasant. It stated:

> When people have the courage to take a long look
> at their lives *and their own part in creating them*
> they may make a commitment to change. When
> people are willing to see what they have done—to
> become disgusted with their own behavior—with the
> pain it has caused so many—then change is possible.

The underlying notion is that prisoners have to be strongly motivated to change, or change will not take place. Motivation is generally thought to be "the first principle" of good education. It's often said that the motivation to change can come from a significant life experience (like being incarcerated). But, of course, everyone in prison has the incarceration experience, and the poor recidivism rate suggests that something more is necessary. The failure of counseling and other such programs to produce the hoped-for results has led to the prevailing attitude that people can't really change.

One good test of whether a self-help program works is whether the inmates like the program. You can assume that if they don't like it, they're not going to get much out of it. Unfortunately, many prisoners don't like counseling. Don McMichael, an inmate at Folsom State Prison in California, described counseling sessions that he said didn't have the intended effect.

> Every group counseling session I've ever been involved with always ended in a fiasco. They always turned out to be "please the headmaster" situations. Hearing the remarks of how 99% of convicts feel about counseling, it's a wonder it still exists.

Behavior Modification

If motivation is felt to be the first principle in education (actually stress reduction and the concurrent development of the mind and emotions should be the first principle), then the next, according to many educators, is reinforcement. Reinforcement as a teaching mechanism is simply the idea that in order to have a successful educational experience, or to change our behavior, we need to receive feedback as to how we are doing. Behavior modification is a reinforcement approach commonly used in the prison environment to bring about a change in behavior.

When I toured the Mount Pleasant prison during my campaign, I was surprised at the degree to which the counselors considered behavior modification as the basic way to get prisoners to comply with the prison rules. In its simplest form, behavior modification means that if you don't follow the rules, you spend some hours or days in "lock-down," meaning you only come out of your cell for an hour of recreation and spend the rest of the time isolated from the other prisoners.

Behavior modification uses either negative reinforcement like lock-down, or positive reinforcement, which is known by educators to be more effective. In prisons, positive reinforcement means receiving various privileges such as opportunities for the prisoner to be out of his cell in the evening, allowing him to take his arts and crafts into his cell, or improvements in living conditions. There are a number of important rules concerning behavior modification that include the need for consistency, and for a reinforcer to be timed to closely follow the actual behavior.

There is no question that we all use reinforcers in getting along with others. However, in situations where complex human behavior is involved, behavior modification has had limited success. Even when it's been successful in prisons, there's a big difference between getting a prisoner to follow the rules when he's under the warden's watchful eye, and changing him from within so that he is naturally self-disciplined and continues to be motivated when he gets out. Pat Corum described his experience with behavior modification in prison. He said:

> For all the years they had a gun on me, they had a tendency to control my outward behavior, but there was no change within, no change in the thinking, no change in the attitude, only the threat of punishment for aberrant behavior.

Jerome Bruner, one of the leading educational psychologists (and an expert on the use of reinforcers in education), insists that while reinforcement and external factors can have importance in developing the motivation to change and to learn, it is only through intrinsic motivation that the desire to change will be sustained. A prisoner, for example, can have a momentary catharsis, but intrinsic development, he says, has long been the key to bringing about sustained change. The real question, of course, is how to bring about the intrinsic development.

Therapy

In Iowa, substance abuse programs use group therapy, which often amounts to the same type of sensitivity training that businesses experimented with in the 1970s. In these sessions a group of ten or twelve prisoners are monitored by a trained group leader and encouraged to analyze each other's attitudes and behavior. They also compare how they see themselves with how others see them.

The emphasis may be on learning about feelings, as much as getting facts, and experimenting with new ways of relating to others or using the insights of others to help you understand yourself. The hope in these programs, of course, is that self-knowledge gained from the training sessions will unlock inner resources and motivate the prisoners to better behavior.

In business, where executives were not under any political pressure to do something, they did away with these techniques, believing that the group sessions did more harm than good, because of their stressful nature. In some instances the techniques caused emotional experiences that even so-called normal people couldn't handle. Despite years of using group therapy, there isn't much in the way of research to show that it has a lasting value, and obviously it doesn't change the physiology to make it resistant to future stressors.

James Fleming, M.D., Co-Director of the Mount Pleasant Mental Health Institute in Iowa, was formerly a psychiatric consultant to the District of Columbia Department of Corrections. He says, that therapy, whether with individuals or groups, is not going to succeed in prisons because approximately 70% of the prison population consists of "anti-social" personalities, who aren't candidates for therapy. Anti-social personalities, he says, "don't tell the truth and they manipulate the situation," which makes them unresponsive to psychiatric approaches. Dr. Fleming had this to say in comparing the current approaches used in prisons with the Transcendental Meditation program:

> "We are in a real dilemma. In California, for example, a federal judge recognized that the mental health care of prisoners in one maximum security prison was woefully inadequate and violated fundamental rights. But what do we do about it? Counseling and psychotherapy, while they may be helpful for some acute situations, will do little to change the thinking and behavior patterns of hardened criminals. Prisoners, for example, don't respond well to authority figures or external controls over them. In my

experience, the Transcendental Meditation program is the one tool that can effect a major alteration in the thinking and behavior of inmates. The change here is self-generated, rather than coming from outside, so there is no resistance to any efforts of those in authority."

Alcoholics Anonymous

One popular approach that combines counseling, the use of reinforcers and elements of group therapy and group persuasion, is the Twelve Steps approach of AA (Alcoholics Anonymous) or NA (Narcotics Anonymous), which is free, popular, and largely unresearched (see chapter 6).

During my campaign, I had a meeting with Bill Reichardt, who ran against Bonnie Campbell in the Democratic primary race for Governor of Iowa in 1994. Reichardt, a former Iowa legislator and an all Big Ten football player, ran a single issue race focusing on preventing crime by taking truants off the street and rehabilitating them. Governor Terry Branstad then promised financial support for Bill's youth programs, and Reichardt made the front pages of the *Des Moines Register* by breaking with the Democrats and endorsing the Republican governor's candidacy. I had wanted to meet Reichardt since we seemed to be part of a small group of candidates who believed rehabilitation was possible.

At our meeting I gave Bill a copy of a videotape explaining the success in rehabilitating prisoners in Senegal. Five minutes into my speech about this new approach, Bill interrupted me. "Let me stop you, Jay," Bill said. "I have to tell you, you're preaching to the choir." Reichardt explained that I didn't have to persuade him, and that he was already very interested in using the Transcendental Meditation program if he ever obtained the pilot program that the governor had promised. Bill explained that his approach to rehabilitation was much like the Alcoholics Anonymous approach, which he believes works better than anything else he has tried. But he acknowledged that six months after the youths left his program, they were back on the street and in trouble again. Bill said he was interested in Transcendental Meditation because it continues to help youths on a daily basis, even after they are out from under supervision —a process of self-recovery.

How Government Allocates Crime Money to Treatment or Prevention Programs

Government recognizes that all the current approaches to prevention and rehabilitation have limited success rates, so it takes a "multi-modality" approach. Because there is no one conventional approach that works, to obtain government funding your prevention or rehabilitation program needs to combine several approaches such as counseling, behavior modification, group therapy, and mentoring, in an attempt at holistic treatment. And in funding sociological programs, the money is also spread among urban enterprise zones, community policing, midnight basketball and whatever other politically correct programs are suggested. But is there any theoretical basis for deciding which programs will be more likely to succeed?

How Business Would Analyze Crime Solutions

Two books that have guided business people for years in their effort to change employee behavior and motivate workers to better performance are *Work and the Nature of Man* and *The Motivation to Work* by Frederick Herzberg. These classic books relate the motivation to perform well in a job to general theories of human nature. Interestingly, Herzberg's ideas of human nature were not much different from those of the classical crime theorists who said that human nature concerned itself with a need to avoid pain and maximize pleasure. Like the theories underlying behavior modification, Herzberg also recognized that pleasure as a motivating factor was more important than pain, and that avoiding punishment didn't motivate people very well. Most importantly, Herzberg, and later Abraham Maslow, determined from their studies that changing environmental factors such as poor working conditions, bureaucratic personnel policies, and lack of job security or job opportunities did-n't motivate employees because they were extrinsic factors that at best affected dissatisfaction. While Herzberg said that the removal of these factors can momentarily eliminate dissatisfaction, he rec-ognized that it didn't produce lasting inner satisfaction, and there-fore didn't motivate people to better and more productive behavior on the job. Instead Herzberg said that businesses had to create solu-tions that provided intrinsic rewards. Businesses tested Herzberg's theories over the years. It is now well accepted that opportunities for intrinsic growth and inner rewards have a more lasting impact than the extrinsic factors, because of their more intimate connection to the individual—their deeper significance in the hierarchy of human needs.

Modern Crime Strategies: Going Beyond the Buzzwords (to More Buzzwords)

Many criminologists recognize these principles and at least some have attempted to apply them. The Justice Department's Office of Juvenile Justice *Programs for Prevention* publication clearly recog-nizes the Herzberg/Maslow hierarchy favoring the intrinsic factors. Unfortunately, while they employ the Herzberg buzzwords, the more you look at the solutions the government advocates, the more you see superficial recommendations. These authors say that chil-dren need to *bond* with the family, and therefore need opportunities such as "making dinner once a week, or researching where the family can get the best buy on a VCR."[3] While no one objects to children being given responsibility or being recognized for their achieve-ments, we're in big trouble if our principal strategies simply identify the details of how to interact with kids, rather than giving both the kids and the adults something that naturally makes them more loving and well-behaved from within. Any number of criminal justice pro-grams call for "going beyond the buzzwords" to find deeper answers, but solutions like letting our children make dinner and describing it with a fancy name like *bonding* just takes us from the old buzzwords to new ones.

New Prisons and Other Extrinsic Solutions

Applying a Herzberg analysis to crime, "extrinsic" or "environmental" factors can have an impact, but improving the job opportunities or housing in urban areas, or removing the graffiti, or closing the parks at night, as Herzberg would say, won't have the same impact as improving more intrinsic factors. Better housing may eliminate dissatisfaction for the moment, but it won't produce a lasting internal state that reliably motivates people toward socially acceptable behavior on the job, or law-abiding behavior in society. In terms of general stress theory, the reason that better housing or job opportunities, or urban enterprise zones, could have some impact on crime is that fixing these problems, if we can, trickles down and causes people to experience less stress in their lives. If, however, we could do something to attack stress directly from a more intimate level, the effect will be much more beneficial. An analogy in medicine would be the difference between the old approach to preventing the spread of polio—telling people to avoid public swimming pools or other situations that especially put them at risk (a difficult approach when the virus may be everywhere)—and inoculating people with a polio vaccine. Polio was beaten when we focused on the *milieu intérieur*, not on the external circumstances. While the external levels of the crime problem are addressed with the best of intentions, these are often expensive experiments that only address stress in a superficial way, and can't have lasting success.

Quarantine or Inoculation

In the U.S. and other countries, governments are spending millions to build new prisons to relieve overcrowding and prevent un-rehabilitated prisoners from having to be released to make room for new prisoners. In some countries new prisons are also being constructed for inmate rehabilitation. In 1991, for example, France's Minister of Justice recognized the deplorable conditions that resulted in 51,000 inmates being incarcerated in prisons designed to house 32,000. Intending to reverse the "revolving door" situation that resulted in inmates repeatedly being returned to prison, the Ministry of Justice turned to the classic external approach—a new prison. In an article in *Paris Match* (July 31, 1991), the French Minister said that "prison should have a punitive and deterrent value; but it should also prepare the inmate for his return to society." To accomplish his laudable reform objectives, the Minister was able to construct a new "luxury" prison with classrooms, workshops, recreation halls and a gymnasium. It provided educational and vocational training, there was no overcrowding, and psychiatrists and psychologists were readily available to attend to the inmate population. But despite all the outer trappings of reform, the experiment failed miserably. Changing the environment won't have the same rehabilitative effect as changing the *milieu intérieur*, and shortly after the prison was built, the inmates rioted and burned the prison to the ground.

At a cost of about $10 million to build a new 100-inmate prison, and an operating cost of about $25,000 per inmate per year, it doesn't make sense to ignore a proven rehabilitation program dealing with stress—the Transcendental Meditation program—which costs only about $1,500 to $2,000 per inmate. Unfortunately, even the generally assumed benefit of a longer prison sentence—that the offender is prevented from committing crimes while incarcerated—has a serious downside in the absence of effective rehabilitation. Without stress reduction, prisoners have a longer period to associate with hardened criminals, and the longer incarceration results in a greater stigma and reduced opportunities upon release. Since 99% of prisoners will be released at some time, rehabilitation is absolutely necessary.

Moreover, the get tough approach of longer prison sentences is actually nothing new. In the U.S. the prison population has doubled in the past ten years, and California, for example, quadrupled its prison population over the same period, but without an appreciable reduction in crime. A 1994 article in the *New York Times Magazine*[4] pointed out that the overall mathematics in criminal justice produces a "crime funnel," which explains why the effect of new prisons and longer sentences isn't greater. For every person incarcerated in prison for a serious offense, from 75 to 100 or more serious crimes are committed. In the U.S. an estimated 34 million serious crimes each year result in only about 277,000 felony sentences to prison (in my own state of Iowa, an estimated 185,000 Group A serious offenses resulted in 1,850 sentences to prison in 1992).

USA Crime Funnel

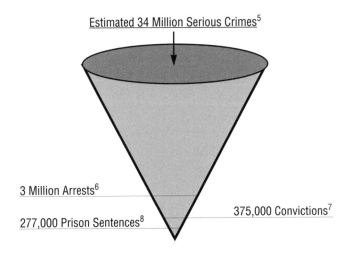

Estimated 34 Million Serious Crimes[5]

3 Million Arrests[6]

375,000 Convictions[7]

277,000 Prison Sentences[8]

Obviously, the maximum impact on the crime rate will come from preventing people from entering the criminal justice system at the large end of the funnel, as opposed to longer sentences for those relatively few persons at the short end who are caught, arrested, tried, convicted, and finally sentenced to prison.

The effort to incarcerate more individuals for longer periods is not unlike efforts to quarantine those with communicable diseases in an attempt to control an epidemic. While a quarantine will have some effect, the large number of carriers relative to those who are cases requires an immunization program. In modern times, epidemics have been overcome with vaccines that change the physiology of the general population, allowing each immunized individual to resist the infection. Quarantines are recognized in medicine as a limited and cumbersome remedy. Similarly, ending the crime epidemic requires a new effort to immunize the physiology of the individual (and to immunize the society as discussed in chapter 12), increasing the individual's natural resistance to stressful encounters and allowing him to be more fulfilled from within.

Psychological and Interpersonal Solutions

Compared with environmental solutions, the psychological and interpersonal strategies attempt to deal with deeper levels of the individual. But this, by itself, provides no guaranty that these strategies work. For example, interactions with counselors may be helpful or harmful, depending on the attitude and skill of the counselors and how they handle the offenders' stress. Midnight basketball as a solution is based on the environmental approach of keeping kids off the streets at 2:00 A.M. by occupying their time, as well as the interpersonal approach of promoting healthy interactions (opposing gang members may play on the same team), and giving counselors an opportunity to make their pitch after the game. But while basketball is fine, in terms of general stress theory the midnight sessions are likely to do more harm than good, because they rob both the players and fans of the sleep that helps to counteract stress. Midnight basketball advocates say that these youths will be up until all hours of the night anyway, so we may as well give them something constructive to do. But midnight basketball encourages entire communities to stay up until the wee hours. In doing so, we're just creating communities that are full of carriers of stress, when we should be educating the community about the importance of deep rest in eliminating stress and crime.

In general, the purely psychological programs described in this chapter (counseling, behavior modification, group therapy, and Alcoholics Anonymous) use the thinking process, but they don't develop it—which requires developing the ability of the nervous system to resist stressful situations and improving brain functioning. The psychological approaches have limited success because using the mind to think about things is fundamentally different from creating orderliness in the mind, just as using a knife is different from sharpening it.

The stress epidemic and the failure of psychological approaches to effectively address the problems of stress, has caused a rapid growth in what are often called "mind-body" stress reduction clinics. These offer a variety of meditation and relaxation procedures, some created by physicians and academicians who studied the Transcendental Meditation research, saw the growing popularity of the technique, and thought they could accomplish the same results. But do the programs of the new mind-body clinics produce the same benefits as the Transcendental Meditation program? And how effective are they at reducing stress in the general population, and particularly in dealing with the highly stressed populations in penal institutions and drug rehabilitation centers?

Chapter Nine

Academia's Crime: Repressing or Demonizing Programs that Originate East of Cambridge

Ironically, one reason research on Transcendental Meditation gets ignored is that so much of it emphasizes physiological or biological changes. Although this provides confidence that the psychological and behavioral changes are real and will be long lasting, biological factors get into a touchy area as far as criminology is concerned. In a chapter in the book *The Causes of Crime: New Biological Approaches*,[1] David Farrington summarizes the politics in the early 1980s behind academia's rejection of biological influences on crime. He points out that criminology has been dominated by sociologists since World War II (it is actually a subdiscipline in the sociology department at most colleges), and sociologists are trained to look at social interactions as causes and solutions to problems. Biology to them is largely a taboo topic. A similar analysis is provided in *Taboos in Criminology*, where Edward Sagarin states that any linking of crime to biology suffers the same fate as linking it to genetic differences or race. It "risks jeers and hissing when the issues are debated in public and a torrent of abusive letters when they are debated in print."[2] Another researcher points to how "younger colleagues skirt controversial issues for fear of not receiving research funds or otherwise damaging their careers."[3]

While psychologists, in general, have been more open to biological solutions than sociologists, their biological solutions to crime have been largely pharmacological, and this gets into a controversial area where there are sound objections to managing violent individuals by keeping them artificially sedated. Librium, Valium, and other drugs have been used in the medication of inmates since the 1960s, occasionally resulting in reductions in aggression, but the use of these pharmacological agents is not without serious problems. While injections of various sedatives can be used effectively to calm individuals in emergency situations (where the debilitating effects are not so much a concern), the prolonged treatment of violent individuals with drugs produces tolerance to their sedative effects, raises ethical issues, creates harmful side effects, encourages chemical solutions for "better living" and, at best, blocks the symptoms but does little to change the underlying condition.

Superficial Mind-Body Techniques

Partly because of the many problems with trying to control behavior and stress through drugs, and partly because of the extensive research on the Transcendental Meditation program dating back to the early 1970s, many academic institutions have begun stress management clinics or mind-body institutes, which teach relaxation or meditation procedures. The basic approach of many of these institutions is that taken by Dr. Herbert Benson, an associate professor of medicine at Harvard's Mind/Body Medical Institute. Dr. Benson recognizes the value of the Transcendental Meditation technique, and was a "second chair" co-author with Dr. Robert Keith Wallace, the principal researcher, on some of the earliest studies on physiological changes during the practice. After finding extraordinary changes with Transcendental Meditation, Benson decided to develop his own technique. Within a year or so after this early TM research was published, and without ever learning to meditate himself, Benson wrote a few brief meditation instructions for what he calls his "Relaxation Response" technique, and he developed an interesting marketing strategy. Dr. Benson does not claim that the technique he developed is better than the Transcendental Meditation technique or any other meditation or relaxation technique. Instead, Benson says that "there is no best way of eliciting the relaxation response."[4] In fact, in the twenty years he has been offering his technique, he has avoided conducting any significant research comparing the effects of his technique with the TM technique, and he has ignored the comparative research done by others, which repudiates Benson's assertion of equivalency for virtually all techniques. To my knowledge, Dr. Benson has even avoided conducting research on his own technique that would investigate basic physiological measurements of stress, such as blood lactate concentrations or cortisol, which would allow others to compare his technique to Transcendental Meditation.[5] Since Benson routinely acknowledges that the TM meditators he initially studied showed "some of the lowest levels of blood lactate concentrations ever recorded,"[6] and says that reduced arterial blood lactate is a prime characteristic of the relaxation response,[7] it is surprising that he would not, for example, publish results of blood lactate changes in his own technique, unless he studied this basic marker and simply did not find comparable changes.

Instead of conducting such comparative research, or acknowledging the differences among the various meditation or relaxation techniques that others have found, Benson claims that numerous methods of relaxation and meditation, including ancient forms of prayer and practices of Zen, Yoga, Shintoism, Taoism, progressive muscle relaxation, mindfulness training, autogenic training, and other techniques, are all simply different ways to elicit what he calls a "relaxation response," and that his technique is as good as any. Dr. Benson repeats this litany whenever he has an opportunity, and since he claims that virtually all techniques produce the same response, he considers himself justified in using research on the Transcendental Meditation technique as evidence of the efficacy of his own technique. But this is like saying that a Cadillac and a Model T both produce a "power response," and then citing research on the Cadillac's internal combustion engine to sell the Model T. In fact, the research shows that different relaxation or meditation techniques produce significantly different results,[8] and the Transcendental Meditation technique is consistently found superior whenever comparative research has been conducted.

Maharishi University or Harvard:
Who's the Real Expert in Meditation?

Early comparisons of the Transcendental Meditation technique and Benson's relaxation response technique were undertaken by a Pennsylvania psychologist who investigated changes in skin resistance.[9] In chapter 5, we discussed how increased skin resistance is one measure of increased relaxation in the nervous system. Twenty-six subjects, half of whom learned the TM technique and half of whom learned Benson's technique, were measured over a seven-day period, three weeks after the subjects began their respective techniques. The mean rise in skin resistance for the Benson subjects was 25K (kilohms), whereas the mean rise for the TM group was 138K, over five times as great. The Pennsylvania study also attempted to determine the practical differences between the two techniques by comparing the subjects' behavior over the ensuing eight months. The researchers found that only one of the Benson subjects was able to reduce his need for tranquilizers, whereas in the TM group all ten who were taking prescription tranquilizers reduced their usage. In addition, subjective reports indicated improved control over impulsive behavior in the TM group, but not in the Benson group. Finally the Benson group said that after six weeks they became "extremely bored" with the practice, whereas in the TM group all the subjects were still meditating after eight months.

A similar early finding was made at Princeton in a comparison study of the Transcendental Meditation technique and Benson's.[10] Tolliver set out to compare the personality traits of those who might prefer the TM technique with those who might prefer Benson's technique. She administered a personality inventory to twenty-six subjects, after which half were first taught Benson's technique and the other half started the Transcendental Meditation technique; then, two weeks later, each group learned the other technique. After several more weeks, the subjects completed a detailed questionnaire describing their experiences. To Tolliver's great surprise, no comparison could be made because every one of the twenty-six subjects reported that they liked the Transcendental Meditation technique better. It didn't matter whether the subjects were rated "high-anxious," "low anxious," "extroverted," "introverted," "dependent," or "independent," *they all preferred the Transcendental Meditation technique.*

One physiological change Dr. Benson noted from his technique, which sparked his marketing strategy, was the observation of reduced oxygen consumption. Reduced oxygen consumption was first noted in early research on the Transcendental Meditation technique, as one component of a broad range of physiological changes during the practice. According to Dr. Robert Keith Wallace, who conducted much of the original research, oxygen consumption is actually a fairly crude physiological measurement compared to the biochemical and other changes that take place during Transcendental Meditation. However, Dr. Benson has used this physiological marker to make his claim of equivalency of all techniques, so it merits further analysis here.

Several early studies on Transcendental Meditation, including those conducted by Dr. Wallace and Dr. Benson, reported a mean 16% to 17% decrease in oxygen consumption during the practice, compared with an *eyes closed resting period before the practice.*[11] Another study by Dr. Wallace reported many TM subjects with individual decreases in oxygen consumption of 20% to 27% during meditation.[12] Based on his initial study of his own technique, Benson claimed it produced a 13% decrease in oxygen consumption, but this claim only passes muster with those who are unfamiliar with the way this research should be conducted. The 13% decrease with Benson's technique was in comparison to a prior control period in which the group was sitting with their *eyes open reading.*[13] In the part of the study that compared the decrease to an *eyes closed resting period* before practicing the technique (the control used in the TM study that Benson participated in), there was only a 10% decrease. Obviously, the activity during the control period makes a great difference. You could probably find a 90% decrease in oxygen consumption while reading a newspaper or watching television, if your comparison period was a sprint around the block.

In all events, it is inappropriate for a scientist to equate a 10% decrease in oxygen consumption with a 17% decrease, and argue that the techniques produce the same changes.

Studies of Reduced Anxiety (Meta-Analysis)

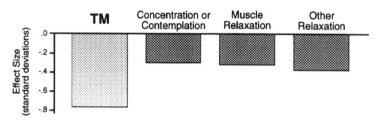

p < .001

More recent research now shows even more clearly the specious nature of the Benson claim that his technique and others produce the same results as the Transcendental Meditation technique. Using meta-analysis, which we have now learned is probably the most effective method of comparing the usefulness of different techniques, Dr. Kenneth Eppley of Stanford University and his co-researchers reported on their analysis of all studies that could be obtained through hand and computer searches of the literature through 1982, involving relaxation and meditation strategies and their effects on trait anxiety (see chart above).[14] Trait anxiety is the variable most frequently examined in studies on relaxation, and it measures the general tendency to be anxious. The studies are based on self-report measures, frequently using the Spielberger State-Trait Anxiety Inventory, which has been validated in hundreds of studies and is thought to be one of the most reliable self-report measures. The Eppley report analyzed 223 studies. The criteria for selecting studies to be compared excluded those with defective designs; ultimately the analysis compared 17 biofeedback studies, 22 progressive relaxation studies, and 70 studies involving some form of meditation, including the Transcendental Meditation technique, Dr. Benson's relaxation response, concentration forms of meditation, and other meditations that attempted to mimic TM, as well as placebos. The results showed that for TM the magnitude of the effect was twice as large as any of these other forms of meditation or relaxation.

In addition, a number of carefully controlled studies have shown that TM produces clinically beneficial results in the reduction of hypertension—results that differed significantly from those of active control groups practicing other relaxation techniques, and those groups given placebo techniques.[15] Other techniques of relaxation and meditation have simply not been found to produce this magnitude of results. Dr. David M. Eisenberg and his co-researchers, for example, conducted a meta-analysis of twenty-six hypertension studies that evaluated Dr. Benson's relaxation response technique, progressive muscle relaxation, biofeedback, meditation techniques *other than TM*, and other "stress management" procedures. They found that the efficacy of all these approaches in reducing hypertension was merely equivalent to that of placebo techniques.[16]

There are no studies that I am aware of where Dr. Benson's technique has been used with inmates or in drug treatment centers. However, Dr. Benson and Harvard (upon being asked to stop citing the Transcendental Meditation research as evidence of the efficacy of Benson's technique) acknowledged in 1995 through their attorneys that "TM has carried out numerous studies which have shown its effectiveness in the alleviation of substance abuse, and there is a paucity of literature on other techniques demonstrating that they can be used as effectively to treat that condition."[17]

Benson's Folly

Dr. Benson developed his technique by reading what had been written about meditation in the existing literature and modeling his technique on popular notions about how to meditate. But the reason meditation has been perceived as impractical for centuries is that these popular notions about how to meditate don't work. The proper procedure of meditation has never been effectively taught by a book or audiotapes; and inventing a technique after reading the popular literature on the subject just perpetuates the errors of the past. The successful practice of the Transcendental Meditation technique is based on a total absence of concentration or effort, whereas every other technique I have ever read about, including Dr. Benson's, requires an effort to do something with the mind—an effort that is counter-productive to the mind settling down and transcending all mental activity to experience a least excited state. And while the TM technique is simple, the instruction to allow the mind to experience its most settled state is highly specific. Each step of instruction is based on the meditator's experience, and the results are vastly different from Dr. Benson's technique.

Instead of pointing to comparative research, Dr. Benson touts his program by making false statements that the same relaxation response may be induced by "either traditional meditational practices or by the simple, *noncultic* technique" he teaches.[18] But this isn't science, it's a marketing strategy. Demonizing all meditation techniques that originate east of Cambridge, calling them *cultic* practices, serves merely to repress effective new crime strategies, or attempt to taint them, in an effort to discourage their use.

The U. Mass. Program

Dr. Jon Kabat-Zinn is another who developed his own meditation program and started a stress reduction clinic at the University of Massachusetts Medical Center. According to a recent magazine article, Dr. Kabat-Zinn began his program after first having taken a yoga class in a church basement, then starting to practice a Zen form of meditation, ultimately evolving his own method after reading books on Zen.[19] He then combined the yoga stretching exercises with his Zen meditation and began his clinic. His "mindfulness meditation" is also vastly different from the TM technique.

Transcendental Meditation is not a process of analyzing your thoughts. That is like swimming on the surface of a pond, rather than diving to the silent depths and experiencing the most settled state of mind. According to Dr. Kabat-Zinn, in his technique, you focus on thoughts, sensations, or physical discomfort.[20] He sometimes calls his mindfulness technique an "insight" meditation, and you are encouraged to note or be mindful of the content of your thoughts, and the feelings and reactions associated with them, in an effort to gain insights.[21] But searching for insights and focusing on thoughts and feelings keeps the mind active at the surface level of thinking, and is in the opposite direction to the mind settling down to experience its least excited state.

The key aspect of the Kabat-Zinn practice is trying to be a silent witness to your thoughts and attitudes, first in meditation, and then outside of meditation in activity, in an effort to train yourself to enjoy your moment-to-moment activity. For example, Dr. Kabat-Zinn says "mindful eating," part of his mindfulness training approach, involves looking at what you're about to eat, asking what is it, how it looks, where does it come from, how do you feel about putting it into your body, and how does your body feel anticipating eating at this moment? Then before swallowing, he tells us to be aware of the intention to swallow, then feel the actual process of swallowing, etc[22] (be careful teaching this technique to inmates, unless you're prepared for some flying spoons and forks).

Kabat-Zinn's approach incorporates one of the classical errors about meditation, which is repeated throughout the ages, often by those who get their knowledge from books rather than experience. Many years ago, Maharishi pointed out this misunderstanding. The ability to spontaneously enjoy your moment-to-moment activity in a settled state of mind that is not distracted by the "noise" of random thoughts, is the end result of a number of years of the practice of Transcendental Meditation. This is an aspect of the state traditionally known as "enlightenment," in which the individual uses his full mental potential, and naturally maintains an inner silence and stability of attention that serves as a platform for daily activity.

But gaining a settled state of mind during one's daily activity—a state which is not distracted by intruding thoughts—cannot be achieved by *trying* not to be distracted. The attempt to remain calm and to be mindful of your daily activity, which Dr. Kabat-Zinn advocates, interferes with a natural spontaneity in life (next time you eat, try asking how you feel about putting the spoon in your mouth, etc.). Consequently, such techniques can be highly counter-productive, and Maharishi has said that they may actually lead to mental dullness and inertia.

In the more than ten years Dr. Kabat-Zinn has been teaching his technique, there are no studies showing that the technique produces changes in the characteristics of the crime prone physiology, such as increased serotonin, decreased cortisol or blood lactate concen-trations, increased skin resistance, or EEG brain wave coherence. *Without these basic physiological changes, there will not be any lasting changes in pro-social behavior from Dr. Kabat-Zinn's pro-gram or, for that matter, from any other program.* That is why Dr. Kabat-Zinn's approach has not produced results with the severely stressed individuals that make up the inmate population.

Mindfulness Training and the Hard Reality of Teaching Prisoners to Be Less Hostile

Because of Dr. Kabat-Zinn's public recognition in Massachusetts, and probably also owing to the confused notion that all forms of meditation and relaxation produce the same response, in 1992 the Massachusetts Department of Corrections began a large prison pro-gram involving Dr. Kabat-Zinn's mindfulness training and his insight meditation. The program was paid for by the government, and was modeled on the one taught at the Stress Reduction Clinic at the University of Massachusetts Medical Center. As of the end of September, 1995, I was told that approximately 2,000 inmates had participated in the program at medium security, minimum security, and pre-release prisons in Massachusetts. Besides meditation, the program included stretching and yoga exercises selected by Dr. Kabat-Zinn, although his staff told me that they don't use the term "yoga" with the prison program, because it is "politically incor-rect." The program also had a research component, utilizing a con-trol group that did not practice these techniques. The inmates were measured with a number of psychological inventories to determine whether there were changes in their levels of hostility and anxiety, and, as is customary, the research measured the inmates before and after they began Dr. Kabat-Zinn's program.

No Results: No Changes from the U. Mass. Program

Dr. Janet Knight, then Director of Research at the Massachusetts Department of Corrections, told me in September 1995 that she had just recently reviewed the research on the first 1,500 inmates. She acknowledged that there were no results—no reduction in hostility or anxiety in the inmates (at least there were no reports of flying forks and spoons). I wasn't surprised. In prisons and drug rehabilitation centers, many of the residents are likely to be chronically stressed individuals, and techniques that don't change the physiology and amount to little more than placebos will not produce significant effects. One indication that mental techniques like Dr. Benson's and Dr. Kabat-Zinn's won't work over time is the lack of satisfaction derived from the practice of the technique itself. As we saw earlier, the Benson subjects in one study all became "extremely bored" and stopped practicing his relaxation response technique. And when Dr. Kabat-Zinn's staff tells his patients (as they do) that his technique is "going to be hard, it's going to be boring, it's going to require homework, but you don't have to like it, you just have to do it,"[25] it's a dead giveaway that there is much that is lacking in the technique.

Origins of Maharishi's Program

The Transcendental Meditation program is one of many approaches that Maharishi has introduced to promote human development. They all derive from the world's oldest tradition of knowledge, the Vedic tradition of India. Maharishi's education in this body of knowledge is not based on reading popular books, or even a few years of practice. As a young man, Maharishi was accepted as a student of Swami Brahmananda Saraswati, who was largely unknown in the West, but was recognized in India as one of its greatest sages and teachers.[24] Maharishi explains that from 1941 to 1953 his teacher (called "Guru Dev" by Maharishi) held a position known as the Shankaracharya of Jyotir Math in the Himalayas. This is a position of great honor in India established by the great Indian philosopher and sage Shankara many centuries before. Shankara's teachings had revived the ancient Vedic knowledge of how to attain the perfect functioning of mind and body that is known as enlightenment.

In order to perpetuate his teachings, Shankara set up four seats of knowledge in different parts of India. Each of those seats would be occupied by a Shankaracharya (a person occupying the chair of Shankara); and Guru Dev, Maharishi's teacher, became the Shankaracharya of the north in Jyotir Math. Because the position of Shankaracharya of Jyotir Math is so important, if there is no one whom the sages of India generally believe to have attained that pinnacle of inner development worthy of occupying the position, then that particular chair of Shankara goes unoccupied. This was the state of affairs for 150 years prior to when Guru Dev agreed to become the Shankaracharya of the north.

Maharishi describes how Guru Dev left home at age nine to learn meditation and other yogic practices, and lived most of his life in the remote forests of India, perfecting his own state of enlightenment. Although he was not known by the general public during this period of his life, Guru Dev became widely recognized by the yogis of India as having obtained a very elevated state of inner development. As a result, in 1943 he was persuaded to abandon his reclusive way of life in order to become Shankaracharya.

Shortly after finishing his university studies, Maharishi became a student of Guru Dev. This is where he learned Transcendental Meditation. On the basis of his own deep experiences in meditation, it became clear to Maharishi that the generally prevailing ideas about how to meditate were wrong. When Maharishi began teaching the Transcendental Meditation technique in the West in 1958, he corrected many misunderstandings about meditation prevalent in the minds of both educated Indians and Westerners. At that time, meditation was thought to involve concentration or control of the mind. Because the technique was wrong, meditation was generally considered to be very difficult and not many continued to practice it on a regular basis. Maharishi also restored the proper understanding that the repeated references in the popular texts to withdrawal from activity or to silently "witnessing" your activity (references misunderstood by Dr. Kabat-Zinn and many others), really were describing the goal, not the path—they were a description of the inner state of silence of an already enlightened mind. But Maharishi pointed out it was not productive to withdraw from life or to practice witnessing your moment-to-moment activity (such as eating or swallowing).

Most importantly, Maharishi's Transcendental Meditation technique reestablished the practical usefulness of meditation. The simplicity and effectiveness of this technique enables it to be used by anyone, regardless of his background or educational level.

The Repression of New Knowledge

Throughout history the fate of new knowledge is often *misinterpretation*. The errors now being made at Harvard, the University of Massachusetts, and other institutions are not much different from those that have occurred in the past to prevent or delay new knowledge and new paradigms from solving the problems of their day. The misinterpretations arise for several reasons. For one, people often don't understand new knowledge, and see it only in terms of what they already know or what they have read about. In a classical psychological experiment illustrating this tendency, a group of subjects consistently misidentified certain anomalous playing cards in a deck of mostly normal cards. A few irregular cards were placed in the deck, such as a red six of spades, and a black four of hearts. Each experiment consisted of flashing a card for a few seconds and asking the subject to identify it. For the normal cards the identifications were usually correct, but the anomalous cards were almost always misidentified as normal. The red six of spades might be identified as a six of diamonds, and the black four of hearts as a four of clubs. Moreover, some of the subjects were never able to make a correct identification no matter how long they looked at the cards.

Professor Thomas S. Kuhn of Princeton believed that this psychological experiment had significance far beyond its immediate context. In his celebrated book *The Structure of Scientific*

Revolutions, Professor Kuhn asserted that the difficulty of under-standing something new, and the disincentives (financial or profes-sional) within the existing disciplines toward accepting new knowl-edge, have been the principal cause of resistance to new scientific achievements throughout history. According to Kuhn's analysis, major scientific paradigms are developed and defended by those working within their own academic disciplines. Each discipline has one or more major themes that govern the discipline and what is published, taught, and promoted. Thus, even though by now quite a lot of evidence has accumulated to support the idea of biological or physiological causes of crime, because criminology is still dominated by psychological and sociological viewpoints, many academics in these fields refuse to accept the idea, and some still ridicule it. And now when universities are competing for students and grants, and academicians for prestige, many of those at stress management clinics have invented their own meditation or relaxation techniques, or they use those that can be learned from books or tapes. They then teach these techniques themselves, and ignore programs that have been proven more effective.

Most of the academic community has remained in deliberate ignorance of the value of the Transcendental Meditation program. When they investigate different relaxation or meditation strategies, they may ignore the Transcendental Meditation program, or they lump all forms of meditation together, refusing to recognize their distinct differences. And most criminologists don't care to look much at any meditation program. C. Ray Jeffrey, former President of the American Society of Criminology, tells us why: the academic community, he says, is committed to existing theology.[25] Professor Jeffrey says those who pursue new ideas are often ridiculed, and those who preach orthodoxy are rewarded. He points out numerous examples of how scientific achievements were opposed by ortho-doxy, beginning with Socrates, and including the so-called "Science for the People" movement at Harvard and MIT. This movement attacked E.D. Wilson (both physically and intellectually) over the publication of his book *Sociobiology*, which began to make a case for the biological basis of behavior.

Many people today recognize that politicians have long prevented new but unpopular knowledge from emerging, but in the press and perhaps even more in academia, there are equally culpable groups that serve to maintain the status quo and prevent new and effective crime solutions from becoming popular. Academics, unfortunately, may represent the most formidable opposition to the emergence of the new strategies since, unlike many politicians, who have no or few ideologies, academics live and die for theirs and are therefore more threatened by unorthodox approaches.

Chapter Ten

The Complementary Crime Vaccine Strategies: Giving the Offender a New Identity

In lectures on physics and consciousness at Maharishi University of Management, physicist Lawrence Domash pointed out that much of life can be understood in terms of several fundamental laws of nature. One of these is the Second Law of Thermodynamics. The Second Law says that all non-living systems become disorderly over time. The Second Law is the familiar law that makes buildings depreciate and bicycles turn into junk piles, when left to the elements of nature. For the non-living system, nature works in only one direction, towards greater disorder (or greater "entropy"). It can't happen, for example, that the various molecules in the junk pile rearrange themselves in an orderly way, and the junk pile suddenly becomes the bicycle again. But living organisms, on the other hand, can maintain order and even become more orderly over time.

How does this happen? As Dr. Domash explained, another law of nature—the Third Law of Thermodynamics—is the law that restores order to physical systems, and Domash explained the relevance of this law to understanding the benefits of the Transcendental Meditation technique. The Third Law states that *when the temperature of a given system is reduced, the entropy (disorder) is reduced; and when the temperature reaches zero, the entropy will be zero.* "Temperature" is just a technical synonym for activity. A high temperature means a high rate of activity and a disordering influence. A lower temperature means a lower rate of activity and an ordering influence. This is nature's primary way of producing order.

The Third Law of Thermodynamics therefore tells us why the Transcendental Meditation technique can be such a powerful tool for ordering the mind and body. As the "mental temperature" or activity of the mind is reduced, it produces a corresponding ordering effect in the brain physiology and the entire body. And as the mental temperature is reduced to its least excited state, it produces the maximum degree of orderliness.

In addition, there are other mechanisms by which living systems maintain order. In his search to identify how living organisms could maintain order in an environment that was tending to disorder and decay, physicist Erwin Schroedinger, a Nobel laureate, said:

> How does the living organism avoid decay? The obvious answer is: by eating, drinking, breathing, and (in the case of plants) assimilating. The technical term is metabolism. The Greek word (meta-ballein) means change or exchange. Exchange of what? Originally, the underlying idea is, no doubt, exchange of material . . . . that the exchange of material should be the essential thing is absurd. Any atom of nitrogen, oxygen, sulphur, is as good as any other . . . . For awhile in the past, our curiosity was silenced by being told we feed upon energy, but this is just as absurd . . . . Surely any calorie is as good as any other calorie. What then is that precious something contained in our food, which keeps us from death? That is easily answered . . . . what an organism feeds upon is negative entropy.[1]

We eat food, change it into necessary building blocks for the body, and then excrete the waste. Food gives us energy, but this isn't the primary reason for eating. The primary reason, says Schroedinger, is to obtain high quality or highly orderly energy. We're really eating the orderliness ("negative entropy" to Schroedinger) found in the environment. The notion that we take in food, burn it up, and transform the heat into energy is an oversimplification. More accurately, we are nourished by the orderly structure of the food we consume. This is why, ideally, we eat fresh food, and if our food isn't fresh from the farm, then at least it's refrigerated to arrest the decaying effect of the Second Law of Thermodynamics (as we've seen, lowering the temperature maintains order by virtue of the Third Law of Thermodynamics). This, then, is a helpful key to understanding possible mechanisms by which the natural strategies of Maharishi Ayur-Veda also help to increase physiological orderliness and resistance to stress. Of the many approaches of Maharishi Ayur-Veda, I'm presenting here just a few, focusing on broad principles of diet, exercise, and other strategies, as examples of how this ancient system of natural medicine can be successfully applied in crime prevention and rehabilitation. Maharishi Ayur-Veda includes not only the Transcendental Meditation technique, but also numerous other natural approaches that help the individual, in Shroedinger's terms, "feed on negative entropy"—to overcome the disordering effects of stress.

Overcoming Crime That Begins in the Kitchen

Many crimes "begin in the kitchen," as Thomas Marsh says in his book *Roots of Crime*.[2] Based on the preceeding discussion, the reason crimes can begin in the kitchen is that the foods being eaten are not creating an orderly effect in the functioning of the mind and body, and, instead, may be contributing to mental and physical disorder. Over the past fifteen years, a significant number of studies have shown the connection between crime and diet and, to a certain extent, this issue is now being discussed in the crime literature, but many criminologists still don't pay much attention because it is outside the traditional disciplines of psychology and sociology. Also, dietary changes haven't lived up to their potential as a means of modifying criminal behavior because our dietary understandings have been so incomplete. Still, as Marsh points out in his book, deficiencies in vitamin B_1 are known to cause symptoms that can include depression and irritability; deficiencies in vitamin B_2 also cause depression; deficiencies in vitamin B_{13} can cause pellagra, a form of schizophrenia; deficiencies in vitamin B_{12} and other vitamins can cause difficulties in concentration, depression, and manic and paranoid behavior; and vitamin C deficiencies are common among schizophrenics. And, according to Dr. Linus Pauling and others, adding vitamin C to the diet helps to combat stress.

Minerals also significantly contribute to the character of our emotions and behavior. Marsh reports that tests of a large group of emotionally disturbed children showed that half of them were suffering from a zinc deficiency.[3] Studies at the College of Medicine at the University of California at Irvine and at Appalachian State University in North Carolina showed that elevated manganese levels were present in the hair of violent subjects.[4] And among the many components in our diet, none has been more condemned than sugar, which is sometimes blamed for irritability, depression, drug and alcohol addiction, and anti-social behavior. Researchers frequently have shown a correlation between sugar and violence or other anti-social behavior.[5] The popularity of this idea has led many correctional institutions to lower the levels of sugar provided to inmates as a potential means of curbing disciplinary infractions. In 1993, the National Research Council funded a study to analyze the relationship between diet and violence. The Council concluded, however, that the understanding of the relationship between diet and behavior is still in its infancy.[6]

The Natural Medicine Approach to Diet

While an understanding of the relationship between diet and behavior may be in its infancy in the West, the connection has long been understood and explained by the classical texts of Ayurveda. This understanding is now being put into practice by the numerous physicians who have been trained in the Maharishi Ayur-Veda approach to health. According to this system, the remedy for the innumerable dietary and nutritional disorders that may contribute to crime is actually the same as the Western remedy—a balanced diet to create order in the physiology. However, the notion of what constitutes a balanced diet and what facilitates order in the physiology takes into account the characteristics of every food, and how food affects the specific characteristics of the individual's physiology. Some people have temperaments (and underlying physiologies) that are hot-blooded and fiery, while others may be cold and calculating like the psychopath. As a result, the process of determining what is a balanced diet in Maharishi Ayur-Veda involves a medical assessment of the state of the individual's physiology, to determine what specific imbalances may be present.

The Offender's Imbalances Determine the Treatment

The Maharishi Ayur-Veda physician analyzes three principles of nature, elements of which are present to a greater or lesser degree in the body of every individual, in food, and throughout the environment. Dietary and other recommendations are made based on the degree to which these various principles are in or out of balance in the body. Unlike most other systems, there is no one diet recommended for everyone—all recommendations (including diet and other approaches) are made on the basis of the functioning of the individual's physiology at that time, and the recommendations may change over time, especially as the physiology begins to function in a more orderly way. The three fundamental principles are known in Maharishi Ayur-Veda as *Vata, Pitta*, and *Kapha*.

Imbalances That Can Lead to Depression and Crimes of Greed

The characteristics of the *Kapha* principle are that it is heavy, sweet, and slow. A person with a predominance of Kapha would have a tendency to gain weight and typically displays an affectionate nature, slow movements, slow speech, and deliberate thinking. When Kapha is in balance in the body, it contributes to easygoing, good-natured, and caring behavior. When Kapha is imbalanced, however, the "heaviness" aspect of Kapha can lead to dullness, mental inertia, depression, procrastination, an inability to accept change, possessiveness and greed. Health disorders stemming from Kapha imbalances typically relate to fluid retention in the tissues, chest congestion, asthma, high cholesterol, cysts and other growths, diabetes (if too much sweet food is added to the body), and obesity, among others. In Western medicine, the prescription for colds, congestion, asthma, and other Kapha disorders involving fluid retention involves the use of antihistamines that dry the system. And in severe cases of bronchitis (an inflammation of the mucous membrane in the bronchial tubes), tuberculosis, or respiratory wheezing, the Western physician may even recommend moving to a dry climate such as Arizona. This symptomatic approach is, in certain respects, not unlike the extrinsic approaches to crime that we discussed earlier (see chapter 8). The antihistamines have an effect in placating the symptoms, but they do little to correct the underlying conditions within the physiology, which cause the fluid retention in the first place. On the other hand, the Maharishi Ayur-Veda approach uses the nourishing and balancing effect of different foods to correct the imbalances. The physician prescribes a diet to create balance among the three basic principles. This is accomplished based on his knowledge of the greater or lesser degrees of each of the principles in different foods.

An understanding of how food can create balance and order is difficult for many people to appreciate, simply because in the West we eat a range of foods that have such a variety of effects on our system that we never appreciate the particular effects that would result from a more systematic approach. Over the course of a week or two, we eat some foods that help the body to overcome imbalances, and others that are harmful, without any net positive effect. But if we consistently eat correctly, we will notice the difference.

Imbalances That Can Lead to Hot-Tempered Crimes

According to Maharishi Ayur-Veda, someone who is hot tempered and excitable has an overabundance of the *Pitta* principle in the physiology. While everyone has some Pitta, a person with a predominance of this principle would usually be of medium build and medium strength and have a good intellect and precise speech. However, he lives by his watch, and often displays a tendency to be demanding, sarcastic, and critical—that is, "intense." One of the main characteristics of Pitta is this "hot" element. When Pitta goes too far out of balance, it shows up in a tendency toward hot-tempered reactions, tyrannical behavior and anger; and physically in inflammatory disorders such as ulcers, excess acidity, and rashes or acne. Again, the proper foods can help correct the Pitta imbalance, resulting in significant reductions in tempers and hostility.

Imbalances That Can Lead to Implusive Crimes

Finally, a predominance of the *Vata* principle produces a light, thin build, and the tendency to perform activity quickly. Vata contributes to changeable and unpredictable moods, bursts of mental and physical energy, love of excitement, and constant change. Vata also promotes short-lived emotions and irregular habits. When Vata is in balance, it leads to being imaginative, sensitive, spontaneous, and exhilarated. Too much Vata, however, leads to worry, impatience, depression, irritability, insomnia, restlessness, and impulsive behavior. Physically this may be accompanied by constipation, intestinal gas, weight loss and other physical signs.

Correcting Dietary Imbalances in Prisons: Do You Need a Chef from the Ritz Carlton?

The dietary guidelines in Maharishi Ayur-Veda are applied in a common-sense way and are not so much strict rules as behaviors to be favored. In prisons and other residential settings, where the daily menu may offer fewer choices than in other circumstances, combinations of certain spices can be used along with the regular menu to counteract these different imbalances. A physician trained in Maharishi Ayur-Veda can identify the imbalances that are present, and then recommend the appropriate foods and spices to help correct the different imbalances.

This dietary approach is a much-needed complement to Western understandings of diet. Western knowledge pretty much begins and ends with a measurement of calories, an injunction to avoid fats, and a recommendation that we eat something daily from each of the different food groups. There's virtually no knowledge of these principles of physiological functioning, how certain foods may be healthful or harmful, or how diet can overcome the imbalances that can lead, for example, to hot tempers, greed, and impulsive behavior. In addition, special food supplements from this ancient system have now been found to play a major role in the prevention and treatment of disorders manifesting in the physiology.

Natural Supplements to Combat Stress, Free Radicals and Disease

Hari Sharma, M.D., Professor of Pathology at the Ohio State University College of Medicine, has written a book, *Freedom From Disease*, describing a new medical paradigm that identifies very small oxygen-based molecules—*free radicals*—as the prime cause of degenerative disease and disorder in the physiology. He states:

> Most researchers studying free radicals estimate that these deadly molecules help to cause 80% to 90% of the degenerative diseases that afflict the human race. We once thought that cholesterol was a major cause of heart disease, but new research indicates that the real culprits are free radicals. We have long known that arthritis comes from constant inflammation, but free radicals cause such inflammation. It is clear that cancer is caused by gene mutation, but free radicals cause most gene mutation. When we thought there were many causes there is often only one.[7]

If free radicals cause disorder and disease, what role might they play in causing the physiological disorder and "dis-ease" that leads to crime? One connection with crime is that free radicals are dangerously increased by stress. Dr. Sharma says that some researchers now even suggest that *stress should be given a new definition as that which accelerates the production of free radicals.*[8] Dr. Sharma says that constant stress generates a constant flow of free radicals.

The high levels of cortisol in the bloodstream that are associated with stress cause cells to shut down most of their normal activities and focus on energy creation. All that energy, he says, causes people under stress to pace up and down or exhibit other forms of hyperactivity.[9] According to the research described by Dr. Sharma, free radicals created by stress, cause damage to the enzymes in the body, to DNA, to the structure of cell membranes, and are a major causative factor in heart disease and stroke, cancer, arthritis, oesteoporosis, diabetes, premature aging, immune system deficiencies, and numerous mental disorders. Perhaps most importantly to crime researchers, membranes in the brain, warns Sharma, are especially rich in the type of polyunsatured fats that free radicals attack. This suggests, he says, that free radical damage, over time, interferes with the ability to secrete crucial neurotransmitter chemicals, such as serotonin;[10] and as we saw in chapter 5, low levels of serotonin are associated with hostility and aggression.

How to Fight Free Radicals

The body naturally fights free radicals in a number of ways. Dr. Sharma explains that the first line of defense is the enzyme systems of the body, which have *anti-oxidant* properties. However, the body's own defenses against free radicals are often not sufficient to maintain a steady state of emotional and physical health, especially for those who are most at risk for stress and therefore crime. Certain pharmaceutical agents, such as probucol, are sometimes prescribed for their anti-oxidant effects, but they are not without dangerous side effects. But certain substances that are available without a prescription actually scavenge free radicals effectively. The most famous of the anti-oxidants that can be useful in eliminating free radicals is vitamin C. Dr. Sharma states that the free radical research has now shown that Nobel laureate Linus Pauling was correct when he attempted to convince the medical establishment of vitamin C's therapeutic effects.[11] However, Dr. Sharma concludes that taking high levels of vitamin C, by itself carries a serious risk of side effects, similar to the taking of prescription drugs, and large amounts of vitamin C taken when one is under stress actually may help to create free radicals.

As the director of Cancer Prevention and Natural Products Research at the Ohio State University, Dr. Sharma has investigated many vitamins and herbal supplements in an effort to determine whether there are natural solutions to disease and impaired mental and physical functioning. After meeting Maharishi Mahesh Yogi and deciding to investigate some of the ancient food supplements of Maharishi Ayur-Veda, Dr. Sharma believes he has now discovered the most effective anti-oxidant known. Named Maharishi Amrit Kalash (or MAK for short), Dr. Sharma says it is *1,000 times more effective than vitamin C*, or probucol in its ability to rid the body of free radicals, without causing adverse side effects.[12]

This supplement was discovered as a result of Maharishi's efforts to complement the health benefits of Transcendental Meditation with other strategies derived from the Vedic literature. One of the great Indian physicians who worked under Maharishi's guidance was Dr. Balaraj Maharshi, the leading expert in the use of medicinal plants in Ayurveda. Dr. Balaraj Maharshi brought forth the formula for MAK, which consists of two substances, one contained in a tablet and the other in a paste. The two combine more than forty beneficial herbs and fruits, some of which only grow in very remote areas of the rainforests and Himalayan mountainsides of India. This combination of natural ingredients creates a synergistic effect in the physiology, which Dr. Sharma believes is responsible for the restorative properties of MAK.

The MAK Research

At this time nearly forty research studies have been conducted on MAK worldwide by fifty or so investigators at different universities and research institutions. Dr. Yukie Niwa at the New Institute in Japan has been researching free radicals for more than twenty years and has tested over five hundred compounds for their effectiveness. He found that MAK scavanged free radicals more effectively than any other substance.[13]

Researchers from medical schools at the University of Kansas, Indiana University, and Ohio State (including Dr. Sharma) conducted immune studies with animals receiving MAK. The results indicated that when the immune system is challenged, the effect of MAK is to "markedly strengthen the immune response."[14]

Researchers at South Dakota State University and the Ohio State University found that a group of animals receiving MAK daily for one week before and one week after a potent carcinogen was administered had signficantly less cancerous tumors. After eighteen weeks only 25% of the animals receiving MAK showed tumors, compared with 67% of the control animals who received the carcinogen but not MAK.[15]

In another study at Indiana University, Dr. Vimal Patel and his colleagues found that animals with advanced lung cancer showed a 45% to 65% reduction in both the size and number of lung cancer nodules when fed MAK in their diet.[16]

And Dr. Jeremy Fields at Loyola University tested the anti-aging properties of MAK after theorizing that it would not just reduce the incidence of specific diseases, but would also increase the lifespan. Dr. Fields' research found that mice receiving both of the herbal supplements that make up MAK lived an average of 20% longer than controls who were fed a standard diet.[17]

Finally, Dr. Robert Keith Wallace (mentioned in chapters 5 and 8), who conducted the earliest research on the physiological changes during the Transcendental Meditation technique, reported in his book, *The Physiology of Consciousness*, on a study that may have direct implications in the crime area. Wallace's study showed the effects of MAK on what is called the imipramine receptor in the brain. Imipramine is a major drug prescribed for depression, and its effect is to increase the activity of serotonin. In Dr. Wallace's study, MAK was found to have an effect similar to imipramine in its interaction with serotonin in human white blood cells, thus suggesting its role in reducing violence, and naturally influencing mood and mental health.[18]

Dr. Sharma states that new discoveries are usually just small extensions of previous ones, and that a sudden, spectacular leap, like that from the results on MAK, is extremely rare.[19] To Sharma, MAK challenges some of the most fundamental conceptions in modern science. The Western medical approach looks at medicinal plants, and tries to isolate the active ingredient. Then pharmaceutical companies attempt to duplicate the natural ingredient with a synthetic substance so they can obtain patent protection (a natural substance would not be granted patent protection). But Dr. Sharma says that the research on MAK shows that the "magic bullets" of the pharmaceutical companies don't work nearly as well as the natural formulations. In Maharishi Ayur-Veda, there are many natural herbal remedies for different imbalances which are based on formulations that utilize the whole plant, and not just what may be considered the active ingredient. And often the ancient formulas recommend not just one plant, but a combination of many plants, since the different components work together synergistically.

In the criminal population, we know that the stress levels are many times higher than in the general population. Because MAK has been shown to eliminate the free radicals associated with chronic stress, and because it affects such a broad range of disorders, it can be an important complement to this new approach to crime prevention and rehabilitation.

Exercise for Stress Reduction, Not Exhaustion

Maharishi Ayur-Veda also understands how exercise can best be used to reduce stress and rejuvenate the body. In many respects, Western habits of exercise do not properly contribute to the rehabilitative goal of allowing the mind and body to function in a more orderly and integrated fashion. When many people exercise, their minds are doing something different from what their bodies are doing. Many joggers and other fitness buffs wouldn't think of exercising without listening to music on their Sony Walkmans, and even the so-called experts on television would have us bobbing and weaving to the latest exercise discos. On the other hand, Maharishi Ayur-Veda physicians point out that for exercise to contribute to coherence in the mind and body, the attention should not be distracted by music or television from what the body is doing. Watching TV or listening to tapes while exercising contributes to the mind and body being out of balance rather than functioning in an integrated fashion.

In addition, in the name of health, many people exercise to the point of exhaustion. The Maharishi Ayur-Veda approach to exercise is opposed to this "no strain, no gain" philosophy. Instead, it recommends exercising only to a comfortable level (about 50% of capacity), and letting the comfort level naturally become expanded over time. Maharishi Ayur-Veda also recommends special stretching and balancing exercises that can be done inside, in a small area (wardens may find it perfect for lock-downs), providing the necessary stimulation to all the major muscle groups in the body. This natural approach is being adopted more and more by professional athletes, along with dietary recommendations, and the breathing and neuromuscular exercises later described.

Neurorespiratory Techniques (Breathing Exercises)

In our Western understanding, as physicist Schroedinger pointed out, breathing is another way that we consume the orderliness from the environment to sustain the inner orderliness that is the essential characteristic of the living organism. On every level, breathing is critical to life. The body is essentially billions and billions of living cells, which are in a constant state of activity, forever changing in ways that can be good or bad for mental and physical functioning. Within the cell, new materials are manufactured and old materials are broken down and eliminated as waste matter. This process requires oxygen, which allows the cells to "burn" their food, and gives off carbon dioxide.

Because of the importance of oxygen in human functioning, breathing techniques have been used for centuries to create specific physiological effects. In the special issue of the *Alcoholism Treatment Quarterly* referred to in chapter 7, physician James Brooks reports on his use of neurorespiratory breathing techniques that, like certain foods, can balance Vata, Pitta or Kapha imbalances that both contribute to substance abuse and are caused by it.[20] These various breathing techniques are known in the Vedic literature as *pranayama*. For centuries, the Vedic tradition of India has used these techniques both to produce specific effects and to generally improve the respiratory system, overcome stress, and enhance physical health. Some of the recent research on how such breathing exercises can affect the physiology has measured their influence on brain waves. In his book on the physiological changes that support higher consciousness, Dr. Wallace describes research showing that one breathing technique allows the individual to create almost instantaneous increases in the EEG activity alternately in one hemisphere of the brain, then in the other.[21] Since this particular exercise has traditionally been said to balance the physiology and psychology, Dr. Wallace theorizes that it establishes "better integration between the two hemispheres of the brain, between our so-called scientific and artistic modes of psychological functioning."[22]

Neuromuscular Techniques (Yoga Asanas)

There are many practices that fall under the general definition of yoga, including stretching or balancing exercises, procedures for internal cleansing, and breathing techniques. Whereas most American systems of physical exercise build muscles, and certain aerobic exercises may promote cardiovascular efficiency, *yoga asanas* are postures that a person assumes, traditionally valued for their ability to promote balance or order in the functioning of the nervous system and in the principal organs.

Many people who have learned the Transcendental Meditation technique also receive instruction in the yoga asanas that Maharishi has determined would be most suitable for good health and mental balance. These postures are performed in a set sequence, and a basic set of asanas takes about ten minutes. As these programs begin to be used more specifically for crime reduction and in prisons, the particular asanas selected will likely differ depending on the criminal tendencies or imbalances to be remedied, in the same way that certain asanas are now prescribed for certain physical ailments. Some

Senegalese inmates learning yoga asanas

asanas result, for example, in the sacral nerves receiving an extra supply of blood, while others are said to remedy problems with abdominal organs, such as the liver or kidneys. Still others may have value in treating sex offenders by relieving the sexual tension that is part of the disorder.

Offering the Offender a Positive New Identity

The philosophy of providing the offender with a new lifestyle and a new sense of identity, in part, underlies the growing use of boot camps for juveniles. Boot camps use elements of the military lifestyle in an effort to rehabilitate. While some aspects of the boot camp program are attractive (the emphasis on exercise, the healthier atmosphere, and the outdoor experience), research evaluations of these programs has not been encouraging.

Jean Bottcher, a research specialist with the California Youth Authority, was given the assignment of evaluating California's boot camp programs. She described the California programs as involving physical exercises, military drill and ceremonies, conventional education, and Twelve Steps AA drug abuse programs in the evening.

Speaking in March, 1995, at a major criminology conference, she said, "the programs do a lot of different things, but have no overall theme of treatment, and no one has put together an underlying treatment strategy that would make a difference." She said that in her heart, based on her preliminary evaluation, she felt the handwriting was already on the wall, and she didn't expect much of significance from boot camps. She said that "for all the short term benefits, it [the boot camp program] is an over-touted program, quite superficial and shallow."

An overall treatment theme is critical, and the goal should be to make the individual *self-sufficient* in his daily progress toward a healthy, productive, and fulfilling life. This new approach from the world's most ancient system of natural medicine provides the offender with a new self-image and a healthy lifestyle that is in sharp contrast to the lifestyle of the streets. Merely offering the offender the conventional lifestyle that he has already rejected will not have the same effect. Once the inmate learns the Transcendental Meditation technique, the dietary considerations, exercise system, and the neuromuscular and neurorespiratory techniques, he has taken a major step toward self-sufficiency. He has a new daily routine that is both enjoyable and healthful, creating order at the deepest level of the mind and body.

Chapter Eleven
Prisons of the Future

In the summer of 1994, Robert Barker, age fifteen, shot and killed two men in the course of a hunting incident in Iowa. Barker and several teenage friends were hunting and crossed a fence line onto private property. Barker knew he was supposed to get permission to go on the property, and that he should have left his rifle at the fence. The property owner and a relative confronted Barker, and, according to the police, Barker admitted shooting the men after a confrontation. At trial Barker said the men "had their guns kind of aiming at me." He says he fired because he was "scared," and he "flipped out." The jury refused to find Barker guilty of first degree murder, which would have meant life in prison without parole. Instead, they found him guilty of manslaughter, and the judge sentenced him to twenty years in prison. He will be up for parole in about five years.

This was a case that Janet from my office and I had talked about on several occasions. It was a troubling case because of the tragedy both for the victims, and for young Barker and his family. Barker, by most accounts, had been a pretty good kid before this incident. He was described at the trial as polite, well-liked, and a high school jock. If Barker had been tried as a juvenile, under Iowa law he would go free at eighteen no matter what crime he committed. When it was decided that Barker would be tried as an adult, the initial discussions between Janet and me revolved around the possibility that a fifteen-year-old might spend the rest of his life in prison, with no possibility for parole. This was the case that led me to conclude that if juveniles were tried as adults for murder, Iowa needed to modify its laws so that they didn't have to receive *mandatory* life

155

sentences without the possibility of parole, as is now the case. As it turned out, the jury probably felt the same way and refused to convict Barker of murder. Instead they found him guilty of manslaughter with a lesser penalty that permitted parole.

But now that Barker will have a chance to show parole authorities that he deserves to get out of prison, how are we going to make a sensible decision five years from now? And how can we best structure a suitable rehabilitation program to help him change so he is no longer a danger to society? One way to help us determine this is to clearly understand *what we are changing him from.* We don't really know, for example, whether Barker's crime resulted from a hot temper, impulsive behavior, poor judgment (cognitive defects), or a lack of self-esteem (wanting to impress his buddies), or whether the crime could have been precipitated by chronically high cortisol or low serotonin levels, or EEG abnormalities. If we are going to make criminology and rehabilitation more of a science, we need to know what abnormality or combination is likely the cause of young Barker's crime, so that we can determine, first of all, the most appropriate rehabilitation program for him, and second, the degree to which he has changed when he comes up for parole. In addition, Barker's rehabilitation will be enhanced by his understanding his psychophysiological profile at the onset of rehabilitation—so he feels confident that he is changing for the better (or, if change does not occur at a fast enough rate, his routine can be modified).

Beginning the Process of Change

The process of change for Robert Barker should start as soon as possible, and requires a series of tests to identify his psychophysiological profile. Ideally, defense counsel would cooperate (with confidentiality of the tests to be maintained). However, if we couldn't do testing before trial, then upon incarceration after trial, a variety of tests would need to be administered to give an objective measurement for later comparison.

At this time, the law in most jurisdictions prohibits physiological testing (other than perhaps urine tests), so the prisoner's consent might be needed, or a change in the law. Many prisoners, however, would want to participate, once they knew that an effective rehabilitation program was available, and that an improvement in their test scores could be an aid in achieving early parole, as well as providing objective evidence of rehabilitation for prospective employers and others. The idea for such an index or profile was first conceived of some years ago by scientists at Maharishi European Research University following an international conference on rehabilitation in Seelisberg, Switzerland. The principal elements of the profile (known as the MERU Rehabilitation Index) as presently constituted are:

1. Brain wave coherence
For this variable EEG testing is administered to determine the level of coherence in the offender's brain functioning. The testing is done by attaching electrodes to the scalp and measuring the brain's electrical activity. As previously indicated, EEG brain wave coherence has been significantly correlated with creativity, concept learning, intelligence, grade point average, principled moral reasoning, mental health factors, and neurological efficiency.[1] This measurement requires special equipment (i.e., an 8-channel EEG recorder, analog-to-digital converter, and computer), but once installed, it can be operated by a trained member of the institution's staff.

2. Biochemical balance and drug and alcohol use
Hair samples and standard urine and saliva tests can be used to monitor illicit drug and alcohol abuse in the previous year, and urine and blood tests can measure biochemical aspects of stress levels in the physiology. Drug and alcohol abuse creates imbalance in the biochemistry, and is highly correlated with criminal behavior. The urine samples would also be used to measure levels of the major stress hormone, cortisol, and 5-HIAA, the principal metabolic end-product of serotonin. Low levels of cortisol predict more harmonious behavior, and many studies show low levels of serotonin are correlated with aggression and hostility (see chapter 5). The cortisol testing should include stress tests, since healthy functioning requires an appropriately strong physiological response to stress.

Little or no responsiveness to stress may indicate either a fearless psychopath or habitual criminal.

3. Autonomic stability and flexibility

Electrodermal (skin resistance) responses measure the stability and flexibility of the autonomic nervous system. Testing the degree to which the individual is relaxed, as measured by fewer spontaneous fluctuations, is one important indicator. However, since psychopaths can exhibit GSR signs of relaxation, it is again important to find an aversive or stressful reaction in the GSR under appropriate conditions. It is important that the individual score high on both stability and adaptability, and not just exhibit dullness or lack of responsiveness.

4. Diet

A number of studies have examined the diets of juvenile delinquents and found vitamin and mineral deficiencies, correlations between anti-social behavior and excessive food additives, and other dietary contributors to crime. As a result, a questionnaire and physiological testing should be administered to identify problem dietary situations that may be corrected. In addition, a medical consultation with a physician trained in Maharishi Ayur-Veda can determine imbalances, and make dietary recommendations to help restore order to the system (see the discussion later in this chapter).

5. Ego development

Ego development is an important factor determining how an individual sees himself and his relationship to society. Teenagers and immature adults are often excessively self-conscious. They may view themselves as the center of the universe and may have a belief that everyone else is watching their every move; this may lead to the feeling they can't "back down" from anything. Using the Loevinger Scale, researchers can determine the level of growth of the overall personality and ego of the offender. This is a test that cannot be manipulated.

6. Field independence

Field independence is believed to be a major indicator of healthy psychological functioning by many researchers.[2] People who are field independent are able to maintain stable attitudes and judgments, without continuous reference to external standards, and they tend to have more interest in taking responsibility. They have what is called "cognitive clarity," a more developed ego, and higher self-esteem. Field independence is measured by Witkins' Embedded Figures Test (you look for the hidden figure embedded in a complex picture), and by the Rod and Frame Test (you rotate a bar and make it vertical within a frame that may be tilted to different angles). Field independence is also positively correlated with coping ability.

7. Impulsive behavior

A significant body of research shows impulsive behavior is often correlated with criminal behavior. To measure impulsivity, offenders would be tested on the Porteus Maze, which requires the subject to patiently trace pathways through a complicated maze. Research has shown that those prone to delinquent behavior do not perform very well on this measure.

8. Moral development

A number of tests measure the growth of moral reasoning. These tests sometimes ask you to analyze a situation where a crime is committed under mitigating circumstances (e.g., stealing medicine from a greedy pharmacist, who alone possesses a curative drug for a desperately ill relative). More important than the individual's determination of whether it is right or wrong to steal in any particular instance, is the reasoning given. At lower levels of moral reasoning, people act for purely physical reasons (you don't harm someone, so that he doesn't harm you). At higher levels of moral reasoning, people refrain from wrongdoing for reasons of conscience, or because they identify with the social order.

9. Frequency and severity of violence, misbehavior, and rule infractions
This variable could be used with prison populations or with those in other residential treatment facilities.

10. Communication with family
Good communication is important between the offender and those he will depend on once he is released. It is considered an important indicator of the degree of the offender's socialization. This variable may be measured on the basis of information received through interviews with family members or others, and it focuses on the frequency and quality of communications.

Testing with the MERU Index

The developers of the MERU Index caution that any rehabilitation index should be applied in the light of the background and overall history of the offender. In using such an index, consideration should be given to the offender's physical condition and general behavior and demeanor. Adjustments may need to be made for physical illness or disabilities, neurological disorders, and psychiatric conditions. When an offender takes these tests, each individual measure discussed above is assigned a score, and the individual scores are combined into a single average score. In addition, each offender's test scores can be compared to a range of normal scores on each measure, now being developed.

Applying the Rehabilitation Index

As originally conceived, the tests should be administered in a manner that provides continuing encouragement to the offender. After the initial testing (as close as possible to the offender's crime or incarceration), regular tests twice a year during incarceration would enable the inmate to monitor his own progress towards rehabilitation and release, and would encourage him to participate fully in the new programs being offered. If he isn't regular in his practice of the Transcendental Meditation technique, for example, and he sees that his own progress is less than the regular meditators are experiencing, it should encourage him in the right direction.

As an aid to parole, the traditional interview and other procedures to determine parole eligibility would be reinforced by the use of the MERU Index, since the index tests are difficult to fake. If inmates merely pretended, for example, to participate in the Transcendental Meditation program, but didn't really practice the technique, the lack of progress should be reflected in the index. There would be serious ethical issues, however, if the index were used to discriminate against certain inmates, or classes of inmates, to justify continued incarceration. Every crime therefore should have a fixed, maximum sentence.

Finally, parole officers could use the index to determine which parolees would require the most intensive post-release supervision. This would allow parole officers to use their time more efficiently, and should result in more positive parole outcomes. Reports from parole officers would also enable the index norms to be continually refined. Ongoing research will aid administrators in determining which test scores are most indicative of complete rehabilitation for particular offenders, and how the index can be improved.

Haphazard or Scientific Parole Decisions: What is the Cost of Our Mistakes?

Certainly one concern in using the MERU Index is the cost to administer the periodic tests. But what is the cost of all the mistakes we make in our parole decisions in the absence of such a measure? And what is the cost if we abolish parole? Without an index that uses objective, scientific measurements of rehabilitation, confinement and parole decisions are haphazard. This results in corrections officials getting blamed when prisoners con the officials and either get discharged or obtain prison privileges, then promptly commit new crimes. A good example of the mistakes made under our current system occurred in Iowa in August, 1995.

In the mid 1980s, Todd Allen Heard escaped from a juvenile training school when he was sixteen and raped two women. He was convicted in 1986 and imprisoned for up to twenty-five years on each count at the Iowa State Penitentiary in Fort Madison. After completing the sex offender program in Iowa, and earning his high school equivalency diploma, in 1995 the twenty-four-year-old Heard earned privileges that included assignment to a minimum security prison farm with little supervision. A month after achieving his new "low-risk" status, Heard walked away from the farm, and allegedly broke into a house where he found a shotgun, and raped again before he was caught.

In the furor over the incident, the *Des Moines Register* reported that Sally Chandler Halford, the director of the Iowa Department of Corrections, said that she and her staff "had been doing a lot of discussion in an attempt to analyze whether there was anything that anyone should have seen" in advance, but "the warning flags just weren't there." But if we're only using the naked eye to look for rehabilitation, we will repeatedly make these mistakes. Like Ms. Halford, most of the correctional heads in our state governments are conscientious administrators, but they'll never see what's wrong with an inmate until they use standard physiological and other testing to aid in their decisions.

The unfortunate reality is that the incident involving Mr. Heard is not an isolated situation. While the consequences of a mistake aren't often so immediate, offenders who don't deserve parole or minimum security gain that status on a daily basis; while others who would be more deserving (based on objective measurements) occupy space that could be used for high-risk persons. The determination to give Heard minimum security status should have been based on stress levels and changes in index scores. Probably anyone, however stressed, could at least "complete" the sex offender program as prisoner Heard did; and a high school equivalency diploma doesn't teach how to overcome a sexual addiction or even simple sexual tension. Moreover, sex offender programs such as those in Iowa are so misguided, it is likely that they merely reinforce the problem (see "Prison Education: What Not to Do" later in this chapter).

A New Classification of Prisoners

Present systems for classifying inmates are based largely on the nature of the crime, the prior record, and partly (but inexpertly) on the nature of the offender. In addition to the MERU Index, another new aspect of the initial classification of inmates that I would recommend would consist of a detailed medical consultation with a doctor trained in Maharishi Ayur-Veda. The offender would be classified based on his psychophysiological imbalances. This would enable the offender to better understand why he has certain behavioral tendencies, and the kind of health routine best suited to create inner order or balance. Many people value a physician's recommendations, even when they ignore the advice of others. A trained physician who understands the rehabilitation program will help the offender appreciate that he is beginning a program to become healthier and more successful, not merely a program to protect others from him. Classifying inmates based on their imbalances will also aid in the administration of this new rehabilitation program. The program has a number of elements, some of which are briefly discussed below.

Sufficient Sleep

Inmates suffer not only from daytime anxiety, but from the nighttime anxiety we call insomnia. And even those without insomnia rarely get the rest they need to overcome stress due to the noise and disorder of prison life, and the fundamental failure of our society to appreciate the value of rest. When I toured the Iowa prisons at Fort Madison and Mt. Pleasant, I was struck by the absence of any strict lights-out policy. In Fort Madison, a maximum security prison, the attitude is that the inmate's cell is his "home," and when he is home, he can do as he pleases. As a result, many inmates stay up until midnight or later listening to music or watching television. If they make too much noise, they may be asked to listen with earphones, but neighboring prisoners often don't complain for fear of retaliation.

To enhance sleep, Maharishi Ayur-Veda physicians often make numerous recommendations based on the imbalances in the inmate.

These prescriptions generally include going to sleep at an early hour, and advice about proper diet and evening activities that facilitate sleep. In the West, most people get into bed, close their eyes, and hope for the best. But this ancient system of natural medicine recognizes that everything we do during the day, and especially in the hours before getting into bed, greatly affects our sleep. One inmate at the Fort B prison in Senegal had this to say after the entire prison learned to meditate and began a more orderly routine:

> The most surprising effect is the change that has taken place at night. Previously, the atmosphere was tense, the inmates would talk loudly, shout, and hammer at the bars. Now the only noises we hear are snores.

Meditation, Yoga, and Breathing Exercises

The Transcendental Meditation technique is practiced twice daily for fifteen to twenty minutes. If possible, those in prison or other residential communities should meditate together in one or more groups. Group meditations have been found to produce a more profound physiological effect for individuals in the group. Initially, prisoners may be fearful of closing their eyes in a group (when the program was first introduced at Folsom State Prison, everyone wanted to meditate in the last row with his back to the wall), but they soon learn to be trusting, and the group influence helps avoid the sense of alienation that inmates experience. In addition to the TM session, inmates may also practice ten to fifteen minutes of yoga asanas (stretching postures) and pranayama for balanced breathing, which can be performed in the rooms or cells.

Habituation: It's the Routine That Brings Peace and Harmony

One principle that allows this holistic program (Transcendental Meditation, natural food supplements, diet, sound sleep, yoga, healthful breathing, and other procedures) to be highly effective is the principle of *habituation*. With this integrated approach, the prisoner is balancing and relaxing his physiology many times a day using a number of different modalities. With such a daily routine, the mind and body soon begin to function habitually in a more settled and orderly manner, even when the prisoner is not performing one of the activities. This is the way the development of human potential occurs, and how you naturally begin to enjoy your moment-to-moment activity. It doesn't happen by *trying* to watch your activity or be mindful of it. With this change in the physiology to a more settled state, the chaos and excited states characteristic of the criminal lifestyle become *unenjoyable*. This is why one juvenile said that he started to enjoy quieter activities after learning the Transcendental Meditation technique.

> I used to get my kicks by doing things that were wrong and destructive . . . . I used to get high and drank a lot, but I have found [after TM] that just doesn't turn me on any more. I don't know why, though. Now I am happy just being with friends or having a good time horseback riding.[3]

Prison Education: What Not to Do

Situations like the Todd Allen Heard case are likely to result in prison officials looking at a myriad of superficial solutions. But they are still likely to defend their sex offender program, even though its value has obviously been called into question. Acknowledging that the program is flawed would only compound the immediate problem faced by the correctional administrators. But putting the best face on the existing prison program, or even expanding the program with more hours of the same kind of instruction, just perpetuates a program that has never had *measurable* success.

The current sex offender programs in prisons, as just one example of a flawed approach, try to educate the offender about the nature of his problem, constantly reminding him of his deviant tendencies. This is the same approach often used in group therapy and in counseling for criminals of all types. The focus is on the offender's sickness, and on teaching the offender about various aspects of his deviance. The sex offender programs at Mt. Pleasant, Iowa, are modeled on those in other states. They require offenders to write a detailed twenty-five-page account of their sordid past, and the inmates read books explaining their sexual addiction. These books are filled with numerous examples of explicit accounts of deviant practices. One book I looked at contained more than a hundred such accounts, many being detailed case histories.

This approach is based on a classical error derived from a fundamental misunderstanding of human nature, at least according to Maharishi Ayur-Veda. Maharishi has summarized the understanding that should guide our rehabilitation approaches in the aphorism, "That which you give your attention to grows stronger in your life," which appears to be a universal truth. Repeatedly focusing on negative thoughts or emotions just serves to ingrain these qualities in your personality. Instead, the focus should be on health and positive thoughts and emotions, and the habituation should be achieved by a balanced routine that helps the offender become fulfilled and more integrated from within. The offender's attention is uplifted, rather than being encouraged to dwell on the behavior that characterized his prior lifestyle. Putting the offender's attention on wrong tendencies also habituates, but in the wrong direction.

The New Prison Education Program

Once effective stress reduction lays the groundwork for more effective education and vocational training, the training available in different institutions could be tailored more to the skills and interests of the inmates. Japan is one country that takes very seriously the characterization of its prisons as "correctional institutions." Virtually all Japanese prisoners work, but even more important than just keeping the prisoners busy is the kind of vocational training that is offered. Japanese vocational training is designed to enable the prisoners to pass national examinations in various occupations, and to secure licenses that will enable them to apply their new skills when they are released. In many states in the U.S., the inmates learn skills, but in most prisons we have not yet reached the desired stage where there's a certified apprenticeship program enabling an inmate to be given a U.S. Department of Labor Certification, which would be of assistance in gaining employment.

Character Education

In addition, the new educational approach I recommend supplements conventional schooling and vocational education with character education. The strategies described earlier in this book are the primary strategies for developing character in inmates. As the offender becomes more relaxed and fulfilled, he feels better about himself and naturally behaves better toward others. But this inner development should be accompanied by an intellectual component that gives the inmate the encouragement to gain the most from his new routine, and to avoid backsliding when he is released. For this, the inmate needs to better understand himself and his tendencies as well as a renewed appreciation of the importance of the traditional values of education and work.

The injunction to "know thyself" has long been understood as being intimately connected in some way with human growth. This new educational program aims at what is probably the most important self-knowledge for inmates—giving the offender an understanding of the physiological imbalances that contributed to his behavioral tendencies (e.g., those that lead to a hot temper, anxiety, negative thoughts, etc.), and how to counteract them in a natural way. The offender would learn how stress is caused, and how it can be eliminated through the deep rest of Transcendental Meditation, adequate sleep, diet, yoga asanas, and proper exercise. The new education aims to help the offender understand the interrelationship between the mind and body, and the role of each in maintaining health, overcoming problems, and human development. This should be an enjoyable program that focuses the offender's attention on the positive transformations taking place in his own life.

Adding Relevance to Education and Work

The second component of this educational program aims to give the offender a basis for deriving greater success and satisfaction from conventional education and work. These are two critical areas to which an inmate must be attracted to help him avoid returning to a criminal lifestyle after being released. Typically, the average adult inmate has not had a full-time job before his incarceration. And even in Iowa, one of the better states in educating the general population, in 1994 the inmate entering prison read on average at the ninth grade level, with perhaps 10% to 20% of inmates reading at a fifth grade level or less. In other words, many inmates are functionally illiterate.

The program to rehabilitate the inmate begins by reducing his stress, thereby allowing him to concentrate better and to be more open and relaxed about the learning process and more interested in acquiring basic skills. But this process can be enhanced by an educational program that deals with the alienation inmates feel toward education, which is an expression of their alienation from the social environment.

What is the cause of this alienation? First, to many people, including those who tend toward criminal activity, education is not interesting because it doesn't seem relevant to their lives. And, second, education in one field doesn't seem to have much, if anything, to do with education in any other field. To remedy these basic problems, educators have sought to make education broadly based or interdisciplinary, but it is obvious that this is still a goal and not a reality. Educators still haven't come up with any coherent means of relating one field of knowledge to another, or of making knowledge more relevant to the student's own life. The apparent disjointed nature of different fields of knowledge has naturally led educators to question whether there is any knowledge that can relate the different fields to one another and to the student, and make them all more comprehensible? In other words, is there any underlying thread that is common to agriculture, business, electronics, physics, psychology, sociology, criminology, and the student's own physiology?

In 1970 a course of study called the Science of Creative Intelligence (SCI) grew out of Maharishi's explanation that, from the Vedic perspective, there is a common integrating factor in all the disciplines of knowledge. The common factor is a pervading orderliness or "creative intelligence" underlying all the laws of nature; and SCI is a study of the most fundamental laws of nature governing human life and the society at large. The approach of SCI is to systematically study the orderliness of growth in human life and nature with reference to the student's own development from the strategies described in this book. Because this program accelerates individual growth, an inmate can more readily appreciate that certain fundamental principles are responsible not only for human growth, but for all evolution. He appreciates the basic principles because they are part of his own experience.

One example of these principles, which are explored in depth in a standard thirty-three lesson SCI course, is that *rest is the basis of activity.* This is a universal principle found in plants, in animals, and everywhere throughout nature. The world, in essence, is a pulsating world of contractions (rest periods) and expansions, whether we are talking about the beating of the heart, night and day, winter and spring, or wave functions in physics. Another lesson explores the principle that *the inner structure of life supports and is the basis of outer growth.* The outer depends on the inner, whether we are considering the plant being dependent on the root, or the house on the foundation, or our activity depending on the functioning of consciousness and the nervous system.

Inmates, regardless of their formal level of education, readily understand these principles, because they are part of their daily experience. When the inmate comes to appreciate the common elements in different natural phenomena, and also sees them in his own life and his own physiology, for many it can be the dawn of a new day. The feeling of alienation—that everything is foreign and that "the world is my enemy"—starts to recede, and the inmate gains a new interest in learning things. All fields of knowledge become more interesting and understandable once the common principles are perceived.

The SCI course has been taught with great success at Transcendental Meditation centers throughout the world, as well as in grade schools, secondary schools, and universities. An entire educational system—kindergarten through the Ph.D. level—applying this approach to the study of the traditional academic disciplines in the sciences, arts, and humanities, is offered at Maharishi University of Management in Fairfield, Iowa. I have taught these basic principles to people from all walks of life (students, as well as white, pink, and blue collar workers), with varied educational backgrounds, and with similar success. The attitudes people have toward work and education often change dramatically when the SCI course is combined with this experience of growth from within. One construction supervisor who took the course told me:

> With SCI, I was able to see more clearly how the construction planning sessions, which went on just in the mind, were the foundation for the success on the job. Then even in the actual construction, the physical foundation for the building provides the support for the entire structure . . . . The SCI knowledge that what is inside supports the outer aspects of life made me appreciate the necessity for paying close attention to the initial stages of a project. It's easy sometimes to lose track of the need for completeness and planning because the job situation often puts great pressure on you to get the job started.

Should Inmates Study Deviance or the Lives of Great Men and Women?

The classroom component to aid in character education also shows how order in consciousness and the physiology manifests in the lives of great historical figures. Instead of reading about deviant individuals and deviant acts, the inmate should study the lives of great men and women who embody noble traits. Studying what makes people great, and seeing the common basis of greatness, has an uplifting quality.

In general, the SCI course gives the inmate a renewed appreciation of the fundamental values in our society that are associated with education and work, and it helps the offender appreciate that whatever his life has been, the program he is now involved in can help him make it better.

Chapter Twelve

The *Extra Strength* Crime Vaccine: The Critical Mass That Can End the Epidemic

E pidemics of smallpox, poliomyelitis, diphtheria, mumps, measles, and other diseases have responded to vaccination programs in a way that has sometimes been called magic."[1] Their ability to do so is based on the phenomenon known as *herd immunity*, which makes it possible to eliminate a disease without everyone being vaccinated. This concept has been discussed for years, and has gained new popularity as a result of the historic success of the global smallpox eradication program, and the determination of the World Health Organization to eradicate poliomyelitis from the world by the year 2000.[2]

The concept of herd immunity is that if a threshold percentage of individuals in a given area have immune systems resistant to a particular microbe, then it is possible to essentially eliminate the microbe in that area. This concept was behind the initial World Health Organization aim to eliminate smallpox in 1959, when the 12th World Health Assembly concluded that the eradication (reduction of both infection and disease to zero) of smallpox in a given area could be accomplished by successfully vaccinating 80% of the population within a period of four to five years. For other diseases the necessary percentage of individuals vaccinated may be higher or lower. Paul Fine, of the London School of Hygiene and Tropical Medicine, recently summarized the research on herd immunity; he states that "wild polio viruses ceased to circulate in most of the United States by 1970, at which time only some 65% of children were receiving a complete course of live oral polio vaccine." [3]

173

The mechanics of herd immunity are not completely understood, but it is well recognized that immune individuals provide *indirect* protection to non-immune individuals in their proximity, preventing them from getting the disease. Some researchers have explained the "magic" of herd immunity by analogy to the physical concept of a *critical mass*. This chemical principle holds that when the accumulation or density of molecules in a gas exceeds a certain threshold, an explosion occurs. And Fine tells us that when the number of persons susceptible to a disease reaches a certain density in a given area, it produces "an explosive increase in the incidence of an introduced infection."[4] If, on the other hand, you keep the number of at-risk individuals below the threshold level by vaccinating a certain percentage of the population, the incidence of disease starts to decline and continues to decline until no one or nearly no one gets the disease.

The theories concerning herd immunity and epidemics hold that an epidemic can be stopped by inoculating a critical percentage of persons, since individuals are assumed to remain infectious for only a given time period. If, during that time period, those who have already become infected come in contact with only a limited number of people who are at risk (because the others they contact are immune), over time the threat of the epidemic is eliminated. It is also thought that important indirect protection is provided by immunized individuals to those who are not immune by the spreading of the *vaccine virus* (the virus triggering the immunity) throughout a community through a myriad of contacts, in the same way that bacterial infections spread (e.g., sewage, foodstuffs, fecal matter, or airborne transmissions).

Immunizing the Community Against Crime

In 1977 researchers reported surprising findings about crime in relation to the Transcendental Meditation program, which bear striking similarities to the phenomenon of herd immunity.[5] In eleven cities where 1% of the population had been instructed in the Transcendental Meditation technique by 1972, significant decreases in the crime rate were found from 1972 to 1973 (a mean decrease of 8.2%), and a decreased trend in the crime rate was discovered in the subsequent five years (1972-1977) in comparison to the previous five (1967-1972). This finding contrasted sharply with an overall increase in crime of 8.3% from 1972 to 1973 in eleven control cities, which had been matched for geographic region, population, and crime rate, and with statistical controls for other demographic variables; crime also increased during this period in the nation as a whole.

Change in Crime Rate per City 1972-1973

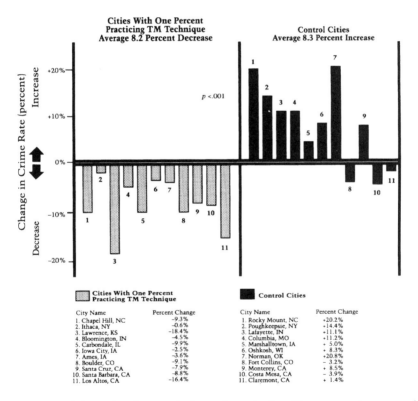

Cities With One Percent Practicing TM Technique		Control Cities	
City Name	Percent Change	City Name	Percent Change
1. Chapel Hill, NC	-9.3%	1. Rocky Mount, NC	+20.2%
2. Ithaca, NY	-0.6%	2. Poughkeepsie, NY	+14.4%
3. Lawrence, KS	-18.4%	3. Lafayette, IN	+11.1%
4. Bloomington, IN	-4.5%	4. Columbia, MO	+11.2%
5. Carbondale, IL	-9.9%	5. Marshalltown, IA	+ 5.0%
6. Iowa City, IA	-2.5%	6. Oshkosh, WI	+ 8.3%
7. Ames, IA	-3.6%	7. Norman, OK	+20.8%
8. Boulder, CO	-9.1%	8. Fort Collins, CO	- 3.2%
9. Santa Cruz, CA	-7.9%	9. Monterey, CA	+ 8.5%
10. Santa Barbara, CA	-8.8%	10. Costa Mesa, CA	- 3.9%
11. Los Altos, CA	-16.4%	11. Claremont, CA	+ 1.4%

Percentage of change in crime rate is shown for each city with one percent or more of its population practicing the TM technique and for each control city. Crime decreased an average of 8.2 percent in the one percent cities and increased an average of 8.3 percent in the control cities.

This first study on what the researchers had termed the *Maharishi Effect* (after Maharishi, who first predicted this phenomenon thirty-five years ago) showed what is known as a "correlation" between increased participation in the Transcendental Meditation program and reduced crime. But finding a correlation between two variables (the TM population and crime) doesn't necessarily mean that one caused the other. It could, of course, be that a third factor (such as unemployment or a change in the percentage of college students in the area) caused the changes in both the TM numbers and crime.

A subsequent study by researchers at three universities (Maharishi University of Management, Southern Illinois University, and West Virginia University) analyzed whether the increased number of individuals participating in the Transcendental Meditation program was the *cause* of changes in the crime rate.[6] In a study completed in 1982, these researchers used what is known as a *cross-lagged panel* correlation in an attempt to determine causation. (It is one of those cosmic coincidences that sometimes *cross-legged* meditators have to be measured by *cross-lagged* correlations.)

This procedure measured the two variables—TM participation (the x variable) and the crime rate (the y variable)—at two points in time, comparing the number of TM meditators in 1993 with crime in 1994, and also comparing crime in 1993 with the number of TM meditators in 1994.

1993	1994
TM Participation (x) ⟶	Crime (y)
1993	1994
Crime (y) ⟶	TM Participation (x)

This method of analysis says that if a third variable (such as a change in the number of employed persons in the area) is the actual cause, the correlation of TM participants with the crime rate would be equal no matter which variable is placed in the earlier year. On the other hand, if the cross-lagged correlations are *unequal,* it indicates that the relationship between the number of TM participants and the crime rate is not due to any unmeasured variable.

The researchers found that, applying the stringent statistical criteria involved in cross-lagged panel correlation, the correlations were unequal, and since the crime decreases *followed* increases in the numbers practicing the TM program and not vice versa, it supported the causal influence of the Transcendental Meditation program on decreased crime. The percentage declines in crime weren't as large as in the eleven-city study described above because of the smaller percentage of meditators (on average less than one-half of 1% in the various cities), but this study used a random sample of 160 U.S. cities, which comprised 25% of the total U.S. metropolitan population, providing substantial confidence in the findings.

The Less Than One Percent Solution

The finding that just 1% of the population practicing the Transcendental Meditation program can have an effect on crime is similar to other natural phenomena where an analogous one percent effect is seen. Scientists who have studied the relationship of the TM program to crime have pointed out that as soon as 1% of the elements of many natural systems begin to function in a coherent way, the whole system undergoes what is known as a "phase transition" to a higher level of coherent functioning. They state that "examples of this are found in magnetism, laser light, crystallization processes, pacemaker cells in the heart, and primary organizer cells in the embryo, etc."[7] And beginning in the late 1970s it was found that an advanced aspect of the Transcendental Meditation program called the TM-Sidhi program (described more fully later in this chapter), could produce a reduction in crime when just the square root of 1% of the population participated in that program.

Forty-Two Studies

One of the first tests of the advanced TM-Sidhi program in the United States occurred in Rhode Island during a three-month period from June to September, 1978. Rhode Island has a population of about one million, so it was predicted that some measurable reduction in crime and other expressions of stress could result with a hundred or more participants in the TM-Sidhi program (one hundred is the square root of 1% of one million). The Rhode Island experiment tested this hypothesis with three hundred TM-Sidhi practitioners after the predictions were published in the *Newport Daily News* on June 2, 1978. Using an index that measured eight variables, including crime, traffic accidents, mortality rates, and environmental pollution, the researchers found a significant overall improvement in the quality of life in Rhode Island during the experimental period, as compared to a control state matched for geographic and demographic variables. (The statistical analysis was at the $p = .01$ level.)[8]

After the relatively small Rhode Island study, a major test of the phenomenon was undertaken the next summer in Amherst, Massachusetts. (A number of these studies have been conducted at summer assemblies when participants in the various TM-Sidhi groups were able to take vacations from school or work.) This time, the goal was to assemble enough TM-Sidhi practitioners to affect negative trends in a more populous state and in the nation as a whole. Over the forty-day experimental period, a group that ranged from 1,570 to 2,770 participants gathered at the University of Massachusetts, a number in excess of the 1,530 participants that would have constituted the square root of 1% of the approximately 234 million population of the United States. There were two general hypotheses to be tested. First, that crime and other fatalities could be reduced in Massachusetts as well as in the nation, and that greater effects would be found in Massachusetts, as compared with other populous states and the nation, because of the relatively compact population surrounding the demonstration site.

The researchers measured the effects of the assembly on motor

traffic fatalities, violent crimes, and eleven categories of fatal accidents, as well as deaths from suicides, homicides, and undetermined causes. These categories were selected because fatalities and
violent crime were likely to represent an occurrence with a stronger
connection to stress, and also because publicly available data on a
monthly basis could be obtained for specific states as well as
nationally. The study design compared the actual crimes or fatalities
during the forty-day period of the assembly with the predicted level
of crimes and fatalities for that period, both in Massachusetts and in
the nation. The predicted levels were based on the mean level of
fatalities and violent crimes for the corresponding six-week period
over all other years for which data were available at the time of the
analysis (both the prior years from 1973 to 1978, and the years after
the experimental period from 1980 to 1981).

The researchers state that the results confirmed their hypotheses.
For the nation as a whole, motor vehicle traffic fatalities were
reduced 6.5% from the predicted level; in Massachusetts the reduction was 18.9% from the predicted level. And comparing
Massachusetts during the forty-day assembly to all other states with
populations over four million, the researchers found that in the
other states, the mean reduction in traffic fatalities was 7.6%, which
was predictably less than what occurred in Massachusetts. For violent crime, there were similar results. In the nation as a whole, the
reduction during this period was 3.4% from the predicted level; in
Massachusetts the reduction was 10.1%. And again, the mean
reduction for the other populous states was only 2.6%, supporting
the finding that something unique was happening in Massachusetts
to cause a reduction in crime and other fatalities. The researchers
also discovered that for each of the eleven categories of fatal accidents, and for the three categories of deaths from suicides, homicides, or undetermined causes, there was again a reduction from the
predicted level, which ranged up to 26%.[9]

Other such studies were then published, some in major scientific
journals where the studies were subjected to the intense scrutiny of
peer review. A series of studies on the occurrence of this phenomenon
in different cities around the world was published in *The Journal of*

Mind and Behavior. One study found, for example, a decrease in violent crime in Washington, D.C., during periods of high attendance at the group practice of the Transcendental Meditation and TM-Sidhi program in that city.[10] Dr. Raymond Rusk, Professor of Psychology at the University of Maine, and the editor of *The Journal of Mind and Behavior*, commented on one of the studies published in his journal, saying that "the hypothesis definitely raised some eyebrows among our reviewers, but the statistical work was sound. The numbers are there." Another study was published in the *Journal of Conflict Resolution*,[11] prompting Dr. Juan Pascual-Leone, a respected psychologist at York University in Ottawa, Canada, and a member of the *Journal's* review board, to say that "the possibility is that we have made one of the most important discoveries of our time."[12] Other studies have shown significant reductions in the average number of casualties caused by terrorism during large assemblies of individuals practicing this program; and, in a study conducted by researchers in Holland, significant decreases in crime in Holland were found on three occasions during a ten-year period, *all three times occurring when assemblies of people practicing the TM-Sidhi program in Holland exceeded the square root of one percent of the Dutch population.*[13]

Because this research challenges conventional paradigms, it often strikes people as impossible, especially in view of the relatively small number of individuals needed to produce a decrease in crime. But in the twenty or so years since the initial studies, this phenomenon of decreased violence and increased positivity has been demonstrated in a total of forty-two studies, known to the editors and staff of the principal journals dealing with sociological issues, but largely unknown to others. Now, the weight of evidence that has accumulated from the number of studies, the similar findings in the studies, the independent review of many studies (by independent review boards or peer review processes at the journals publishing the studies), and even the dramatic nature of the advanced TM-Sidhi program (what I call the *extra strength* crime vaccine), requires a change in our thinking about how to most effectively *prevent* crime.

Decreased Crime in Holland

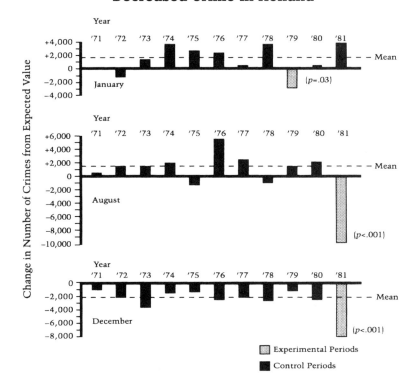

The *Extra Strength* Crime Vaccine: Yogic Flying

People who have been practicing the Transcendental Meditation technique for at least six months have the opportunity to learn the advanced TM-Sidhi program. The TM-Sidhi program also comes from the Vedic literature, and was derived by Maharishi from the *Yoga Sutras* of Patanjali, a great sage of the Vedic tradition.

Successful practice of the Maharishi TM-Sidhi program is based on the individual's practice of the Transcendental Meditation technique. Maharishi explains that the TM technique is a procedure whereby the mind arrives at the experience of transcendental consciousness, the most settled state of mind. Maharishi describes this as the most powerful level of the mind and also explains that this is the experience in human consciousness of the deepest and most powerful level of nature's functioning. The TM-Sidhi program makes use of the Yoga Sutras of Patanjali to train the mind to *function* from this level of transcendental consciousness, which has some rather dramatic consequences.

As we discussed before (see chapter 5), the same field of transcendental consciousness which underlies the mind's activity also underlies physiological functioning and gives orderliness and structure to the functioning of the body. But now this understanding is carried one step further. This same underlying field of transcendental consciousness, Maharishi explains, is also at the basis of the functioning of all of nature. It is the deepest level of nature's intelligence, from which the laws of nature govern the universe. When the mind experiences this fundamental field, it is like dropping a pebble into a pond, to use one of Maharishi's analogies. The pebble produces a ripple, spreading throughout the pond in all directions. And when not one, but a number of individuals experience this field together at the same time, the ripple becomes a wave, producing a powerful influence of coherence and orderliness throughout the whole society.

Of course, if the collective consciousness of society is to be changed by such a small group of individuals, it would have to be on the basis of a profound experience in the consciousness and physiology of those triggering the effect.

The technique to produce this experience is known as Yogic Flying, which has been found to be the most important TM-Sidhi technique for creating an orderly influence in the collective consciousness. *As predicted by Patanjali, the first stage of Yogic Flying results in the body lifting or hopping off the ground, based on a simple mental performance.* The practice, however, is not valued for this outer effect, but for the changes it produces in the individual's consciousness and brain physiology. Internally, the practice produces the maximum mind-body integration, as reflected in highly coherent EEG brain wave patterns at the moment of lift-off during Yogic Flying (see charts on next page); and, subjectively, those who practice the technique often experience intense inner happiness. The important point for our purposes is that this "extra strength" crime vaccine creates such an enhanced coherence in the individual, it requires correspondingly fewer individuals (compared with the Transcendental Meditation technique) to spread coherence and reduce stress in the collective consciousness of the population.[14]

Increased EEG Coherence During Yogic Flying

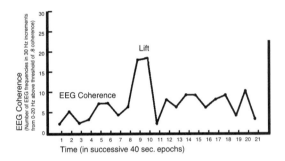

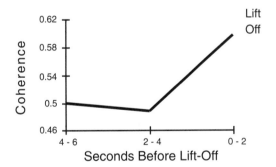

During Yogic Flying, immediately before lift-off and before any movement artifacts were produced in the EEG, broadband coherence (5-20 Hz) significantly increased compared to the two earlier periods.

Reference: 1. F.T. Travis and D.W. Orme-Johnson, "EEG Coherence and Power During Yogic Flying," *International Journal of Neuroscience* 54 (1990): 1-12.

Another aspect of Yogic Flying is that during group practice of the technique, participants often experience that the larger the size of the group, the greater the effect of the program in producing

feelings of exhilaration and of being connected to the other participants in the group at some fundamental level. Both this experience
of *connectedness,* and the understandings of the Vedic literature
shed light on what physics is now telling us about nature's functioning, which may also make Yogic Flying and these forty-two
studies more understandable.

Quantum Physics and Field Effects

In the nineteenth century, physics viewed the world as composed of
solid bits of matter, which affected each other mainly through direct
physical contact. Psychologists and sociologists then developed similar
models, which picture individuals as wholly separate, and capable of
influencing others only through direct contact. But while matter is dis-
crete and separate on some levels, twentieth-century developments in
quantum mechanics and quantum field theory have shown that *connectedness* can be found at deeper levels, at the level of underlying fields.

Physicist David Bohm, who wrote a classic textbook on quantum
theory, conducted landmark research showing the interconnectedness
of small particles at subtle levels of creation. As described by physicist
Michael Talbot in his book *The Holographic Universe,*[15] quantum
physics actually sees everything in the universe as connected, as part
of a continuum. Individual things may be separate, says Bohm, at what
he calls the *explicate level*, but his work showed there was an underlying *implicate* level, and that the implicate level and the explicate level
blend into each other.

One example of the interconnectedness that exists at the implicate
level is illustrated by debates that occurred between Einstein and Niels
Bohr, another of the founders of quantum physics. As Talbot points
out, when certain particles (an electron and a positron) come together
they eventually destroy each other and decay into two quanta of light
or two photons" traveling in opposite directions. Talbot, in his book,
says that no matter how far apart the photons travel, they will always
be found to have identical angles of what is known as polarization, the
angle of the photon's wave-like aspect as it travels from its point of
origin. Bohr, says Talbot, theorized that the only way the angles could

always remain the same was that the two photons were instantaneously communicating with each other. Einstein disagreed because that would require faster-than-light interconnections to exist. Bohr countered that instead of faster-than-light communication, the two photons were not independent particles, but were part of a single invisible system. Now most physicists agree with Bohr.

Action at a Distance

Physicist John Hagelin, who has published some of the most widely read papers in physics and was the 1992 winner of the prestigious Kilby Award, has explained more about the implicate level, and how it relates to the Yogic Flying phenomenon. Hagelin says that the particles of nature are now understood as fluctuations of underlying, continuous fields which pervade the universe. For example, due to the earth's magnetic field, a compass anywhere will automatically align itself with the field and point to north. And a central broadcasting station propagates electronic waves through the electromagnetic field, permitting receivers in the area to show televised images. Fields such as gravity and the electromagnetic field allow for what is known as *action at a distance*. This is a fundamental attribute of a field through which an event at one location can exert an influence that carries information through the field, causing almost immediate long-range effects (the central broadcasting station sends an instantaneous signal to everyone with a TV in the area).

Viewed from this perspective, Dr. Hagelin believes that the coherence generated by the Yogic Flyers produces a coherent effect on the society at large because consciousness also displays field-like attributes and thus can generate field effects, including *action at a distance*. When those involved in the Transcendental Meditation and TM-Sidhi program experience what Maharishi describes as the deepest level of nature's functioning, they radiate a society-wide influence of *harmony and coherence* (these are the properties at this implicate level, as the Third Law of Thermodynamics suggests—see chapter 10). Dr. Hagelin says that since all other natural phenomena produce field effects and action at a distance, the field effects of consciousness should not be surprising unless we are prepared to adopt a view of life that says that somehow consciousness is fundamentally different from all other natural phenomena.

Laughter at a Distance and the Home Court Advantage

The idea that consciousness is capable of producing field effects has also been the subject of investigation by scientists at Princeton University. Researchers at the School of Engineering have found that high degrees of intellectual cohesiveness, shared emotions, or other *coherent qualities of groups* can produce an observable effect at a distance. Their studies utilize a device that produces white noise, which is transmitted to a computer and is transformed into bits of information forming a predictable pattern. When the researchers placed their device in the presence of a humor conference, and at other conferences where the groups engaged in significant shared emotional activity, there was a significant deviation in the white noise data from what was expected; moreover some of the largest deviations occurred when the group was obviously in synchrony (as, for example, during a particularly funny session at the humor conference). In nine out of the ten conferences, the researchers found deviations that were not predicted by their database, and with five of the groups the differences were statistically significant at the $p = .05$ level. While the researchers acknowledged the preliminary nature of their findings, they theorized that there is a "salient role for group consciousness . . . having significant impact on our values and the possibility of creating new forms of constructive human interactions."[16]

Another phenomenon familiar to many that may have something to do with the ability of consciousness to create action at a distance is the *home court advantage* in sports. This phenomenon is usually attributed to the fans uplifting or inspiring the home team with their cheers (or deflating the visitors with their jeers), but I suspect that the field effects of consciousness are at least partially responsible. Everyone who has played competitive sports knows that you are oblivious to the fans during most of the game, and especially during the key moments as, for example, when you are shooting the basketball or guarding the man with the ball. As a player, if your attention is on the fans and the cheering, you can't perform at your best. The home court advantage, then, may really be a function of the home town fans generating a cohesive state of consciousness that causes some greater degree of cohesiveness for the home team.

The research at Princeton, and phenomena like the home court advantage, actually illustrate several points previously discussed. First, there can be a group or collective consciousness composed of the sum of the individual states of consciousness, capable of producing some effect at a distance. But it also illustrates that varying effects will be found, depending on the quality of consciousness of the group triggering the effect. There are different levels of the mind, as there are different levels in nature, and as we've seen the deeper levels are more powerful, both in nature and in consciousness. For this reason, the research at Princeton on shared experiences at more excited levels of the mind, and other phenomena based on excited mental states (like the home court advantage), will produce relatively superficial action at a distance, compared with the deep inner experience of the participants in the TM-Sidhi program.

Becoming Peaceful, Not Just Wishing for Peace

The crime-reducing effects of the Transcendental Meditation and TM-Sidhi programs, according to a field theory of consciousness, have nothing to do with the social interactions of the participants with others in society. The Yogic Flyers are creating an influence of coherence in the collective consciousness of society, based on their contacting a fundamental field underlying all of nature including everyone's consciousness, and based on fundamental field behavior.

This is a new concept, which may account for some of the skepticism over research that, based on results, should have already resulted in large scale crime reduction programs. Even those who are open-minded to the new ideas have difficulty appreciating the new paradigm. During my 1994 campaign, I talked to one

Democratic Party candidate who had previously heard this crime research described in general terms. Like many people, however, she considered the group TM-Sidhi program to be some loose equivalent of people getting together and praying for peace or for less violence. My wife Susan pointed out the flaw in that analysis. When a group of meditators come together they are not trying to think of anything in particular. The purpose of the group program is to allow the mind to experience more settled states and, ultimately, transcendental consciousness. This produces coherence, and when a critical mass generates coherence in their own consciousness, the collective consciousness of the community (i.e., everyone's consciousness) receives an *instantaneous* influence of coherence.

Increasing Serotonin in the Community

If the consciousness of the community is in fact influenced positively by the critical mass of "coherence carriers," this should be supported by an improvement in the physiological functioning among community members (as described earlier, profound changes in consciousness should produce corresponding physical changes). Studies have now found this to be the case. One of the most important physiological changes contributing to reduced violence in the individual may be the increase in serotonin through the practice of the Transcendental Meditation technique (see chapter 5). Accordingly, several researchers determined to find out whether a relatively large group of Transcendental Meditation and TM-Sidhi participants could have a positive effect on serotonin levels of individual members of the group, causing their serotonin levels to increase as the size of the group increased.

A dissertation study[17] by Sarah Loliger evaluated eleven volunteers ages twenty to forty. These individuals practiced the TM-Sidhi program daily with large groups in the Maharishi University of Management community in Fairfield, Iowa. The design of the study covered a fifty-day period and measured the experimental subjects' moods, sleep habits, and their serotonin changes (as indicated by the metabolite 5-HIAA—see chapter 5) as a result of the large group program. To measure changes in their moods and sleep habits, the subjects completed questionnaires four times a day during the fifty-day period. To measure changes in serotonin, the subjects collected all their urine over the entire twenty-four-hour period of each of the fifty days.

The findings supported the theory. As the size of the large Yogic Flying group increased, serotonin increased for those individuals who were being studied. The statistical analysis showed that for each hundred-person increase in the size of the group, there was approximately a 9% improvement in mood, a 17% increase in 5-HIAA, and a 31% improvement in the quality of sleep in the experimental subjects.

Another study on the Fairfield community, conducted by Dr. Kenneth Walton and his colleagues, was presented at the Society of Neuroscience in Toronto in 1988.[18] This study is even more striking since serotonin was measured in people in the community who were not part of the meditating group. Walton measured 5-HIAA excretion rates over a period of fifty to eighty-six days, comparing the daily numbers of the people in Fairfield who were participating in the TM-Sidhi program with the serotonin levels of those participating in the program, as well as people in the general community who were not participating in the program. The study involved four groups of subjects and found increases in serotonin in all four groups when the daily TM-Sidhi group program numbers increased, including two groups (eight subjects) who simply resided in the area. *In other words, a relatively large meditating group increased the serotonin levels of non-meditators in proximity to the group.*

An Important Study with Public Predictions and an Independent Review Board

Based on forty-one earlier studies, Dr. Hagelin and the Institute he directs organized a large-scale Yogic Flying project to reduce crime in Washington, D.C. in the summer of 1993. If good results could be achieved in the nation's capital, a major crime center of the world but also a major power base, it was hoped that government leaders could not ignore the findings. In addition, a program to increase coherence in the collective consciousness of Washington, D.C. was felt to be urgently needed because of the hazards of major governmental decisions being made in such a highly stressed atmosphere. The stress in the collective consciousness of our nation's capital has a negative effect on the thinking and behavior of the entire Washington, D.C. community (maybe you've noticed that the Republicans and Democrats in Washington don't always see eye to eye), and the daily decision-making of that community affects the lives of everyone in the world.

The Washington, D.C. demonstration project was a highly publicized experiment, and the predictions of violent crime reduction were made publicly in advance (as other studies had done). Moreover, a distinguished panel of more than twenty sociologists and criminologists, representing a wide range of universities and institutions, as well as members of the D.C. government and police department, and civic leaders, served as an independent advisory board to oversee the study design and the analysis of the crime data.

As with some of the previous studies, the research protocol specified a sophisticated *time series analysis* of violent crime data (violent crime for these purposes was homicides, rapes, and aggravated assaults). Time series methodology has the effect of controlling for previous trends and cycles or other factors that can affect the crime rate. For example, analysis of the relationship in prior years of violent crime to temperature, precipitation, and weekly crime cycles showed that these variables needed to be taken into account (more violent crime occurs on the weekends, and when it's hot, and when it doesn't rain). Using time series analysis, the researchers developed a model of what the D.C. crime rate should have been during this period based on previous trends, as well as the actual temperature, precipitation and other factors that occurred during the experiment. Then the analysis assessed whether crime significantly decreased compared with what should have been the case without the group of Yogic Flyers. This was felt to be a better test than merely measuring crime during the experiment as compared with the previous months or the previous year, which would be misleading because of other factors that influenced the various trends. According to time series analysis, for example, if during the two-month period of the D.C. project, it had been much cooler overall, the *predicted* level of crime would have been much less, and the TM-Sidhi group would have had to achieve a decrease in crime below that predicted level.

In the Washington, D.C. project, the group of TM-Sidhi program participants ranged in size from about 1,000 at the beginning of the experiment in early June, 1993, to about 4,000 for the last two weeks. Many of the participants came from all parts of the world at their own expense to spend their summer at several colleges and hotels in the area, to show that this technology could work. Including these financial contributions, the demonstration project is said to have cost over $5 million.

The results again supported the theory. By the end of the two-month period, when the group of Yogic Flyers was the largest, there was approximately a 20% decrease in crime from what was predicted, which was statistically significant ($p = .027$ for daily crime analysis and $p = .0006$ for weekly crime analysis). The results indicated that the effects could not be attributed to temperature, rainfall, weekend effects, previous trends in the data, or police surveillance in certain districts. The analysis also predicted that there would have been a much larger long-term crime reduction (over 40%) if the group of 4,000 had been maintained in the District for one hundred days. (This is similar to the herd immunity effects in disease, where it is recognized that "achieving a herd immunity threshold does not mean immediate disappearance of the infection, it only starts a downward trend.")[19]

In the Washington, D.C. project, as the theory predicts, the 20% decline occurred in the two-week period when the group was largest, with lesser results when the group was smaller. In one week, when the group was relatively small, there was an unusually high level of homicides, but Dr. Hagelin says analysis of the data showed that homicides were not significantly higher during the demonstration project than in previous months and were not significantly related to the group size.

Violent Crime Decreased as Attendance Increased

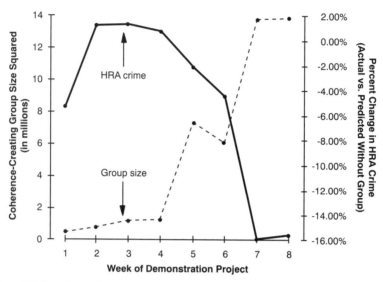

The solid line shows the percentage change in HRA crime from the levels predicted without the coherence-creating group. In the first weeks of the Demonstration Project when the coherence-creating group (broken line) was relatively small, HRA crimes continued the rising trend of earlier months. As the group size increased, however, violent crime decreased significantly (p=.003, daily HRA data).

Dr. Beverly Rubik, a biophysicist and Director of the Center for Frontier Sciences at Temple University, a member of the project review board, said that "the data showed an impressive, statistically significant correlation." Dr. John Davies, Research Coordinator for the Center for International Development and Conflict Management at the University of Maryland, another member of the review board, stated that "the project design was rigorous, the analysis was conducted in a highly competent manner, and the results are impressive." And Dr. David Edwards, Professor of Government at the University of Texas at Austin, another member of the project review board, has commented on similar research that "the promised practical societal impact of this research significantly exceeds that of any other ongoing social-psychological research program." Dr. Edwards felt that the research deserved "the most serious evaluative consideration by the social science community."

The Naysayers at Work

Despite the impressive results, others tried to take credit for the reduction in violent crime. The District of Columbia mayor said the reduction was a result of an increased police watch, but this was contrary to the statistics. Of the seven police districts in Washington, police shifts were significantly increased during the demonstration project only in district 1 and in districts 5-7. Yet the reduction in violent crime occurred throughout the District of Columbia, and the decreases were statistically significant even in districts 2-4, where there was virtually no increase in police anti-crime activity during the demonstration project. Moreover, after the TM-Sidhi group left Washington, D.C. on July 30, 1993, the crime rate soon resumed its previously high level, even though the police continued their increased activities in each district through August and September, and in some cases until December.

While the research again confirmed the hypothesis, indicating a discovery of the greatest social significance, the novelty of the research and the highly political nature of crime strategies resulted, for the most part, in institutional apathy, as well as predictable jeers from at least one prominent member of the academic community. MIT's Museum and its *Annals of Improbable Research* journal awarded Dr. Hagelin one of its "Ignoble Peace Prizes" in 1994 as a result of his study. That was the kind of award Iowa's *Des Moines Register* and other papers couldn't resist, and they prominently featured the story. The press, of course, never checked the reason Hagelin was selected, or if they did, they ignored what they found since that would have ended the story. When I called the editor of the Annals, he readily acknowledged that no scientific analysis had been done of Hagelin's work. Hagelin was vilified just because his conclusion sounded improbable. The editor of the *Annals* also said that some of the research that wins their dubious awards "are wonderful things that just sound unusual," and that MITs publication "just wants people to *ask questions*," a statement that should qualify for next year's *baloney* award. When a prominent university ridicules research just based on how it sounds, it causes people to come to negative conclusions about the project and to dismiss it, rather than to ask questions.

Our Choice: An Explosion in Crime or an Upsurge of Peace

We are at a major crossroads today in our fight against crime. Those who study crime data can foresee a significant explosion in crime as the population in the critical fifteen-to-nineteen age bracket (the group with the highest offense rate) will grow disproportionately over the next ten years. The total population is projected to increase about 12% by 2005, but the number of teens between fifteen and nineteen will increase 21%, and young black and Hispanic men, who have the highest crime rates, will increase 24% and 47%, respectively.

In addition, Harry Allen, the 1995 President of the American Criminal Justice Society, points out that there are massive changes taking place in America that will also increase the mass of at-risk people. He points out that the American dream of working hard and saving for old age or a rainy day doesn't apply to an increasing segment of the population. The increasing disparity between haves and have-nots in the U.S. has come about as a result of the downsizing of organizations, the knowledge explosion, and the increasing need in the work force for those who can understand computers, e-mail, and the Internet, and a drastically reduced need for unskilled labor. Consequently, a large proportion of Americans are becoming economically and politically disenfranchised. We are becoming a nation and a world of haves and have-nots, and now virtually everyone has access to assault weapons, bombs, and the tools of germ warfare.

The herd immunity concept in epidemics suggests that if we don't keep the number of carriers of stress (including criminals, as well as stressed individuals in the general population) below the level that would constitute a critical mass, we will experience a huge explosion in crime. On the other hand, if we first reach a critical mass of coherent minds, general stress theory predicts we can have a great upsurge of peace and a truly successful conclusion to the war on crime. Those advocating the Transcendental Meditation and

TM-Sidhi program over the years have been a relatively small number, an oddity to those entrenched in looking to more conventional solutions. But based on any logical risk/reward analysis, and the dangerous explosion in crime that may be coming, we can't now afford to ignore this new approach. It's ludicrous to believe that anti-terrorism legislation, for example, or longer prison sentences, or more crimes punished by the death penalty, are the solutions for preventing future bombings, nerve gas attacks or the like. If we bomb-proof all the federal buildings, those who are driven to such acts can attack the state buildings, or the public libraries, or the subways. Crime begins in the human mind, and that is the most effective place to prevent it from occurring.

The Annual Cost of Crime to Society

The cost of training and maintaining a relatively small group of Yogic Flyers in each major city, or in the nation as a whole, is exceedingly small in comparison to the rewards. Excluding the cost of incarceration, and just looking at the cost of crime caused by criminals at-large, a year ago *Business Week* and *U.S. News & World Report* placed the annual cost of crime in the United States at approximately $685 billion.[20] This includes $175 billion to $200 billion as the economic value of loss of life and work (this category is referred to as "victimization" in the chart below), $120 billion as the cost of crimes against businesses, and $110 billion as the cost of persons driving while intoxicated.

Annual Cost of Crime: $685 Billion

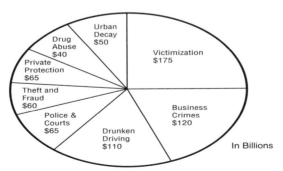

The Cost to Reduce Crime in Society

On the other hand, the cost of training and maintaining a group of 4,000 Yogic Flyers in a city with a population of about one million would be about $5,000 per person or $20 million for training, and an equal amount for salaries and for maintaining the group for the first year. There may be a need to pay a salary to at least some of those involved in the program, since their attendance would be needed for most of the morning and for two hours at the end of the day. Based on, for example, the Washington, D.C. study, such a group should be able to produce approximately a 20% to 40% decline in crime in the city (20% was achieved, and 40% was predicted if the group had been maintained for 100 days), and a 10% decline in crime in the state (in the Amherst study there was a 10% state-wide reduction in crime with a smaller group).

The foregoing reductions in crime would decrease the city's crime costs by perhaps 25% and the state's costs by perhaps 5%, since part of the crime costs, such as the infrastructure and personnel devoted to crime, could not immediately be allocated to other areas of society. A city like Boston, as an example, has a population of about 550,000, which is similar to the population of Washington, D.C. If Boston incurred a proportionate share of the total $685 billion cost of crime to society (based on the number of FBI Index crimes in Boston compared with the nation as a whole), the city and its residents incur a crime cost of approximately $2.7 billion each year, and (based on the Washington, D.C. study) save 25% of that sum or $675 million. The state of Masssachusetts, with a population of six million people would derive further savings of 5% of the crime costs outside of Boston (again based on the number of crimes in the state in relation to crimes in the nation) or $578 million, for total savings throughout the state of approximately $1.25 billion.

The Risk/Reward Ratio We Can't Ignore

The actual benefits, of course, are not just in the savings from reduced crime in the city and state. Crime decreases as a result of stress decreasing and coherence increasing. Thus, as we've seen, fatal accidents and other negative occurrences would decrease, and positive business and social interactions should increase. But just considering the reduced crime in the city and state (and ignoring any reduced crime in the nation), the total annual benefit in the above example is $1.25 billion in the year after the group is trained, with a cost of approximately $40 million for the first year. This is a risk/reward ratio of 31.25 to one, and the ratio improves dramatically in subsequent years. After several years, for example, it should not be necessary to train people at government expense, or pay salaries. The increased number of Yogic Flyers should make it possible for a stable group to produce the same or better results in fewer hours each day, enabling the group members to hold regular jobs. *The chart below is therefore comparing annual savings in the city and state with what may be only a cost for the first year or two.*

Annual Crime Savings

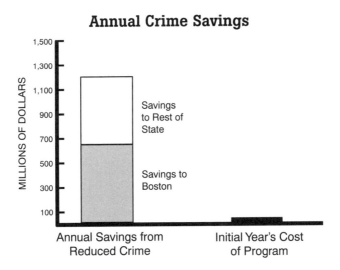

How would an investment analyst view this program? I think he would say that even if we believed there was only one chance in a thousand that the program would work (and the research shows that the odds are more like one chance in a thousand *that it won't work*), government should begin a number of these programs as soon as possible. Unfortunately, while this is the kind of risk/reward ratio that makes Wall Street analysts light up their cigars, politicians are not very interested where unconventional solutions are concerned.

We're Looking for a Few Good Men and Women

Since governments move so slowly in utilizing strategies from outside the mainstream, individuals and other institutions need to adopt this program to end the crime epidemic. Individuals, for example, can learn the TM-Sidhi program and join with existing groups of Yogic Flyers to increase the number of coherence carriers. Businesses can make these programs available to their employees, and the media and academic institutions can seriously evaluate the forty-two research studies on this phenomenon. And those who are influential in society can encourage governments and the military to sponsor crime prevention wings made up of those already being employed with our tax dollars. Because of the immediate reward for joining this new war on crime (personal stress reduction and the growth of fulfillment), participating is in no sense a sacrifice. Like the U.S. Marine Corps' television ads, we're looking for a few good men and women—those who aren't afraid of unconventional solutions and are interested in changing the course of history.

Afterword

The Failure of Government: Limiting the Search for Solutions to What is Popular

A few months after the 1994 elections, I flip the channel past *The Terminator* to C-Span, where Newt Gingrich is speaking before the American Legislative Council. He is quite inspiring in his characterization of the goals of the Republican Party. This is not the first time I have seen Gingrich on television, but previously he was testy and unappealing. Gingrich is advocating a five-point platform for reform, and he is supposed to be the opposition party, so I am wondering why I identify so much with his speech. A half hour later it dawns on me. First, Gingrich's talk is about what's wrong with America, something most of us can agree on. Second, it's about the need for reform, and since everyone identifies with reform messages (especially when government isn't working), Gingrich is pushing the right buttons, as long as he doesn't get too specific.

The Rhetoric of Reform

Gingrich says we need to recognize that we are in an Information Age, and we need to enable every American to take advantage of the vast amounts of knowledge now available to help us live better. I can agree with that, but it strikes me later that *how* we educate Americans to be able to take advantage of the Information Age is the real question. Gingrich's education point is that we have to "renew American civilization, recognizing that we are multiethnic, but one civilization," and Gingrich ridicules some of the "nonsense" being taught in schools, under the guise of academic freedom. He doesn't go into detail, but reminds us that people from

199

outside America moved here because they wanted to live here.

Gingrich's main emphasis in this talk is on what's wrong with education; but again, figuring out what's wrong is the easy part, whereas real reform would tell us how to make it better. What *should* we be teaching? I agree with Gingrich that we need to focus in education on what we share in common, rather than our differences, but these are empty words in the absence of a concrete plan to change education. I decide that the Natural Law Party knows a lot more than Gingrich about what's needed in education, and about how to promote American civilization and reduce crime. What's missing in education is the knowledge of how to reduce stress and develop consciousness, so people are interested in learning. The functioning of an individual's consciousness will determine his motivation to learn, yet most people can't even define consciousness, don't know how to develop it, or even why they should want to.

Next on Gingrich's list is welfare reform that replaces a welfare society with an opportunity society. Here Gingrich makes frequent references to the writings of psychologist Morris Schectman who distinguishes between "caring" and "caretaking." Our present welfare orientation simply makes government a caretaker of the down and out, as opposed to real caring, he says. Although Gingrich doesn't carry the thought quite far enough, it is a point I have often made about the difference between taking care of people and teaching them to take care of themselves.

But again, what's the Republican proposal to teach people how to be self-disciplined and take care of themselves? The Republican philosophy is to provide economic incentives or disincentives (limiting the duration of welfare) to stimulate a work ethic and strengthen family values. But these solutions won't really get to the heart of the problem, which lies deep within human consciousness and the physiology. You can apply external pressure to encourage people to get jobs, but this is like the extrinsic crime solutions. It will have a limited effect compared with developing the individual from within, so he is naturally interested in education, work and expressing his emerging capabilities (see chapters 8 and 11). The major parties' programs are largely more of what hasn't worked, or less of it; but they are devoid of new knowledge. For the most part, anything fundamentally different from what's been done before is too risky for major parties, which favor whatever seems popular or centrist in order to capture votes.

Among the failures of society Gingrich mentions are twelve-year-olds having babies, fifteen-year-olds shooting one another, and eighteen-year-olds graduating from high school without the ability to read. Gingrich speaks favorably about a program to educate second and third graders who couldn't read. He, himself, takes credit for the innovation of offering those children $2 for every book they read one summer, and he indicates that it worked. This is a jumping-off ground for telling us that there are programs that work (show me the research please), and that we need to "zero out" all the existing education, treatment, and welfare programs, and then have the agencies convince us why they should be reinstated.

Zeroing out all the education, treatment, and welfare programs, and asking the agencies to argue for their reinstatement, may be a step in the right direction, but it only makes sense if Gingrich provides appropriate criteria for determining whether a program should be started or reinstated. Several months later I will hear the Republicans say they want to get rid of the "stupid" programs, which also sounds okay (albeit not particularly articulate), but again how do we decide what is "stupid," when most programs will have *some* logic to recommend them? In crime prevention, for example, is midnight basketball stupid? What about the DARE program, or behavior modification? The Natural Law Party criteria for starting new programs, or for reinstating old ones, would be to adopt those programs that are field tested, researched and proven effective. That's the appropriate test and not many crime programs, I suspect, could stand up to it.

Lastly, Gingrich wants a smaller government, with more leadership and volunteerism. "A tiny government and big people," Gingrich says, recognizing that our investment in professional politicians has failed.

Gingrich makes his points in an inspiring way, but I remember being inspired by President Clinton when he ran in 1992 on a message of change, and I was inspired more than thirty years earlier by John F. Kennedy and his volunteerism message ("Ask not what your country can do for you; ask what you can do for your country"). Gingrich's C-Span speech has sounded the call for reform, but the real test of whether it offers any hope for substantive change is in the effectiveness of the solutions being proposed. Everyone is against government waste and unnecessary government interference. Everyone wants Americans to take advantage of the Information Age. Everyone is appalled by juvenile crime, the erosion of family values, and the caretaking aspects of welfare. And, if only there were no nonsense in education. But these and similar problems have existed for years, and the major parties' solutions have not brought any significant improvement.

The Failure of Major Party Politics

Politicians will say that any failure does not stem from the policies of *their* party, because even when their party was in power, they didn't have *enough* power, and lacked support from one or another of the houses of the legislature; or, if they controlled both houses, they lacked control over the executive branch of government. When he declared his candidacy for the 1996 presidential race, Phil Gramm said that we are now one vote away from real change, and with him as president, we would have it. But over the past thirty or so years, considering state and federal governments, there has been virtually every possible combination of Republican and Democratic heads of state with favorable legislatures, yet no single government stands out as having solved the numerous problems that beset their state or the nation. As a result, in the great tradition of glorifying failure, we now have popular politics proclaiming that it is not the role of government to solve problems, and that people need to solve their own problems (i.e., a tiny government and big people). While this makes sense in many contexts, smaller government is only a partial answer. In many cases, this just means shifting responsibility from the federal government onto the states, yet even if the federal government gets out of education, crime and health care, for example, which will be difficult to do, there's no evidence that the state governments know better how to deal with these problems. States may be closer to the problems, but what state programs are successful at educating our youth, for example, to live drug-free, nonviolent lives? What states know what to do about air pollution, noise pollution, suicides, and the diseases of modern civilization (heart disease, cancer, and strokes)? What states have done anything significant to solve juvenile delinquency problems? And show me a state that knows how to rehabilitate prisoners.

Limiting the Search for Solutions to What is Popular

The vicious circle of failure in government has its roots in the fact that politicians, first and foremost, have an instinct for self-preservation. They want to be reelected, and that means searching for solutions that have popular support. The public only gets government solutions that politicians believe will "play well" to the public, and solutions outside mainstream America are ignored. Being "mainstream" is the goal. As a number of political commentators have stated, the major parties have an unquenchable thirst to be mainstream. They are opposed to innovation since they recognize that most of the votes lie near the middle, and winning is the primary objective.

Just a few months ago, Bob Dole sent me a form letter on behalf of the Republican National Committee asking for a contribution and telling me that "the Republican Party is *the* party of mainstream America." But in 1994, when President Clinton campaigned in Iowa, he called the Democrats the *mainstream* and the Republicans the *meanstream.* In Michigan's 1994 senate race, Republican Spencer Abraham and Democrat Bob Carr both scoffed at recommending Transcendental Meditation for use with prisoners, despite its favorable research, because "it wouldn't play well to the voters." The allegiance to whatever is mainstream is an allegiance to votes, not ideas. The fact that innovative, useful ideas have historically come largely from outside the mainstream, and the fact that mainstream solutions have largely failed, often seems to escape the politicians' notice.

Writing in *The Turning Point*,[1] physicist Fritjof Capra says that traditionally U.S. presidents have turned to academics and "think tanks" that formulate the "mainstream academic view," and advise governments on various policy matters. But, as Capra says, "the mainstream of ideas has split into dozens of rivulets, and in some areas it has dried up altogether." He notes that in one *Washington Post* story under the heading "The Cupboard is Bare," some of our most prominent thinkers admitted they were unable to solve the nation's most urgent problems, and they didn't think anyone else in the mainstream could solve them. If that was true of mainstream knowledge fifteen years ago when Capra wrote his book, it is even more true today.

Why Third Party Candidates Get Ignored

Unfortunately, the preoccupation with what is mainstream and already popular isn't limited to politicians. Just prior to the end of my attorney general race, I decided to call Phoebe Howard, who wrote the *Des Moines Register*'s article on the attorney general debate. I wanted to find out how it happened that I only received one sentence of coverage at the end of her article, a sentence that merely noted that I had "appeared on the program." Phoebe was straightforward. There was no apparent malice toward me, and no hidden agenda, and I wasn't the only third party candidate who merely "appeared" at his debate. The one sentence of coverage at the end of the article was an institutional policy, determined in large part by political editor David Yepsen. Jim Schaefer, for example, the Natural Law Party candidate for secretary of agriculture, and Susan Atkins, an independent candidate for the same office, also received only one sentence of coverage about their debate with the Republican and Democratic candidates, again noting only that they had appeared on the program.

The policy at the *Register* was straightforward, but also unenlightened. Because the polls showed we didn't have popular support, precious column inches weren't going to be devoted to giving us any coverage. The events were news, but the third party ideas were not, irrespective of what we had to say.

We Get All the News That's Popular

There was a time when people at least assumed that the press was giving us "all the news that's fit to print." Whether or not this was ever actually true, now, during political campaigns, we get "all the news that's popular." The failure of the media to report third party views sends a message to the public that our ideas aren't worthy of consideration, when often no such judgment has been made. In political campaigns, some eccentric proposals come from third party and independent candidates, but often there are innovative approaches, too. And when the media ignore the third party perspective, and report only a narrow range of ideas, they become a major force for retarding progress and maintaining the status quo —not exactly what our founding fathers intended by the guarantee of a free press.

When my campaign began, I had thought my particular third party message would be well received. This is an age, I reasoned, when PAC money has given us a government *of* the Republicans and Democrats, *by* the Republicans and Democrats, *for* the Republicans and Democrats, and people were looking for change. My message might have been well received, but the press never gave it the chance. Instead, the press focused on political strategy, and who's ahead in the polls, who's winning.

Winning Elections as an Ideology

It is too obvious to be disputed that the primary objective of the major parties is winning. The Democrats, for example, readily admit that they are trying to figure out "how to appeal to Joe Six-Pack," as one commentator said it, or how to appeal to the angry young men who don't go to college and whose prospects for a rosy future are dim. In Iowa, after the 1994 Republican victories, Democrats engaged in soul-searching to make their message more appealing to the voters. The goal, as always, was to fashion an ideology that captures certain votes, and the major parties would never deny this. What the political process amounts to is fashioning your beliefs and your policies to win, rather than standing up for what you believe, and persuading people that your beliefs will lead to a better life. Winning itself becomes the major ideology. As Professor J. David Gillespie says in his landmark book about two-party America, "The Democrats and Republicans do attract some people for reasons of principle, even ideology; but these major parties mainly seek to win elections and, through winning, to control the political system and its political processes."[2]

One of the ways the major parties maintain their positions, and prevent third parties from encroaching on their territory, is to adopt third party ideology when it gains enough popular support to be useful to the major parties. There is nothing wrong with this. The problem arises when the third party ideas aren't considered—when, for example, third party candidates aren't invited to the debates, or if they get invited, when the press ignores their positions. This is especially unfortunate in view of Professor Gillespie's statement that "many of America's noblest and most far-reaching advances in freedom were third party proposals years before major parties touched them with even the longest pole."[3] The Liberty Party, for example, was against slavery twenty years before the Civil War, and the Populists first demanded equal rights for men and women in 1892. The Populist Party was first to campaign for shorter working hours (finally resulting in the Wages and Hours Act of 1938), a graduated income tax, and legislation through initiatives, which were enacted in many states although not federally. And the Socialist Party called for the abolition of child labor, and backed the Wages and Hours Act, initiatives, referendums, the Social Security Act, and unemployment insurance. The major parties weren't so interested in these reforms until the third parties gave them enough exposure to win some support.

Winning at All Costs

Unfortunately, winning at all costs also involves all those tricks of the trade that help to give politics and politicians a bad name— negative campaigning, maintaining ballot access laws that keep third party and independent candidates from having a fair opportunity to be heard, and expending endless efforts making the representatives of the other party look bad. One of the most interesting insights into winning as the dominant ideology was the revelation of Gingrich's ten-year plan that created his political action committee (GOPAC) in the 1980s to educate new Republicans (the "Newtonians") about how to win elections. One of the most famous of the GOPAC documents is the memo Gingrich titled "Language, a Key Mechanism of Control." As the *Los Angeles Times* reported, after focus group testing, the new guard of Republicans were instructed in their campaigns to characterize Democrats with words such as "corrupt," "decayed," "sick," "pathetic," and "wasteful," while describing Republicans as "optimistic," "positive," "truthful," "moral," and "courageous." (In the Iowa State Penitentiary, putting on this kind of a face is called "walking the walk, talking the talk, and conning the con.") The GOPAC documents also told the new Republican candidates to focus on "wedge issues that tend to divide voters,"[4] and not to "make the mistake of worrying too much what friends and neighbors and the so-called country club set might think if you go negative and get aggressive." As for ideology, they were counseled to invoke issues that would serve as "shields" to prevent them from being characterized as heartless, and to move in on issues like the environment or education that are traditionally Democratic, in an effort to "drive the Democrats nuts," as Gingrich put it.[5]

We're A One-Party America, Not Two

Given the paramount importance of winning, and therefore touting what is popular, the Republicans and Democrats are not so unlike each other as they would have us believe. Reform to Republicans and Democrats traditionally occurs within a narrow range of what is popular, despite wholesale claims by both parties of either "zeroing out" all programs or "reinventing government." Because ideology matters little, both major parties, for example, wanted Colin Powell to join them in late 1994, without knowing where he stood on any issues. And when Dan Quayle dropped out of the 1996 race for

President, he could truthfully say he would support "whomever the Republican party nominated," whether he or she was a conservative, a moderate, or a liberal.

Peg Luksek, who ran in the 1990 Republican primary for governor of Pennsylvania, ran again as an independent in 1994, with the following perspective on major party politics. She said that the Republicans and Democrats represent "one party with two names, and without a lot of difference between them." Bob Dole and Bill Clinton aren't all that different to Peg Luksek, and at the risk of offending my equally invisible third party and independent fellow candidates, even if the ideas of the Socialists, Libertarians, Populists, Greens, Reds, and whatever are thrown into the hopper, we would have many new ideas, but one fundamental way of thinking.

From an ideological perspective, this is probably the most important point in this book. Tax-and-spend Democrats, new Democrats, new Republicans, old Republicans, Libertarians, Populists, and Socialists, despite what seem like major differences in their points of view, all have a fundamentally similar way of looking at the world, which more often than not prevents them from addressing the root causes of problems in our society.

In health care, for example, the 1994 debate was over the financial aspects that result in access or a lack of access to the health care system. But the debate among the left, center, and right on the need for universal coverage; or on how long the phase-in period should be; or on whether business, individuals, or the state should bear the cost of coverage; or on whether we can freely choose our own health care providers or be obligated to use an HMO; never gets to the heart of the matter. All these proposals deal with the problem at a level that never addresses the root cause of the problem, and none will ever be successful. The debate fails to recognize that the reason the health care system is in a crisis is that *people are basically unhealthy.* Fifty percent of all deaths are caused not by infectious diseases or natural aging, but by preventable behaviors such as smoking, drinking, and poor eating habits. Forty-four percent of all Americans suffer from stress-related health problems, including anxiety and hypertension. On any given day, 25% of high school students haven't eaten any vegetables and 24% haven't eaten any fruit. And just in case you think we simply need more conventional education on these matters, 71% of Americans are overweight, a new record despite the current educational emphasis on staying healthy. This is the real cause of a health care system that is in a financial crisis. Lasting solutions will result only by providing people with the education they need to be self-sufficient in *preventing illness from within.*

To repeat a metaphor, if your problem is that the leaves of the tree are dry and flaky, the liberals who would approach the leaves from the left, or the conservatives who would approach the leaves from the right, or the moderates who would approach from the center, will all fail. The solution is not in the leaves, so it's not remedied from the left, right or middle. There is an inner solution—an invisible solution—that alone can remedy the problem. Nourish the root rather than attending to the leaves, and the problem at the surface disappears.

The Natural Law Party Philosophy

The Natural Law Party was founded by scientists to bring the deepest scientific knowledge into politics. The NLP has a distinct philosophy. Wherever possible, government programs should be based on those that have been field tested and scientifically proven to be effective, or at least those common sense approaches that take into account the functioning of the fundamental laws of nature governing growth or evolution.

As a permanent solution to the health care crisis, the NLP focuses on improving people's health through proven, prevention oriented strategies that enable people to develop their innate potential for lifelong health and well-being. The problems of health care, like the seemingly intractable problems of crime and substance abuse, are all "people problems" that cry out for new inner solutions—solutions that are cost-effective but may not be popular with the special interests making good money from conventional solutions, even if they don't work very well.

President Clinton and Speaker Gingrich sound fine when they talk about caring for people rather than caretaking, or when they speak about improving education, or call for an end to teenage pregnancies and youth homicides, but it's easy to identify the problems. It's when they try to do something about the problems that the quest for popularity often leads to superficial solutions, and to what works at getting votes, rather than what works at solving the problems.

This book is about the deeper approaches to the problems that plague us in the area of crime and drug abuse, but the principles can be applied to all the people problems—poor relationships with family members, lack of creativity and productivity on the job, teenage pregnancies, dependence on welfare, abortion, racism, and negative tendencies in general. It's about "moving forward," as President Clinton has said, not moving left or right, but it's moving forward by moving inward, and correcting problems using our innate resources.

What's the Big Deal about Nature?

Perhaps the theme that most distinguishes the Natural Law Party ideologically from the Republican or Democratic parties is the NLP respect for nature, and a belief that in the deepest understandings of nature is the key to solving not just individual problems, but also those we face as a society. Today, our major cities are covered by layers of smog. Our health is threatened as well by the water we drink and the food we eat. Synthetic food additives, pesticides, and other chemicals are marketed at such an increasing rate that they may be destroying the ecological systems we depend on for existence. We take Aspirin, Maalox, Gelusil, Valium, and other synthetic medicines at the slightest provocation to mask our pain and to counter the ups and downs of modern life. And we do it all from a fundamental lack of knowledge about the inherent perfection in the functioning of nature.

The Natural Law Party's understanding of nature results in a genuine concern for the environment, but it goes much deeper. It recognizes, for example, that there are different "layers" of nature (e.g., the physical and the underlying mental, the molecular and the underlying atomic, the leaves and the underlying sap), and that the innermost levels are more powerful and govern the outer layers. This is why the subatomic levels are more powerful than the atomic level, and why the field of intelligence at the basis of nature's functioning is potentially the most powerful level of all.

The functioning of nature contains within it a deep level of intelligence that can't be duplicated by what is man-made or artificial. And this intelligence in nature is the same intelligence found deep within the human mind. When the mind settles down and transcends all mental activity, it brings the mind and body into contact with this underlying field. Maharishi explains that as the mind begins to function from the same level of nature that organizes everything from the movement of the planets to the birth of a child, that same organizing power of nature becomes available to the individual. This is the principle value of the Transcendental Meditation and TM-Sidhi programs. These programs ultimately aim to enable every individual's thoughts and desires to be supported by the vast organizing power of nature. This is the most important result of achieving what is traditionally known as the state of enlightenment, and it has the most profound implications for individual success *and* for success in solving society's problems. Changes in society come from changing the way individuals function, and we have now learned that we can "jumpstart" the process of transformation in society with just a small group of individuals (see chapter 12).

The Coming Elections

In 1994 there was some interest in third party and independent candidates, and a few independents even got elected. However, much of the interest in alternatives to the major parties came from an orientation of disillusionment—over gridlock, partisanship, negative campaigns, and special interest considerations—rather than a positive orientation to any new ideological perspective. The interest in third parties or independents was mostly a protest against what hasn't worked, yet even as a protest, it is clear that most people are disillusioned and want a real change. Many I believe will find it in the

Natural Law Party, and in its candidates. This party was founded in April, 1992, and in just six months before the November elections, it became only the third party in political history to achieve National Party Committee Status from the Federal Election Commission and federal matching funds for its presidential candidate. The party has a broad platform that aims, for example, to promote a healthy economy by cutting taxes significantly (through the cost-effective programs of the NLP in crime, drug abuse, and health care, taxes can be reduced *responsibly*), to reverse declining educational trends by making education more relevant to the student, to encourage the development of renewable energy resources and sustainable farm practices, and to revitalize both rural communities and our inner cities. The party supports election and campaign reforms and a shortened campaign season. And the party upholds the basic rights of women and minorities, proposing to end bigotry and prejudice by instituting programs to eliminate the stress that is at the basis of narrow-minded thinking.

In 1992, the party's 130 or so candidates for federal and state office impressed people with their new solutions to society's problems, and their *unwillingness* to campaign "the old-fashioned way." These are candidates who don't engage in negative campaigning, and seek votes and funding based on their ideas, not any allegiance to PACs or special interest groups. They're intelligent, unpretentious, and they don't put winning above all else. Many of them practice the Transcendental Meditation technique. If they have seen farther than other men, it may be because their eyes have been closed.

Notes

Chapter Two

1. Gottfredson, M.R., and Hirschi, T., *A General Theory of Crime,* Stanford University Press, Stanford, 1990, p. 5.

2. Ibid., pp. 6-7.

3. Ibid., p. 33.

4. Transcript, "What Can We Do About Violence, A Bill Moyers Special," WNET Public Affairs Television, Inc., New York, 1995, p.2.

5. Siegel, L.J., *Criminology,* West Publishing Company, St. Paul, MN, 1995, pp. 10-11.

6. Ibid., p. 150.

7. Ibid., p. 153.

8. Ibid., p. 158.

9. Raine, A., Venables, P.H., and Williams, M., "Relationships Between Central and Autonomic Measures of Arousal at Age 15 Years and Criminality at 24 Years," *Archives of General Psychiatry,* Vol. 45, 1990, p. 1003.

10. Walton, K. and Levitsky, D., "A Neuroendocrine Mechanism for the Reduction of Drug Use and Addictions by Transcendental Meditation," *Alcoholism Treatment Quarterly,* Vol. 11, Nos. 1/2, 1994, p. 101.

Chapter Three

1. Ibid., p. 92.

2. Bloomfield, H., Cain, M.P., and Jaffe, D.T., *TM: Discovering Inner Energy and Overcoming Stress*, Delacorte Press, New York, 1975, p. 50.

3. Siegel, *Criminology* (see note 5, chapter 2), p. 192.

4. Olsen, J., Burgogne, K., Bell, P., Benson, S., Cody, R., Catalano, R.F., Chappell, P.J., and Hawkins, D.H., "Communities That Care: Risk and Resource Assessment Training," presented by the Office of Juvenile Justice and Delinquency Prevention, U.S. Department of Justice, developed by Developmental Research and Programs, Inc., Seattle, 1994.

5. Winslow, C.E., *The Conquest of Epidemic Disease*, Princeton University Press, New Jersey, 1944, p. 346.

6.   Maharishi Mahesh Yogi, *Creating an Ideal Society*, Age of Enlightenment Press, Livingston Manor, NY, 1976, p. 91.

7.   See note 5.

Chapter Four

1.   "What Can We Do About Violence?" (see note 4, chapter 2), p. 27.

2.   Bloomfield, H., and Kory, R., *Happiness*, New York, Simon and Schuster, 1976, p. 127.

3.   "What Can We Do About Violence?" (see note 4, chapter 2), p.1.

4.   Ibid., pp. 2-3.

5.   U.S. Department of Health and Human Services, *Healthy People 2000*, 1994.

6.   U.S. Department of Justice, *Crime in the United States: Uniform Crime Reports 1993*, pp. 11 and 35.

7.   Ibid.

8.   Ibid.

9.   Siegel, *Criminology* (see note 5, chapter 2), p. 192.

10. *Crime* (see note 6), p. 222.

11. U.S. Department of Justice, *Sourcebook of Criminal Justice Statistics 1993*, p. 628.

12. Gottfredson and Hirschi (see note 1, chapter 2), pp. 145-149.

13. Polednak, A.P., *Host Factors in Disease*, Charles C. Thomas, Springfield, IL, 1987.

14. Ibid., p. 64.

15. Gottfredson and Hirschi (see note 12), p. 147.

16. Satterfield, J.H., "The Hyperactive Child Syndrome: A Precursor of Adult Psychopathy," in *Psychopathic Behavior: Approaches to Research*, ed. Hare and Schalling, John Wiley & Sons, New York, 1978, p. 329.

17. Ibid.

18. Ostfeld, A.M., Kasl, S.V., D'Atri, D.A., and Fitzgerald, E.F., *Stress, Crowding and Blood Pressure in Prison*, Lawrence Erlbaum Associates, Hillsdale, NJ, 1987.

Chapter Five

1.   Krebs, H., "On the Overuse and Misuse of Medication,"
      Executive Health, Vol. 11, No. 2, 1974.

2.   Wallace, R.K., Benson, H., and Wilson, A.F., "A Wakeful
      Hypometabolic Physiologic State," *American Journal of
      Physiology*, Vol. 221, 1971, pp. 795-799.

3.   Wallace, R.K., "Physiological Effects of Transcendental
      Meditation," *Science*, Vol. 167, 1970, pp. 751-1754.

4.   Wallace, R.K., and Benson, H., "The Physiology of Meditation,"
      Scientific American, Vol. 226, 1972, pp. 84-90.

5.   Jevning, R., Wilson, A.F., and Davidson, J.M., "Adrenocortical
      Activity During Meditation," *Hormones and Behavior*, Vol. 10,
      No. 1, 1978, pp. 54-60; Werner, O., Wallace, R.K., Charles, B.,
      Janssen, G., and Chalmers, R., "Endocrine Balance and the TM-Sidhi Program,
      *Scientific Research on the Transcendental Meditation and TM-Sidhi
      Programme*: *Collected Papers* (hereafter this reference is to *Collected Papers*),
      Vol. 3, MVU Press, Vlodrop, Netherlands, 1989, pp. 1626-1633.

6.   Bujatti, M. and Riederer, P.,"Serotonin, Noradrenaline,
      Dopamine Metabolites in Transcendental Meditation," *Journal
      of Neural Transmission*, Vol. 39, 1976, p. 257; Walton, K.G.,
      Lerom, M., Salerno, J., and Wallace, R.K., "Practice of the
      Transcendental Meditation and TM-Sidhi Program May Affect
      the Circadian Rhythm of Urinary 5 - Hydroxyindole Excretion,"
      Society for Neuroscience Abstracts, Vol. 7, 1981, p. 48.

7.   Banquet, J., "Spectral Analysis of the EEG in Meditation,"
      Electroencephalography and Clinical Neurophysiology, Vol.
      35, 1973, pp. 143-151; Levine, P.H., Herbert, J.R., Haynes,
      C.T., and Strobel, U., "EEG Coherence During the
      Transcendental Meditation Technique," *Collected Papers*, Vol.1,
      1976, p. 187.

8.   Jevning, R., Smith, R. and Wilson, A.F., and Morton, M.E.,
      "Alterations in Blood Flow During Transcendental Meditation,"
      Psychophysiology, Vol. 13, 1976, p. 168.

9.   Kotulak, R., "How Brain's Chemistry Unleashes Violence,"
      Chicago Tribune, December 13, 1993.

10.   Kotulak, R., "How Brain's Chemistry" (see note 9); and see
      Kotulak, R., "Tracking Down the Monster Within Us," *Chicago
      Tribune*, December 12, 1993.

11.   Ibid.

12.   Ibid.

13.   Coccaro, E., "Central Serotonin and Impulsive Aggression,"
      British Journal of Psychiatry, Vol. 155, Supplement 8, 1989, pp. 52-62.

14. Kotulak, "How Brain's Chemistry" (see note 9).

15. Bujatti, M., and Riederer, P., "Serotonin, Noradrenaline, Dopamine Metabolites in Transcendental Meditation" (see note 6).

16. Walton, K.G., Lerom, M., Salerno, J., and Wallace, R.K., "Practice of the TM and TM-Sidhi Program May Affect the Circadian Rhythm of Five-Hydroxyindole Excretion" (see note 6), p. 48.

17. Jevning, R., Wallace, R.K., and Beidebach, M., "The Physiology of Meditation: A Review. A Wakeful Hypo-metabolic Integrated Response," *Neuroscience and Bio-Behavioral Review*, Vol. 16, 1992, pp. 415-424.

18. Walton, K. G., and Levitsky, B., "A Neuroendocrine Mechanism for the Reduction of Drug Use and Addictions by Transcendental Meditation" (see note 10, chapter 2), p. 89.

19. MacLean, C.R.K., Walton, K.G., Wenneberg, S.R., Levitsky, D.K., Mandarino, J.B., Wazari, R., and Schneider, R.H., "Altered Cortisol Response to Stress After Four Months' Practice of the Transcendental Meditation Program," presented at the 18th Annual Meeting of the Society for Neuroscience, Anaheim, California, October, 1992.

20. Knoblich, G., and King, R., "Biological Correlates of Criminal Behavior," in *Facts, Frameworks and Forecasts*, ed. McCord, Vol. 3, Transaction Publishers, New Brunswick, NJ, 1992, p. 4-5.

21. Janby, J., "Immediate Effects of the Transcendental Meditation Technique: Increased Skin Resistance During First Meditation After Instruction," *Collected Papers,* Vol. 1, 1976, p. 213.

22. Bloomfield, H., Cain, M.P., and Jaffe, D.T., *TM: Discovering Inner Energy and Overcoming Stress* (see note 2, chapter 3), pp. 80-82.

23. Orme-Johnson, D.W., "Autonomic Stability and Transcendental Meditation," *Psychosomatic Medicine*, Vol. 35, 1973, pp. 341-349.

24. Wilcox, G.G., "Autonomic Functioning in Subjects Practicing the Transcendental Meditation Technique," *Collected Papers*, Vol. 1, 1976, pp. 239-242; Berker, B.A., "Stability of Skin Resistance One Week after Instruction in the Transcendental Meditation Technique," *Collected Papers*, Vol. 1, 1976, pp. 243-247.

25. Goleman, D.J., and Schwartz, G.E., "Meditation as an intervention in stress reactivity," *Journal of Consulting and Clinical Psychology*, Vol. 44(3): 1976, pp. 456-466.

26. Magnussen, D., "Antisocial Behavior of Boys and Autonomic Activity/Reactivity," in *Biological Contributions to Crime Causation*, ed., Moffitt and Mednick, Martinus Nighoff, Boston, 1988, p. 143.

27. Venables, P.H., "Psychophysiology and Crime: Theory and Data," in *Biological Contributions* (see note 26), p. 78.

28. Satterfield, J.H., "The Hyperactive Child Syndrome: A Precursor of Adult Psychopathy?," in *Psychopathic Behavior: Approaches to Research*, John Wiley & Sons, New York, 1978, p. 331.

29. Ibid., pp. 334-335.

30. Ibid., p. 329.

31. Ibid., p. 340.

32. Brennan, P., Mednick, S., and Volavka, J., "Biomedical Factors in Crime," in *Crime*, ed. Wilson and Petersilia, Institute for Contemporary Studies, San Francisco, 1995, p. 85.

33. Schalling, D., "Psychopathy-Related Personality Variables and the Psychphysiology of Socialization," in *Psychopathic Behavior* (see note 28), pp. 87-89.

34. Brennan, P., Mednick, S., and Volavka, J., "Biomedical Factors" (see note 32), p. 86.

35. Ibid.

36. Knoblich, G., and King, R., "Biological Correlates of Criminal Behavior," in *Facts, Frameworks, and Forecasts. Advances in Criminological Theory*, ed., McCord, Vol. 3, Transaction Publishers, New Brunswick, New Jersey, 1992, p.2.

37. Banquet, J., "Spectral Analysis of the EEG in Meditation" (see note 7), pp. 143-151.

38. Levine, P.H., Herbert, J.R., Haynes, C.T., and Strobel, U., "EEG Coherence During the Transcendental Meditation Technique" (see note 7), p. 187.

39. Gaylord, C., Orme-Johnson, D.W., and Travis, F., "The Effects of the Transcendental Meditation Technique and Progressive Muscle Relaxation on EEG Coherence, Stress Reactivity, and Mental Health in Black Adults," *International Journal of Neuroscience,* Vol. 46, 1989, pp. 77-86.

40. Seeman, W., Nidich, S., and Banta, T., "Influence of Transcendental Meditation on a Measure of Self-Actualization," *Journal of Counseling Psychology*, Vol. 19, 1972, pp. 184-187.

41. Nidich, S., Seeman, W., and Dreskin, T., "Influence of Transcendental Meditation: A Replication," *Journal of Counseling Psychology*, Vol. 20., 1973, pp. 556-566.

42. Marcus, J.B., *Success From Within*, Maharishi University of Management Press, Fairfield, IA, 1990, pp. 181-188.

Chapter Six

1. Dwyer, D.C. and McNally, R.B., "Public Policy, Prison Industries and Business: An Equitable Balance for the 1990's," *Federal Probation*, Vol. 57, No. 2, 1993, p. 30.

2. Nossiter, A., "Making Hard Time Harder, States Cut Jail, TV and Sports," *New York Times*, September 17, 1994.

3. Evans, B., "Health Check," *A.C.M.I. First Step Newsletter*, Vol. 22, Georgia Dept. of Corrections, 1994, p. 3.

4. Ellis, G.A., *Inside Folsom Prison*, ETC Publications, Palm Springs, CA, 1979, p. 170.

5. Abrams, A.I., and Siegel, L.M., "The Transcendental Meditation Program and Rehabilitation at Folsom State Prison: A Cross-Validation Study," *Collected Papers,* Vol. 3, 1989, pp. 2093-2103; see also Abrams, A.I., and Siegel, L.M., "Transcendental Meditation and Rehabilitation at Folsom Prison: Response to a Critique," *Criminal Justice and Behavior*, Vol. 6, No. 1, 1974, pp. 13-21; and see Abrams, A.I., "A Follow-up Study of the Effects of the Transcendental Meditation Program on Inmates at Folsom Prison," *Collected Papers,* Vol. 3, 1989, pp. 2108-2112.

6. Ramirez, J., "The Transcendental Meditation Program as a Possible Treatment Modality for Drug Offenders: Evaluation of a Pilot Project at Milan Federal Correctional Institute," *Collected Papers*, Vol. 2, 1989, pp. 1118-1134.

7. Ferguson, R., "The Transcendental Meditation Program at the Massachusetts Correctional Institution Walpole: An Evaluation Report," *Collected Papers,* Vol. 2, 1989, pp. 1146-1155.

8. Ballou, D., "The Transcendental Meditation Program at Stillwater Prison," *Collected Papers,* Vol. 1, 1976, pp. 569-576.

9. Cunningham, M., and Koch, W., "The Transcendental Meditation Program and Rehabilitation: A Pilot Project at the Federal Correctional Institute at Lampoc, California," *Collected Papers*, Vol. 1, 1976, pp. 562-568.

10. Gore, S., Abrams, A., and Ellis, G., "The Effect of Statewide Implementation of the Maharishi Technology of the Unified Field in the Vermont Department of Corrections," *Collected Papers*, Vol. 3, 1989, pp. 2453-2464.

11. Bleick, C.R., and Abrams, A.I., "The Transcendental Meditation Program and Criminal Recidivism in California," *Journal of Criminal Justice*, Vol. 15, 1987, pp. 212-215.

12. Alexander, C.N., Grant, J., and Stadte, C. Von., "The Effects of the Transcendental Meditation Technique on Recidivism: A Retrospective Archival Analysis," doctoral thesis of first author, Dept. of Psychology and Social Relations, Harvard University, Cambridge, 1982.

13. *Stress Management for Correctional Officers and Their Families*, a publication of the American Correctional Association, 1984, p. xii.

14. Ibid.

Chapter Seven

1. Presentation by The Sentencing Project at "Crime and Politics in the 1990s: A National Leadership Conference," Arlington, VA, 1994.

2. Blumstein, A., "Making Rationality Relevant: The American Society of Criminology 1992 Presidential Address," *Criminology,* Vol. 31, No. 1, 1993, p. 5.

3. Blumstein, A., "Youth, Violence, Guns, and the Illicit-Drug Industry," *Journal of Criminal Law and Criminology*, 1995 (in press).

4. Nadelmann, E. A., Kleiman, M.A.R., Earls, F., "Should Some Illegal Drugs be Legalized?", Issues in Science and Technology, Vol. 4, No. 4, 1990, p. 46

5. Ibid.

6. Ibid., p.48

7. Ibid.

8. Ibid.

9. U.S. Dept. of Justice, *Sourcebook* (see note 11, chapter 4), p. 228.

10. Tobler, N., "Drug Prevention Programs Can Work," *Journal of Addictive Diseases*, Vol. 11(3), 1992.

11. Wysong, E., Aniskiewicz, R., and Wright, D., "Truth and Dare: Tracking Drug Education to Graduation as Symbolic Politics," *Social Problems*, Vol. 41, No. 3, 1994, p. 448.

12. Ibid.

13. Ibid.

14. Ennett, S.T., and Rosenbaum, D.P., "Long-Term Evaluation of Drug Abuse Resistance Education," *Addictive Behaviors*, Vol. 19, No. 2, 1994, pp. 113-125.

15. Wysong, E., Aniskrewicz, R., and Wright, D., "Truth *and* Dare" (see note 11), p. 448.

16. Ennett, S.T., Tobler, N., Ringwalt, C.L., and Flewelling, R.L., "How Effective is Drug Abuse Resistance Education? A Meta-Analysis of Project DARE Outcome Evaluations," *American Journal of Public Health*, Vol. 84, No. 9, 1994, p. 1394.

17. Alexander, C.N., Robinson, P., and Rainforth, M., "Treating and Preventing Alcohol, Nicotine, and Drug Abuse Through Transcendental Meditation: A Review and Statistical Meta-Analysis," *Alcoholism Treatment Quarterly*, Vol. 11, Nos. 1/2, 1994, p. 46.

18. Tobler, N., "Meta-Analysis of 143 adolescent drug prevention programs: Quantitative outcome results of program participants compared to a control or comparison group," *Journal of Drug*

Issues, Vol. 16, 1986, pp. 537-567.

19. Greaves, G.B, "An existential theory of drug dependence," in
    Theories of Drug Abuse, ed., Lettieri, Sayers, and Pearson,
    Washington, D.C., National Institute on Drug Abuse, 1980, p. 26.

20. *Alcoholism Treatment Quarterly*, Vol. 11, Numbers 1/2 and 3/4, 1994.

21. O'Connell, D.F., "Possessing the Self: Maharishi Ayur-Veda
    and the Process of Recovery from Addictive Diseases,"
    Alcoholism (see note 13), pp. 468-469.

22. Alexander, C.N., Robinson, P., and Rainforth, M. (see note 17), p. 73.

23. Ibid., pp. 40-42.

24. Ibid., p. 73.

25. Schenkluhn, H., and Geisler, M., "A Longitudinal Study of the
    Influence of the Transcendental Meditation Program on Drug
    Abuse," *Collected Papers,* Vol. 1, 1976, pp. 544-555.

Chapter Eight

1. Harer, M.D., "Recidivism Among Federal Prison Releases in
   1987: A Preliminary Report," Federal Bureau of Prisons, Office
   of Research and Evaluation, Washington, D.C., March 11, 1994.

2. Ibid., p. 42.

3. "Risk-Focus Prevention Using Communities that Care," Office
   of Juvenile Justice and Delinquency Prevention, U.S.
   Department of Justice, 1994.

4. Anderson, D.C., "The Crime Funnel," *New York Times
   Magazine*, June 12, 1994.

5. U.S. Department of Justice, Bureau of Justice Statistics,
   *National Crime Victimization Survey: Crime Victimization in
   the United States 1992*, 1994; U.S. Department of Justice,
   Crime in the United States: *Uniform Crime Reports 1993*
   (1990 data).

6. Ibid.

7. U.S. Department of Justice, Bureau of Justice Statistics, *Felony
   Sentences in the United States, 1990*, 1994.

8. Ibid.

Chapter Nine

1.   Farrington, D.P., "Implications of Biological Findings for
      Criminological Research," in *The Causes of Crime: New
      Biological Approaches*, ed. Mednick, Moffit, and Stack,
      Cambridge University Press, 1987, p. 58.

2.   Sagarin, E., "Taboo Subjects and Taboo Viewpoints in
      Criminology," in *Taboos in Criminology*, ed., Sagarin, Sage
      Press, Beverly Hills, California, 1980, p. 8.

3.   Gordon, R.A., "Research on IQ, Race, and Delinquency: Taboo
      or Not Taboo?," in *Taboos in Criminology* (see note 2), p. 47.

4.   Everly, G.S. Jr., and Benson, H., "Disorders of Arousal and the
      Relaxation Response: Speculations on the Nature and Treatment
      of Stress-Related Diseases," *International Journal of
      Psychosomatics*, Vol. 36 (1-4), 1989, p. 18.

5.   Report of the research of Dr. Herbert Benson and his colleagues
      by the Mind/Body Institute, Deaconess Hospital, Boston, Mass.,
      sent to the author July 19, 1995.

6.   Benson, H., speaking on *Inner Calm,* an audio tape produced by
      Freudberg, D., for Public Radio International, Far Reaching
      Communications, Cambridge, Mass., 1995.

7.   See note 4.

8.   Fehrer, P.M., Carr, R., Sargunuraj, D., and Woolfolk, R.L.,
      "Stress Management Techniques: Are They All Equivalent, or
      Do They Have Specific Effects?," *Biofeedback and Self-Regulation*,
      Vol. 19, No. 4, 1994, p. 353.

9.   Lewis, R., study conducted at the Lawrence County Mental
      Health Clinic, Newcastle, Pennsylvania, under the sponsorship
      of the Pennsylvania Governor's Justice Committee, 1976.

10.   Tolliver, D., "Personality is a Factor Determining Response to
      Two Different Meditation Techniques," Senior Thesis,
      Princeton University, 1976.

11.   Wallace, R.K. and Benson, H., "The Physiology of Meditation,"
      Scientific American, 1972, pp. 84-90; Corey, P.W., "Airway
      Conductance and Oxygen Consumption Changes Associated
      with the Practice of the Transcendental Meditation Technique,"
      Collected Papers, Vol. 1, 1976, p. 94.

12.   Wallace, R.K., "The Physiological Effects of Transcendental
      Meditation: A Proposed Fourth Major State of Consciousness,"
      Collected Papers, Vol. 1, 1976, p. 43.

13.   Beary, J.F. and Benson, H., "A Simple Psychophysiologic
      Technique Which Elicits the Hypometabolic Changes of the
      Relaxation Response," *Psychosomatic Medicine*, Vol. 36, No. 2,
      1974, pp. 115-120.

14. Eppley, K.R., Abrams, A.I., and Shear, J., "Differential Effects
     of Relaxation Techniques on Trait Anxiety: A Meta-Analysis,"
     Journal of Clinical Psychology, Vol. 45(6), 1989, pp. 957-974.

15. Alexander, C.N., Langer, E., Davies, J., Chandler, H., Newman,
     R., "Transcendental Meditation, mindfulness and longevity: An
     experimental study with the elderly," *Journal of Personality and
     Social Psychology*, Vol. 57, 1989, pp. 950-964; Schneider, R.,
     Alexander, C., Wallace, R.K., "In search of an optimal
     behavioral treatment for hypertension: A review and focus on
     Transcendental Meditation," in *Personality, Elevated Blood
     Pressure, and Essential Hypertension*, ed. Johnson, Gentry, and
     Julius, Hemisphere Publishing Corp., Wash., D.C., 1992, pp.
     291-312; Schneider, R., Staggers, F., Alexander, C.N., et al., "A
     randomized controlled trial of stress reduction for the treatment
     of hypertension in older African Americans," *Hypertension* (in Press).

16. Eisenberg, D.M., Dilbanco, T.L., Berkey, C.S., Koptchuk, T.J.,
     Kupelnick, B., Kuhl, J., and Chalmers, T.C., "Cognitive
     Behavioral Techniques for Hypertension: Are They Effective,"
     Anuals of Internal Medicine, Vol. 118, No. 12, 1993, pp. 964-972.

17. Letter dated March 13, 1995 from Ropes & Gray, attorneys for
     Harvard Medical School and Dr. Herbert Benson, to Kevin J.
     McDevitt, of Willian Brinks Hofer Gilson & Lione, attorneys for
     Maharishi University of Management (formerly Maharishi
     International University).

18. Benson, H., Greenwood, M.M., and Klemchuk, H., "The
     Relaxation Response: Psychophysiologic Aspects and Clinical
     Applications," *International Journal of Psychiatry in Medicine,*
     Vol. 6, No. 1/2, 1975, p. 96; and see Benson, H., "The
     Relaxation Response and Stress," in *Behavioral Health*, ed.
     Malarazzo, Weiss, Herd, Miller, and Weiss, John Wiley & Sons,
     New York, 1984, p. 335; Benson, H., Marzetta, B.R., Rosner,
     B.A., Klemchuk, H.M., "Decreased Blood-Pressure in
     Pharmacologically Treated Hypertensive Patients Who
     Regularly Elicited the Relaxation Response," *The Lancet,*
     February 23, 1974, p. 289.

19. Garfinkel, P., "Meditation Goes Mainstream," *Yoga Journal,*
     April, 1995, p. 63.

20. Kabat-Zinn, J., "Mindfulness Meditation: Health Benefits of an
     Ancient Buddhist Practice," in *Mind Body Medicine*, ed.
     Goleman and Gevin, Consumer Reports Books, Yonkers, New
     York, 1993, p. 259.

21. Ibid., p. 262.

22. Ibid., p. 266.

23. Garfinkel, P., "Meditation" (see note 19), p. 69.

24. Domash, L., "Introduction," *Collected Papers*, Vol. 1, 1976, pp. 13-31.

25. Jeffery, C. R., "Sociology and Criminology: The Long Lean Years of the Unthinkable and Unmentionable," in *Taboos* (see note 2), p. 122.

Chapter Ten

1. Schroedinger, E., "What is Life," from *The Great Ideas Today,* Encyclopedia Brittanica, London, 1967, p. 415.

2. Marsh, T., *Roots of Crime*, Nelson Publishing Company, Newton, New Jersey, 1981.

3. Ibid., p. 32.

4. Gottschalk, L.A., Tessio, R., Buchsbaum, M.S., Tucker, H.G., and Hodges, E.L., "Abnormalities in Hair Trace Elements as Indicators of Aberrant Behavior," report of the Department of Psychiatry and Human Behavior and Pharmacology, College of Medicine, University of California, Irvine, 1991.

5. Virkkunen, M., "Reactive Hypoglycemia Tendency Among Habitually Violent Offenders," *Neuropsychobiology,* Vol. 8, 1982, pp. 35-40; Virkkunen, M., "Reactive Hypoglycemic Tendency Among Habitually Violent Offenders," *Nutrition Reviews,* Vol. 4498. (supp.), 1986, pp. 94-103; Schoenthaler, S.J., "The Los Angeles Probation Department Diet-Behavior Program," *International Journal of Social Research*, Vol. 5, 1983, pp. 88-98.

6. Kanarek, R.P., "Nutrition and Violent Behavior," in *Understanding and Preventing Violence*, Vol. 2, National Academy Press, Wash., D.C., 1994, pp. 515-539.

7. Sharma, H., *Freedom From Disease*, Veda Publishing, Toronto, 1993, p. 1.

8. Ibid., pp. 66 and 67.

9. Ibid.

10. Ibid., pp. 94 and 167.

11. Ibid., p. 121.

12. Ibid., pp. 147-149.

13. Ibid., p. 146.

14. Wallace, R.K., *The Physiology of Consciousness,* Institute of Science, Technology and Public Policy and MIU Press, Fairfield, Iowa, 1993, p. 126.

15. Ibid., p. 117.

16. Ibid.

17. Ibid., p. 160.

18. Ibid., pp. 127 and 128.

19. Sharma, H., *Freedom* (see note 7), p. 149.

20. Brooks, J., "The Application of Maharishi Ayur-Veda to Mental Health and Substance Abuse," *Alcoholism* (see note 20, chapter 7), pp. 395-411.

21. Wallace, R.K. (see note 14), p. 106.

22. Ibid.

Chapter Eleven

1. Orme-Johnson, D.W. and Haynes, C.T., "EEG Phase Coherence, Pure Consciousness, Creativity and TM-Sidhi Experiences," *International Journal of Neuroscience*, Vol. 13, 1981, pp. 211-217; Dillbeck, M.C., Orme-Johnson, D.W., and Wallace, R.K., "Frontal EEG Coherence, H-Reflex Recovery, Concept Learning, and the TM-Sidhi Program," International *Journal of Neuroscience*, Vol. 15, 1981, pp. 151-157; Haynes, C.T., Herbert, J.R., Reber, W., and Orme-Johnson, D.W., "Psychophysiology of Advanced Participants in the Transcendental Meditation Program: Correlations of EEG Coherence, Creativity, H-Reflex Recovery, and Experiences of Transcendental Consciousness," in *Collected Papers*, Vol. 1, 1976, pp. 639-648; and Orme-Johnson, D.W., "Factor Analysis of EEG Coherence Parameters," Fifteenth Annual Winter Conference on Brain Research, Steamboat Springs, Colorado, January 28, 1982.

2. Werner, H.A., "The Concept of Development from a Comparative and Organismic Point of View," in *The Concept of Development,* ed. D.B. Harris, University of Minnesota Press, Minneapolis, 1957.

3. Childs, J.P., "The Use of Transcendental Meditation as a Therapy with Juvenile Offenders," *Collected Papers*, Vol. 1, 1976, pp. 577-585.

Chapter Twelve

1. Fine, P.E.M., "Herd Immunity: History, Theory, Practice," *Epidimiologic Reviews*, Vol. 15, No. 2, 1993, p. 266.

2. Ibid.

3. Ibid., p. 291.

4. Ibid., p. 269.

5. Borland, C., and Landrith, III, G., Improved Quality of City Life

Through the Transcendental Meditation Program: Decreased Crime Rate," *Collected Papers*, Vol. 1, 1976, p. 639.

6. Dillbeck, M.C., Landrith, III, G.S., Polanzi, C., and Baker, S.R., "The Transcendental Meditation Program and Crime Rate Change: A Causal Analysis," *Collected Papers*, Vol. 4, 1989, pp. 2515-2520.

7. Burgmans, W.H.P.M., Van der Burgt, A.T., and Langenkamp, F.P.Th., "Sociological Effects of the Group Dynamics of Consciousness: Decrease of Crime and Traffic Accidents in Holland," *Collected Papers*, Vol. 4, 1989, p. 2566.

8. Dillbeck, M.C., Foss, A.P.O., and Zimmermann, W.J., "Maharishi's Global Ideal Society Campaign: Improved Quality of Life in Rhode Island Through the Transcendental Meditation and TM-Sidhi Program," *Collected Papers*, Vol. 4, 1989, p.2521.

9. Davies, J.L., and Alexander, C.N., "The Maharishi Technology of the Unified Field and Improved Quality of Life in the United States: A Study of the First World Peace Assembly, Amherst, Massachusetts, 1979," *Collected Papers*, Vol. 4, 1989, p. 2549.

10. See, for example, Dillbeck, M.C., Banus, C.B., Polanzi, C. and Landrith III, G.S., "Test of a Field Model of Consciousness and Social Change: The Transcendental Meditation and TM-Sidhi Program and Decreased Urban Crime," *The Journal of Mind and Behavior*, Vol. 9, No. 4, 1988, pp. 457-486; Dillbeck, M.C., Landrith III, G., and Orme-Johnson, D.W., "The Transcendental Meditation Program and Crime Rate Change in a Sample of Forty-eight Cities," *Journal of Crime and Justice*, Vol. 4, 1981, pp. 25-45.

11. Orme-Johnson, D.W., Alexander, C.N., Davies, J.L., Chandler, H.M., and Larimore, W.E., "International Peace Project in the Middle East: The Effect of the Maharishi Technology of the Unified Field," *Journal of Conflict Resolution*, Vol. 32, No. 4, 1988, pp. 776-812, and see "The Effects of the Maharishi Technology of the Unified Field: Reply to a Methodological Critique," *Journal of Conflict Resolution*, Vol. 34, 1990, pp.756-768.

12. Oates, R.M., "Journals Support MIU Research Claims," *Fairfield Ledger*, Fairfield, Iowa, March 4, 1989, p. 5.

13. Burgmans, W.H.P.M., et al (see note 7).

14. Travis, F.T., and Orme-Johnson, D.W., "EEG Coherence and Power During Yogic Flying," *International Journal of Neuroscience*, Vol. 54, 1990, p. 1; Orme-Johnson, D.W., Clements, G., Haynes, C.T., Bodaori, K., "Higher States of Consciousness: EEG Coherence, Creativitiy, and Experience of the Sidhis," *Collected Papers*, Vol. 1, 1976, p. 707.

15. Talbot, M., *The Holographic Universe*, Harper Perennial, New York, 1992, p. 48.

16. Nelson, R.D., Bradish, G.J., Dobyns, Y.H., Dunne, B.J., and

Jahn, R.G., "FieldReg Anomalies in Group Situations," Princeton Engineering Anomalies Research, Technical Notes 95003, Princeton University, Princeton, NJ, June, 1995.

17. Loliger, S., "Relationship Between Subjective Bliss, 5-Hydroxy-3 Indoleacitis and the Collective Practice of Maharishi's TM and TM-Sidhi Program, Maharishi University of Management, Fairfield, Iowa, 1990.

18. Pugh, N., Walton, K.O., and Cavanaugh, K.L., "Can Time Series Analysis of Serotonin Turnover Test the Theory that Consciousness is a Field," presented at 18th annual meeting of the Society of Neuroscience, Toronto, Canada, Nov. 1988 (Soc. Neuroscience Abstracts 14:372, 1988).

19. Fine, P.E.M. (see note 1), p. 266.

20. "The Cost of Crime," *U.S. News & World Report*, January 17, 1994, p. 40; "The Economics of Crime," *Business Week*, December 13, 1993, p. 71.

Afterword

1. Capra, F., *The Turning Point*, Bantam Books, New York, 1982, p. 25.

2. J. David Gillespie, *Politics at the Periphery: Third Parties in Two-Party America*, University of South Carolina Press, 1993, p. 12.

3. Ibid., p. 24.

4. Rosensteil, T. B., "Gingrich's Power Play 10 Years in the Making," *Los Angeles Times,* December 19, 1994.

5. Ibid.

Acknowledgments

Much of the material in this book is based on accumulated research in different scientific areas. I am therefore indebted to the prior work of numerous researchers.

In the actual writing of this book, I received very helpful suggestions from Dr. Mike Tompkins and from Farrokh Anklesaria and David and Claudia Magill. The interviews from inmates and correctional officers who learned Transcendental Meditation were largely derived from tapes and letters assembled by the Department of Rehabilitation at Maharishi University of Management for its treatise *Total Rehabilitation* (in press), edited by Farrokh Anklesaria. Mr. Anklesaria also provided many of the photos used in this book and helpful advice based on his teaching activities in prisons throughout the world over the past fifteen years. Certain interviews with inmates were transcribed from the tape "The Transcendental Meditation Program in the Criminal Justice System," which was produced by Mark Halberstadt and John Lyons.

In addition, I thank professors John Hagelin, Robert Keith Wallace, Kenneth Walton, David Orme-Johnson, Charles Alexander, Chris Jones and Ron Jevning for their comments or review of certain of the scientific sections of the book, and physicians James Fleming, Stuart Rothenberg, Robert Schneider, David Sands, and Ron David for their help with the medical and other sections.

Professor Harvey Brooks provided comments on much of the book. Professor R. Dean Wright guided me to important reference works in criminology. Professor Robert Agnew provided helpful comments on general stress theory. Professor Kevin Ryan provided a helpful paper and certain insights on prison rehabilitation. Dr. Janet Knight provided advice on the use of the rehabilitation index.

For typing the manuscript (lots of typing) and for their general encouragement, I thank Janet Derby, Becky Ewing, and Christine MacDonald.

I also thank Ken Roseboro for his editing, and George and Felicity Foster for their much appreciated designs for the cover and the book's interior.

Lastly, I thank my wife for her editing and general support, and my daughters, Emily and Kirsi, for their help during my campaign for attorney general and especially for making the parades and signature gathering as much fun as they were.

Resources

For information on crime prevention or rehabilitation programs utilizing the Transcendental Meditation or TM-Sidhi programs or the programs of Maharishi Ayur-Veda, contact:

> Department of Rehabilitation
> Maharishi University of Management
> Fairfield, Iowa 52557
> (515) 472-2857

For information on the Natural Law Party of the United States of America:

> Natural Law Party
> 51 West Washington Street, Suite 100
> Fairfield, Iowa 52556
> (515) 472-2040

Index

About the Author

Jay B. Marcus grew up in New York City and its suburbs. He is a graduate of Rutgers University and the University of Virginia Law School. The author practiced law in New York City and Los Angeles before moving to Iowa in 1982. He is a partner in the law firm of Marcus, Courtade & Thompson in Fairfield, Iowa.

Mr. Marcus has written two prior books and several professional articles on stress management and preventing crime, drug abuse and unethical conduct. From 1990 to 1993 he was chairman of an Iowa Bar Association ethics committee, and in 1994 he ran for attorney general of Iowa as a candidate of the Natural Law Party.

Mr. Marcus is an avid basketball fan and golfer. He was co-captain of his college basketball team, and is still active coaching in his community. He is married and has two daughters.